Underachievement in Gifted Education

T0386626

This book provides an opportunity for researchers, professionals, and practitioners working directly with gifted individuals to engage with and examine the concept of underachievement of highly capable and talented individuals from different perspectives.

Chapters written by experts in gifted education from diverse backgrounds explore underachievement in principle, illuminate underachievement as a response to written and unwritten policy and practice, showcase ranges of intellectual capability outside of traditional academic subjects, shift deficit views of not meeting rigid expectations to honoring interests and cultural values of the individual, and provide suggested and proven practices and services as solutions to bridge the gaps in achievement and performance for gifted and talented students.

Expertly blending theory with practice, *Underachievement in Gifted Education* is a must-read for all practitioners, educators of gifted individuals, and researchers seeking more opportunities to help students align how they choose to exhibit their talent and efforts with external and internal expectations, personal interests, and cultural values to reach their maximum potential.

Kristina Henry Collins is an Associate Professor of Talent Development at Texas State University and the Immediate Past President for Supporting the Emotional Needs of the Gifted (SENG, Inc.). She is an award-winning researcher and nationally recognized expert in identity and talent development of underrepresented and underserved students in gifted, STEM, and advanced academics.

Javetta Jones Roberson serves as the District Coordinator of Secondary Advanced Academics & Gifted and Talented in McKinney ISD in McKinney, Texas. She is an Adjunct Professor in the Teacher Education and Administration Department at the University of North Texas.

Fernanda Hellen Ribeiro Piske is a globally respected expert in giftedness, inclusive and special education with a doctorate in Education from the Federal University of Paraná State, Brazil. She is the founder and President of Institute C&S – Creativity & Giftedness, for gifted students and 2e students, in Curitiba, Paraná, Brazil.

Underachievement in Gifted Education

Perspectives, Practices, and Possibilities

Edited by Kristina Henry Collins, Javetta Jones Roberson, and Fernanda Hellen Ribeiro Piske

Routledge
Taylor & Francis Group

NEW YORK AND LONDON

Designed cover image: © Getty Images

First published 2024
by Routledge
605 Third Avenue, New York, NY 10158

and by Routledge
4 Park Square, Milton Park, Abingdon, Oxon, OX14 4RN

Routledge is an imprint of the Taylor & Francis Group, an informa business

Library of Congress Cataloging-in-Publication Data
Names: Collins, Kristina Henry, editor. | Roberson, Javetta Jones, editor. |
Piske, Fernanda Hellen Ribeiro, editor.
Title: Underachievement in gifted education : perspectives, practices, and possibilities /
edited by Kristina Henry Collins, Javetta Jones Roberson, Fernanda Hellen Ribeiro Piske.
Description: New York, NY : Routledge, 2024. | Includes bibliographical references
and index. |
Identifiers: LCCN 2023005118 (print) | LCCN 2023005119 (ebook) |
ISBN 9781032439549 (hardback) | ISBN 9781032432830 (paperback) |
ISBN 9781003369578 (ebook)
Subjects: LCSH: Gifted children--Education. | Gifted children--Mental health. |
Motivation in education. | Motivation (Psychology) in children.
Classification: LCC LC3993 .U527 2024 (print) | LCC LC3993 (ebook) |
DDC 371.95--dc23/eng/20230223
LC record available at https://lccn.loc.gov/2023005118
LC ebook record available at https://lccn.loc.gov/2023005119

ISBN: 978-1-032-43954-9 (hbk)
ISBN: 978-1-032-43283-0 (pbk)
ISBN: 978-1-003-36957-8 (ebk)

DOI: 10.4324/9781003369578

Typeset in Bembo
by Deanta Global Publishing Services, Chennai, India

Contents

Figures

Tables

About the Editors

Kristina Henry Collins is the core faculty for Talent Development Program at Texas State University, USA. She teaches graduate courses related to program, curriculum, and research design and implementation in the areas of talent development, multicultural gifted education, and mentoring across the lifespan. With an extensive background in STEM identity and talent development, Dr. Collins holds a dual appointment as Associate Director for the LBJ STEM Institute for STEM Education and Research. She is a former member of the NAGC Board of Directors and immediate past president of SENG. She is the proud recipient of NAGC's 2021 Early Leader Award, Special Population Network of NAGC 2020 Early Career Award, Bridges 2e Education 2020 "Person to Watch" Award, and Georgia Association of Gifted Children's 2011 Mary Frasier Equity and Excellence Award, to name a few, all presented for her work in advancing educational opportunities for underrepresented students in gifted education.

Javetta Jones Roberson serves as the District Coordinator of Secondary Advanced Academics & Gifted and Talented in McKinney ISD, McKinney, Texas, USA. Javetta also serves as a lecturing professor in the Teacher Education and Administration Department at the University of North Texas. Her research interests include diverse gifted and Advanced Placement populations, equity in giftedness, Culturally Responsive Pedagogy (teaching, leadership, and curriculum), and professional learning of teachers) (special education and gifted). Previously, she has served as a high school campus administrator, high school Advanced Academics Coordinator, elementary Gifted Campus Coordinator/Liaison, and Gifted dual language teacher. Javetta serves on the Board of Directors for the Council of Exceptional Children – Association for the Gifted and is a past board member of the Texas Association for the Gifted and Talented. She also serves on the Diversity, Equity & Access committee, the Conference Program Committee, the Special Populations Network as Program Co-Chair & G-RACE Sig Co-Chair with the National Association of Gifted Children. Javetta is the recipient of the 2021 SENG Gifted Educator of the year award. She continues to author articles, books, book chapters, and offers professional learning on helping gifted student populations from various backgrounds thrive.

Fernanda Hellen Ribeiro Piske is a globally respected expert in Giftedness, Inclusive and Special Education. Her doctoral degree is in Cognition, Learning and Human Development from the Federal University of Paraná, Brazil. Dr. Piske is the founder and President of the Institute C&S – Criatividade & Superdotação (Creativity & Giftedness) in Curitiba, Paraná, Brazil. The Institute C&S contributes to identifying and assisting gifted and 2e children and adults through pedagogical, psycho-pedagogical, psychological, neuropsychological, and legal advice. She completed postgraduate studies in Special Education and Inclusive Education at the International University Centre, Uninter. As a researcher and well-established author in the field, Dr. Piske has authored and/or edited many gifted and talent development books on topics including, but not limited to: twice exceptionality, autism, creativity, social-emotional development, affectivity, bullying, teacher training, complexity theory and human rights. As a visionary leader in the field, her published work is uniquely positioned as she effectively coordinates the collaborative research and writing efforts of experts from around the world. Dr. Piske has lectured on gifted education and twice exceptionality at congresses and events.

Contributors

Tony D.D. Collins II serves as an Assistant Football Coach at Washington & Lee (W&L) University, Lexington, VA, USA. Collins comes to W&L after earning his Master of Education in Educational Psychology from the University of Georgia. He also earned a Credential of Readiness (CORe) and Master of Business Essentials from Harvard University and a Bachelor of Science degree in psychology from Davidson College, where he played four years of D1 football. While at Davidson, Collins was a four-year member of the Wildcats football team. He earned Second Team All-Pioneer Football League honors in 2019 and honorable mention accolades in 2018, while totaling 205 tackles and 10.0 tackles for a loss in his career. As an identified gifted student-athlete, his background and experience have informed his research foci in gifted multipotentiality and translating athletic and academic gifts and talents for talent development. He was recognized by the National Association for Gifted Children (NAGC) as a Dr. Martin Jenkins Scholar in 2015.

Andrea Dennison is a licensed psychologist in Texas and has published across a number of fields, including school psychology, cross-cultural psychology, gifted education, social-emotional learning, and applied behavior analysis. She is invested in the meaningful application of sciences through implementation research and skillful practice of psychology with youth, the aging, the disabled, and other diverse populations.

Cheryl Fields-Smith is a Professor of Elementary Education in the Department of Educational Theory and Practice at the University of Georgia, USA. She earned her doctorate from Emory University. Dr. Fields-Smith pioneered research conceptualizing contemporary Black home education as resistance, challenging the question of who homeschools and why. She is the author of *Exploring Single Black Mothers' Resistance through Homeschooling* and co-edited, *Homeschooling Black Children in the U.S.: Theory, Practice, and Popular Culture*. Her work has been featured in major multimedia agencies. Dr. Fields-Smith taught elementary school in her native state of Connecticut before she began working on her doctorate.

Jennifer Groman is an Associate Professor and directs the graduate program in Talent Development at Ashland University, Ohio, USA, and she is a visiting lecturer for the

Talent Development Program at McNeese State University. She is a teacher, singer, and songwriter who has worked with students from 2 years old to the graduate level, in general education, talent development education, creativity studies and songwriting, reading, and math intervention. She has worked as a state-level gifted consultant and teacher trainer and at the local level in arts administration. She has four self-produced albums of her own music and big band jazz.

Keri M. Guilbault is an Associate Professor of gifted education at Johns Hopkins University, Maryland, USA, and a former school district supervisor of K-12 gifted and talented programs. She received the 2019 National Association for Gifted Children (NAGC) Early Leader Award and serves on their Board of Directors as treasurer.

Daniel Hernández-Torrano is an Associate Professor at the Graduate School of Education, Nazarbayev University Nur-Sultan, Kazakhstan. Dr. Hernández-Torrano obtained his PhD in Educational Psychology from the University of Murcia in Spain, and has held research positions at University College London , the Universidade do Minho in Portugal, and the University of Connecticut, USA. He teaches courses in quantitative research methodology, educational psychology, and inclusive education. His main areas of interest are gifted education, inclusive education, the intersection between excellence and equity, and young people's well-being.

Josyln Johnson currently serves as a cabinet member of the College of Literature, Science and the Arts at the University of Michigan, USA, and is an instructor in Stanford's Continuing Studies Program. She earned her degree in Adult, Professional, and Community Education at Texas State University in 2017. Her research explored the lifelong, lifewide, and life-deep experiences of high potential individuals who experienced a sense of purpose and career success in early adulthood. Her research has led to several academic recognitions, including the award for the Top Research Paper at Texas State University's International Research Conference and the Graduate Research Award, at the Adult Education Research Conference.

Robin Johnson is a doctoral student in Educational Psychology at the University of North Texas, USA, with a specialization in gifted and talented. Her teaching experience includes 23 years in the elementary classroom with 9 years teaching gifted and talented students. Her research interests include gifted and talented identification and education in rural communities. Other interests include how culture and environment impact learning, talent development, and future aspirations of gifted and talented students.

Ljiljana Krneta obtained her PhD in Psychology in the Faculty of Philosophy in Pale, the University of East Sarajevo, in 2010. In 2018, at the 16th International Conference on Excellence, Innovation and Creativity in Education and Psychology, at the University of Paris Descartes, Paris, France, she was awarded the Excellence in Education Award for her outstanding contribution in the field of education. She has participated in many scientific and professional conferences throughout the region and Europe with written contributions and papers, being a reviewer of a number of papers in the field of psychology and pedagogy as well. She is a president of the Association Together in Europe (2011), Banja Luka, BiH, and certified as a European Talent Point by ETSN – European Talent Support Network. She has published over 140 scientific papers. She is the author of seven books (three as co-author), and she has participated in over 60 scientific gatherings in the field of giftedness (ICIE, ECHA and others). She has published works in France, Portugal, Austria, Germany, Slovenia, Croatia, Serbia, Bosnia and Herzegovina, North Macedonia, and Romania.

Grizelle Larriviel is a doctoral student in Educational Psychology at the University of North Texas, USA, with a specialization in gifted and talented, and an educator in Irving ISD. Interests include sociocultural theory and its impact on underrepresented special populations going through the gifted and talented process, underachievement, SEL development, and building cultural wealth. Additionally, she wants to address the needs of gifted and talented children and their families and transform campus/district culture to reflect today's student bodies' economic and cultural diversity.

Zauresh Manabayeva is a teacher of English at Nazarbayev Intellectual School in Kyzylorda, Kazakhstan, with more than ten years of working experience. Zauresh obtained her Bachelor's Degree from Korkyt Ata State University and an MSc in Educational Leadership at the Graduate School of Education at Nazarbayev University. Her main area of interest is gifted education. Her main goal is to understand giftedness to facilitate the realization of every student's full potential.

Araceli Martinez Ortiz is the Microsoft President's Endowed Professor of Engineering Education in the Department of Biomedical Engineering & Chemical Engineering/Interdisciplinary Learning & Teaching at the University of Texas, San Antonio, USA. Dr. Martinez Ortiz's research investigates teaching and learning approaches that better support student engagement in engineering education. As a result, she has designed and piloted integrated engineering education efforts to encourage young students from diverse backgrounds to excel in mathematics and science courses. These efforts also support professional development for teachers in this focus area. She also received a competitive faculty fellowship with NASA's Office of STEM Engagement in 2022, where she serves as one of NASA's Minority Serving Institute Faculty Fellows (IPA) and advises OSTEM on education program design and research elements with NASA headquarters' teams.

Kimberly M. McCormick is an Assistant Professor in the Department of Early Childhood Education & Human Development at the University of Cincinnati, USA. Her work in higher education allows her to partner with practitioners to facilitate best practices in gifted education, assessment strategies, cognitive engagement, and STEM education.

Christian E. Mueller is Professor of Educational Psychology & Research at the University of Memphis, USA. He received his PhD in Educational Psychology from the University of Kentucky in 2006. Dr. Mueller's research focuses on how context influences motivation, identity, and psychosocial well-being among potentially at-risk or historically underserved student populations (e.g., gifted, adolescents, ethnic-minority youth). Much of his research lies at the intersection of developmental theory, ecological theory, and social-cognitive theory/motivational theory, and focuses specifically on understanding how social supports – family, school, and peers – enhance or impede these processes. He has explored these issues at the student, classroom and at the broader contextual level, and has served as PI, Co-PI or Senior Personnel on over $2 million in funded projects.

Rachel U. Mun is an Associate Professor of Educational Psychology at the University of North Texas, USA. She received her PhD in Education, Learning Sciences and Human Development from the University of Washington. Her research interests are two-tiered and best described as an intersection between culture, gifted education, and socio-emotional well-being. At the micro-level, she explores socio-emotional development and decision making for high-ability students (emphasis on immigrants) within family, peer and academic contexts with the goal of promoting well-being. At the macro-level, she examines ways to improve equitable identification and services for K-12 high-ability learners from diverse populations. She has published in *Gifted Child Quarterly*, *Journal for the Education of the Gifted*, *Roeper Review*, *Journal of Advanced Academics*, *Gifted Child Today*, and *Parenting for High Potential*.

Sally M. Reis holds the Letitia Neag Chair in Educational Psychology, is a Board of Trustees Distinguished Professor, and was the former Vice Provost for Academic Affairs at the Neag School of Education at the University of Connecticut, USA. She served as Principal Investigator of the National Research Center on the Gifted and Talented and as Department Head of the Educational Psychology Department. She has authored and co-authored more than 270 articles, books, book chapters, monographs and technical reports, and worked in a research team that has generated over $60 million in grants in the last 15 years.

Colin Seale was born and raised in Brooklyn, NY, where struggles in his upbringing gave birth to his passion for educational equity. Tracked early into gifted and talented programs, Colin was afforded opportunities his neighborhood peers were not. Using lessons from his experience as a math teacher, later as an attorney, and now as a keynote speaker, contributor to *Forbes*, *The 74*, *Edutopia* and *Education Post* and author of *Thinking Like a Lawyer: A Framework for Teaching Critical Thinking to All Students* (Prufrock Press, 2020) and *Tangible Equity: A Guide for Leveraging Student Identity, Culture, and Power to Unlock Excellence In and Beyond the Classroom* (Routledge, 2022), Colin founded think-kLaw, a multi-award-winning organization to help educators leverage inquiry-based instructional strategies to close the critical thinking gap and ensure they teach and reach all students, regardless of race, zip code, or what side of the poverty line they are born on. When he's not serving as the world's most fervent critical thinking advocate or tweeting, Colin proudly serves as the world's greatest entertainer to his two young children.

Andrea Stewart is a doctoral student in Educational Psychology at the University of North Texas, USA, with a specialization in Human Development and Family Science. She has been a classroom teacher for 12 years at Ursuline Academy of Dallas, where she is currently Chair of the Social Studies Department and teaches a variety of history courses. Her research interests include cognitive and language development, English Language Learners, cultivating talent and curiosity, and improving student learning.

Vanessa Velasquez is a graduate of Texas State University, USA, where she earned a Bachelor of Science with a minor in Interdisciplinary Studies and a Master's of Education with a minor in Elementary Education and a concentration in Talent Development. Ms. Velasquez has enjoyed working with children as an educator for over 10 years.

Denise L. Winsor is Associate Professor of Educational Psychology & Research at the University of Memphis, USA. She received her PhD from the University of Nevada,

Las Vegas in 2007. Using a dynamic or ecological systems framework, Dr. Winsor is interested in student knowledge and learning processes related to parents, teachers, and peers. She has applied this framework in her work related to giftedness in children and adolescent students' cognitive, social, and emotional development; and their relationships to teachers, parents, and peers; specifically, underachievement, bullying, peer victimization; and depression and suicide. Her other research interests include early epistemological development and the impact on interrelated developmental domains and learning; using technology in early teaching and learning. Dr. Winsor's current work has included investigating preschool parent-child conceptions of knowledge; and their developmental process of knowing and understanding the world around them using artful expressions. She has worked collaboratively on projects associated with elementary reading success, engaged in scholarship promoting success with African-American students; and how to use music as a cultural tool. Dr. Winsor teaches graduate courses in child psychology, emotional regulation, culturally diverse students, moral development, personal epistemology, psychology of aging, and lifespan development. Her service activities include professional development in the Memphis community (e.g., Head Start, Early Head Start, Jewish Community, Germantown Library, Shelby County Schools).

Kenneth Wright is pursuing his doctorate in Educational Psychology, with a focus on creativity, giftedness, and talent development at the University of Connecticut, USA. He holds a Bachelor's degree in social science teaching, a Master's degree in school counseling, and an endorsement in gifted and talented education. During his sixteen years as a classroom teacher, he taught history, geography, theater, psychology, and English. He has worked extensively in student leadership, counseling at-risk teens, and in the performing arts. He is the author of three picture books and travels to schools across the United States speaking to young students about the importance of creativity and curiosity.

Foreword

Colin Seale

If this Foreword had a title, I would probably have called it "Reflections of a Recovering Gifted Underachiever." But over the last several years as I've led thinkLaw, an organization I founded in order to give educators and school systems powerful, but practical curriculum, tools, and strategies to close the critical thinking gap in education, I realized that underachiever may not have been the right word.

I was more of a *selective* achiever. If I was into it, I was all the way into it. And if I did not care, I would go out of my way to become the textbook example of what it looked like to not care about something. I love history and I love stories about real-life heroes in our history. But when my third-grade teacher at P.S. 208 in my self-contained gifted class in Brooklyn, NY, assigned us to create a Women's History Month calendar, I was not going to do that assignment. Nope. Never. It didn't matter that I would *enthusiastically* give you a 30-minute verbal presentation on 12 famous women in history in my sleep. I was not going to spend 30 seconds drawing out boxes and labeling the dates and coloring and designing a ridiculous calendar simply because my teacher asked me to.

I was the problem.

This was something my mother could not comprehend. My mother raised my older sister and me in trying times. I was the first generation of my family born in the United States, we were on free and reduced lunch at school, and she raised us by herself after my parents split – a job that became even harder when my father was incarcerated for a decade for selling drugs. Despite all these struggles (or likely *because* of it), here I was: a gifted child who would never have been identified if I wasn't getting in trouble all the time and if I didn't need an evaluation for speech-related services. And I was squandering the opportunity. She forced me to do the calendar after my teacher ratted me out, and through middle school, she continued to have a confidential informant on my case for each of my attempts to avoid unworthy assignments.

But by the time I reached high school at the prestigious, and increasingly-harder-for-Black-and-Hispanic-kids-to-get-into Bronx High School of Science, teachers apparently had joined the stop-snitching movement. No one seemed to raise any flags when I went months without turning in assignments. When I decided to take almost every lunch period almost every day, no teacher ever called my mother to tell her I'd been skipping class daily. They just gave me my zeroes and kept it moving.

I was still the problem.

But was it really all about me? New York City's Board of Education had and still has one of the most segregated school systems in the nation. In elementary and middle school, I attended schools that were essentially all-Black, with the overwhelming majority of students coming from Caribbean countries. I was in self-contained gifted classes from second grade to fifth grade, and in middle school I went to a performing arts magnet school where 100% of students in my academic classes were identified as gifted as well. But in high school, not only did I have a 90-minute commute each way from my Canarsie/East Flatbush neighborhood to the North Bronx, but I was commuting a world away from any school I'd ever known.

Until high school, I'd never even known what "acting white" meant because I didn't know any white students. I had no clue what it meant to be a "minority" when every single child in every school I attended looked like me, and everyone in my community did too. It had never occurred to me that there was anything peculiar about being Black and brilliant at the same time, being poor and brilliant at the same time, or being an immigrant and brilliant at the same time. This new school was a culture shock for me. Prior to this moment, my personal development, racial identity, and academic success all worked in tandem with each other. But in high school, everything changed.

It seems strange that this school – whose sole criterion for admission was a single test that I excelled on – would not have implemented thoughtful and intentional strategies to support struggling students who clearly had the academic capacity to succeed. Especially a student like me, who started high school double-accelerated in multiple subjects. I also wonder why no one recognized that students like me needed extra support for this transition. As a late-blooming ninth grader taking classes with sophomores and juniors – who typically looked like grown men and women by that age – no one addressed any of the obvious social and emotional challenges I would face grappling with this incredible level of change.

I was *not* the problem.

The problem was, and still is, that we are too comfortable with the idea of leaving brilliance on the table. It is a small miracle that I pulled it together to graduate from high school. But I still struggle when I consider that out of the 24 students in my dual-grade self-contained elementary gifted class, three did not graduate from high school. And it is an outright tragedy that stories like these still exist in gifted education globally.

This is why *Underachievement in Gifted Education: Perspectives, Practices, and Possibilities* is such an important read. I no longer have to wonder what would have happened if my mother did not have to continually stress, worrying that her underachieving gifted son was a defective product, because this book has powerful, but practical lessons for understanding the unique ways that gifted learners struggle. And the classification of "unique" is well deserved because this incredible collection goes into depth examining what this looks like for learners in both online and brick-and-mortar school settings, and how this may look different and be addressed differently for culturally and linguistically diverse gifted underachievers.

If I was asked to write the Foreword of any other book, you might as well have asked me to create another Women's History Month calendar. But this book is different. It would already be overachieving by highlighting current, relevant, and meaningful research in this crucial field and matching this research with the very policy and people connections that create the conditions for underachievement to exist. With these two things alone, a world where we no longer left brilliance on the table would seem well within reach.

But *Underachievement in Gifted Education* takes it one step further. In my work with thinkLaw, we often help school systems redesign their curriculum so that our students do not just have the opportunity to analyze and understand the world as it *is*. We go deeper and push them to think critically about how they believe the world *ought to be*. The final Part of this book models this shift with concrete calls to action for changing the way we think about equitable leadership practices in education. Incredible ideas for unique university-school partnership opportunities. Innovative strategies for embedding equity throughout all stages of the gifted identification and program success pipeline. And even tackling the "and then what?" question about challenges around gifted underachievement during the transition to adulthood.

For those educators and scholars, and for families reading this book without a close connection to the gifted education field, I have to add one more important consideration: your learnings from this book have implications well beyond gifted education. We are currently in a space where the presumption that gifted learners will be "just fine" applies to lots of other types of high achievers without the gifted label. The theme of having engaged elementary school students who start checking out in middle school and completely check out by high school is not a problem unique to gifted learners. But like many of the innovative instructional practices and curricular approaches used in gifted education, if it benefits gifted learners, it also has so much potential to benefit each and every child.

Understanding underachievement matters. Doing something about it matters even more. And while I still think my personal experience was more of a *selective* achievement story, the actual name is irrelevant. What is relevant, however, is using this book to create a new reality where school systems know what to do to help gifted underachievers *select* to achieve.

Introduction

*Kristina Henry Collins, Javetta Jones Roberson,
and Fernanda Hellen Ribeiro Piske*

"Underachievement" is a common term used to refer to students who do not meet expectations within the classroom or academic setting. Of particular interest, most discussions about underachievement are centered around gifted students more specifically. It is generically defined as "the fact of doing less well than expected, especially in schoolwork" (Dictionary.com). The National Association for Gifted Children defines it as "the unanticipated difference between accomplishment and ability" (NAGC.org). The *Encyclopedia of Child Behavior and Development* (https://rdcu.be/dazgC) suggests that underachievement occurs when a child's academic performance is below what is expected based on the child's ability, aptitude, or intelligence. Some scholars have postulated the construct of underachievement, using a discrepancy model that establishes it by the relationship (or discrepancy) between effort and outcomes. As an example, a student who scores in the 97th percentile on standardized tests in a given area can be expected to excel in that area, earning As and perhaps some Bs. Similarly, if a student has been identified as gifted, the same expectation occurs across all academic areas of study. If the student does not make mostly As, then one can assume, based on these definitions and model, that the discrepancy that occurs between measured ability and grades as an outcome is the result of the student's effort as the primary factor. Also problematic in a discrepancy model, underachievement is also the given prognosis when both effort and outcomes are low, which does not signify a discrepancy at all. Underachievement is a concept that is as complex as its perceived solutions. In addition, comprehensive discussions and sustainable solutions about why it exists have not been widely addressed.

This text aims to answer the following questions about underachievement:

- What are the major factors influencing underachievement?
- Is it a case of once an underachiever, always an underachiever?
- How is underachievement determined?
- Are there levels of underachievement, and does it matter?
- How does it compare to overachieving?
- Is "underachiever" a preventable status for gifted individuals?
- How does underachievement look in settings beyond the classroom?
- Is it socialized or taught?

DOI: 10.4324/9781003369578-1

These are just a few critical questions that may come to mind as scholars, parents, and educators attempt to unpack the concept of underachievement and its impact on gifted individuals. When addressing and evaluating underachievement within gifted education, we envision *Underachievement in Gifted Education: Perspectives, Practices, and Possibilities* to be a resource for that purpose, and more. Included in discussions for understanding and addressing underachievement as a construct are underlying concepts that must also be understood and addressed. These concepts include, but are not limited to, abilities, learner profiles, latent talents, motivation (defined in terms of expectation and value), potential, perfectionism, and belongingness, to name but a few. This book provides an opportunity for practitioners, parents, and other stakeholders working directly with gifted individuals (formally and informally identified highly talented students) to examine the current concepts of underachievement from different perspectives.

As its subtitle suggests, *Underachievement in Gifted Education* is divided into three Parts: Perspectives, Practices, and Possibilities. Part I, "Perspectives," offers background information on underachievement in principle to include factors and manifestation. A diversity of perspective is provided through a synthesis of empirical research and professional testimonies. Part II, "Practices," illuminates underachievement as a response to policy and practices put in place by stakeholders, written or unwritten, and gaps within well-intended policy, that lead to underachievement. Extending the current understanding of the term, we contend that an understanding of underachievement must also include discussions about "underrepresented" and "underserved" as a contribution to underachievement. Practices to support gifted individuals who experience underachievement are also spotlighted. Part III, "Possibilities," includes a view of gifted students that showcases a range of intellectual capabilities outside of traditional academic subjects, and shifts deficit views of not meeting rigid expectations to honoring the interests and cultural values of the individual. It provides some suggested and proven practices and services within gifted education and advanced academies as solutions to bridge the gaps in achievement and performance for gifted and talented students. While Part I is targeted more toward a professional and research audience, Part II complements Part I with a more practical approach to addressing underachievement. However, because practitioners tend to conduct action research by default through their own efforts to constantly improve pedagogy and instructional practices, Part I is still relevant and will prove to be beneficial to researchers and practitioners to include in teacher preparation programs in gifted education, as well as in-service teachers working in the field.

Underachievement in Gifted Education compels the reader to be reflective of the environment, contexts, and other factors that are in play during student academic engagement. The more meaningful dialogue and awareness we build in the field on this topic, the more opportunities we have to find ways to help students align how they choose to exhibit their abilities, talent, and efforts to external and internal expectations, personal interests, and cultural values so that maximum potential is realized. When mismatch prevails, relevant concerns are not recognized and addressed, proactively or reactively, and this further exacerbates underachievement as we currently define it. This is not only detrimental to students' academic growth and overall success in schools, but can negatively impact a student's self-concept, confidence, and future academic/career decisions.

As editors, we are proud to present a collaborative work of experts of gifted education from diverse backgrounds, including chapters from international scholars, to offer multiple perspectives and to also extend our reach to those abroad. Editorial care was taken to ensure that a DEI (diversity, equity, and inclusion) lens was utilized as the fabric for the many threads (perspectives and social milieus) to design a book that is interconnectedly woven together and cohesive. This book is timely and ideal to address the inequities that arise from misperceptions, preconceived notions, and consequential judgments related to underachievement. It is our hope that gifted coordinators, counselors, and other school administrators who make professional development decisions will also find this book useful when they are choosing resources for their professional development for the teachers who work directly with students. More importantly, we hope that it influences a more inclusive approach to talent and advanced development, whereby the social, emotional, and cultural contexts are prioritized under a true partnership between families and the educational systems that serve them.

Perspectives

Underachieving Gifted Children and Adolescents

What Teachers, Parents, and Researchers Must Know

Denise L. Winsor and Christian E. Mueller

Introduction

Gifted underachievement is a broad and encompassing term that carries with it many connotations for parents and teachers; and anyone working with or concerned for the well-being of gifted individuals. Gifted underachievement carries inherent difficulties in terms of how to define, measure, and develop empirically based intervention strategies to help gifted individuals realize their full potential (McCoach & Siegle, 2018). Our aim in writing this chapter is not to settle the ongoing debate around how to define, measure, and identify causes of gifted underachievement; this may be infinitely difficult (e.g., Reis & McCoach, 2000), and not necessarily useful for those interested in helping gifted individuals achieve to their maximum ability and skill level (e.g., Steenbergen-Hu et al., 2020). Further, many of the other chapters in this edited book explore those topics more in depth. Instead, we build on some of our previous work in this area (e.g., Mueller & Winsor, 2018; Winsor & Mueller, 2020), and recent related research showing that interventions may impact psychosocial well-being for gifted individuals when exploring gifted underachievement (e.g., Steenbergen-Hu et al., 2020). From this collection of research, we put forth a framework, Social and Emotional Scaffolding in the Underachieving Gifted (SESUG), that can be used by parents and teachers, and adapted by those interested in helping gifted individuals achieve to their highest potential at all stages of development (Gagné, 2004; Seligman & Csikszentmihalyi, 2000); and is applicable to administrators when choosing professional development or employers as they seek to assist their gifted but underachieving employees. To understand the context for our proposed framework, we next provide a brief review of some of the more important issues to consider when designing interventions for the underachieving gifted. This is followed by a description of the SESUG framework, which is then most importantly followed by a discussion of how parents and teachers can be creative in social and emotional learning and development with gifted individuals. In turn, these suggestions can be implemented to help underachieving gifted individuals achieve to their highest potential and beyond because the framework emphasizes unique characteristics of gifted individuals through: (1) attention to asynchronous development; (2) stepping

DOI: 10.4324/9781003369578-3

away from intellectual growth, and stressing social and emotional development and learning; (3) demonstrating student-centered approaches, with parents and teachers as the catalyst for learning using scaffolding strategies; (4) defining *what to implement*, based on what the individual can excel at independently versus what they can accomplish with a scaffold (e.g., praise, encouragement, task options, a graphic organizer, extended research); (5) contextual strategies that address the *how to implement* a scaffold (e.g., individual, small group, whole group, designated use of space for interventions); and (6) *where to implement scaffolds* that can be contiguous between home and school with the collaboration of parents and teachers.

Underachievement among the Gifted

Whether one is interested in intervening directly, conducting research with, or has direct experience with gifted underachievers, there are many factors that must be considered under the "gifted underachievement" umbrella. There is the issue of *defining*, *measuring*, and *identifying factors* that correlate with gifted underachievement – what is it, how do we know it when we see it, and what causes it? These are all questions that educators, practitioners, and researchers have wrestled with since the earliest examination of gifted underachievement. For example, Reis and McCoach (2000), which is considered one of the early defining pieces on the topic of gifted underachievement, noted:

> The underachievement of gifted students is a perplexing phenomenon. Too often, for no apparent reason, students who show great academic promise fail to perform at a level commensurate with their previously documented abilities, frustrating both parents and teachers (Whitmore, 1986). The process for defining underachievement, identifying underachieving gifted students, and explaining the reasons for this underachievement continues to stir controversy among practitioners, researchers, and clinicians. Legitimate problems exist in determining whether these students are at greater risk for social or emotional problems than other students, and most interventions to reverse underachievement have met with limited success. Practitioners who responded to a National Research Center on the Gifted and Talented needs assessment identified underachievement as a major research problem (Renzulli et al., 1992). Despite this interest, underachievement of gifted students remains an enigma.
>
> *(p. 152)*

Recent researchers continue to document the enigma that is labeled "gifted underachievement" (e.g., McCoach & Siegle, 2018), and which led Snyder and Wormington (2020) to conclude "it becomes clear that no single case of underachievement is alike" (p. 64). Therefore, trying to determine exact causes for gifted underachievement will likely continue to frustrate educational researchers.

Another concern in identifying gifted underachievement relates to context or outcome. For example, most interventions aimed at helping gifted underachievers focus almost exclusively on academic performance; however, this may be problematic as gifted individuals may not be motivated by school for a variety of reasons (e.g., Snyder & Wormington, 2020). For example, Winsor and Mueller (2020) and others (e.g., Ramos et al., 2021) have noted that the academic subjects, curriculum, or classrooms do not prioritize gifted students' intellectual needs and interests; and are seldom prepared with the knowledge and skills required to assist with asynchronous social and emotional needs that gifted individuals possess. Undetected, unacknowledged, and unaddressed social and emotional delays can be the impetus that lowers levels of motivation and opens the door for gifted individuals to underachieve (Obergriesser & Stoeger, 2015; Schultz, 2010). Winsor and Mueller (2020), drawing from person-environment fit theory (e.g., Eccles et al., 1993; Hunt, 1975), suggested that a mismatch may exist for gifted students in academic settings, because of asynchronous development patterns (i.e., discrepancy between cognitive ability and social and emotional development, and academic setting; Silverman, 1997, 2002). In turn, this may lead to lower levels of motivation and engagement, and other social and emotional issues (e.g., trust, social isolation, depression, anxiety, boredom).[1] In these cases, many gifted students are turned off by traditional schooling, and explore intellectual pursuits on their own or through other non-academic avenues.

It is difficult to estimate the true number of gifted students who underachieve in school, although estimates range from 9% to 28% (Ramos et al., 2021). Furthermore, variable-centered approaches (i.e., trying to determine the most robust predictor variables) have yielded underwhelming results in terms of explaining causes of underachievement (e.g., Steenbergen-Hu et al., 2020). Some have suggested switching to what is referred to as a person-oriented approach in which patterns can be examined more specifically and in relation to academic and non-academic pursuits; for example, the development of the Pathways of Underachievement Model (PUM) (Snyder & Linnenbrink-Garcia, 2013), which draws from motivation theories and concepts to explain patterns of gifted underachievement, such as expectancy-value theory (e.g., Wigfield et al., 2009), self-worth theory (Covington, 1992), and mindset (e.g., Dweck, 2006).

Additional models propose addressing many facets of functioning or taking a holistic approach in studying and intervening with gifted underachievement. With our SESUG framework, we are proposing similar intervention approaches. For example, there exists Rimm's trifocal model, Renzulli and Reis's schoolwide enrichment model, and perhaps best known, the Achievement Orientation Model (AOM) (Siegle & McCoach, 2005), which is like the other models listed here and draws from intrapersonal, interpersonal, and environmental factors to explain underachievement patterns. For our proposed framework, in addition to taking a holistic or ecological approach (Bronfenbrenner, 1979, 2005; see also Collins et al., 2022; Piske et al., 2022) that considers *intrapersonal*, *interpersonal*, and *contextual/environmental* factors, we also suggest that *developmental* considerations are important for effective intervention strategies as children and adolescents will present with unique psychological, social, and emotional needs (Mueller & Winsor, 2018). In turn, each of these factors will function differently for intervening with underachievement patterns, whether inside or outside the classroom.

To illustrate how some of these factors have been conceptualized, we refer to the AOM model. Included in this model are academic self-perceptions, attitudes toward teachers and classes, attitudes toward school, goal-valuation and motivation, and self-regulation. These can be measured using the *School Attitude Assessment Survey-Revised* (SAAS-R) (McCoach & Siegle, 2003; Steenbergen-Hu et al., p. 134). Similarly, in the past, we have advocated taking a holistic approach to examining gifted student development, which we have adapted for the SESUG framework proposed in this chapter (e.g., Mueller & Winsor, 2018). We turn our attention to that framework next.

Creating Social and Emotional Scaffolding in the Underachieving Gifted

The social and emotional scaffolding in the Underachieving Gifted (SESUG) frame-work flows from the premise that it is best to structure any intervention strategies only after other complicating factors have been ruled out to the extent possible, and those working with the gifted individual seeks and comes to know them as more than just their gifts or talents through information gathering or personal interactions. In our recent work, we have drawn from Gagné's Differentiated Model of Giftedness and Talent Development (DMGT; 2004, 2012) and person-environment fit theory (e.g., Eccles et al., 1993; Hunt, 1975) to explore issues related to different aspects of gifted student development (e.g., Winsor & Mueller, 2020). There are four key aspects con-sidered in that work, which are applied under the SESUG framework (see Figure 1.1).

First, we take an ecological approach in understanding underachievement and designing interventions (i.e., the consideration of intrapersonal, interpersonal, and environmental factors). Second, we draw from Vygotsky's (1978) Zone of Proximal Development (ZPD), that at any time, gifted students are capable of growth through their own efforts, but more likely with the help of more capable individuals (i.e., par-ents, teachers, peers) (Fani & Ghaemi, 2011). Third, we take a developmental approach to understanding that gifted students are often more cognitively advanced (but not necessarily socially or emotionally equivalent) than their same-aged peers, and that social and emotional needs change with age. Fourth, we focus on promoting resiliency (hence achievement) through parent and teacher scaffolding approaches.

Referring to Figure 1.1, there are two general components that should be explained prior to introducing the framework in detail. Note the juxtaposition of "potential" (i.e., top-high achieving) with "performance" (i.e., bottom-underachieving). This is important because it is analogous to Gagné's DMGT model, in which, at any given point in a gifted person's life (i.e., childhood, adolescence, adulthood), all the com-ponents within the SESUG framework are coming together to promote or impede growth trajectories. Also embedded in the framework are the three arrows moving from left to right, these arrows that extend from top/bottom left to top/bottom right indicate patterns of growth, either up or down. It is also important to note here that patterns of growth are not linear. In other words, where one starts (e.g., identified at age 10 with IQ of 145) does not lead directly to "performance" or "developed talent"

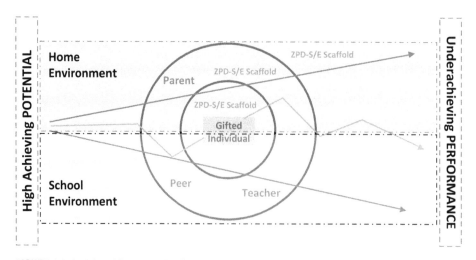

FIGURE 1.1 Social and Emotional Scaffolding in the Underachieving Gifted (SESUG).

in adulthood (DMGT; Gagné, 2004, 2012). The line in the center represents the asynchronous development characteristic of gifted individuals and often underachievers.

For the sake of organization, we will begin at the center of the framework and work outwards. First, from the ecological perspective, the gifted individual is at the heart of it all (i.e., intrapersonal characteristics), there is a dotted circle around the gifted individual to represent their movement in the world and their relationships and interactions with others (i.e., parents, teachers, peers – interpersonal characteristics). Beyond the parent, teacher, and peers, there is another dotted circle to represent contextual influences (i.e., home and school environments). To distinguish home and school, there is slight shading differentiation with each surrounded by a dotted rectangle to indicate how experiences are influential and move with an individual between home and school but can include outside experiences that are age-dependent (e.g., childhood-zoo outing, adolescent-school government, young adult-employment). In terms of the remaining aspect of the framework, there are three points where ZPD-S/E Scaffold appears. The placement of the ZPD-S/E Scaffold is relevant for three reasons. First, it captures how the framework is grounded in Vygotskian theory, using ZPD strategies. The S/E refers to the specific targets being geared toward social and emotional needs of the gifted underachiever. Last, it demonstrates the implementation of scaffolded practices that can be applied to meet unique needs at the intrapersonal level (i.e., autonomous interventions), the interpersonal level (i.e., pair, small group, whole group), and contextually (i.e., creating a space, classroom, or home climate). The scaffold refers to the process of figuring out the *who*, *what*, *when*, *how*, and *where* parents and teachers can provide social and emotional support[2] to underachieving individuals in ways that promote resiliency and higher levels of achievement while meeting social and emotional barriers or risk factors.

Understanding the Ecology and Development

Gifted underachievers have the potential, what is lacking is the demonstrated performance. Gifted students are intellectually and cognitively advanced, however, due to their often, asynchronous developmental patterns, it is advantageous to understand the situatedness of their current social and emotional states. This is because, many times, these issues are often the vulnerable zone where intrapersonal, interpersonal, and environmental factors intersect to put gifted students at risk for underachieving (Sonia, et al., 2018).

Holistic Understanding of Underachievement

Intrapersonal and interpersonal characteristics function independently but should be considered interwoven in how individuals interpret their experiences, respond, and react to opportunities; and develop (e.g., socially, emotionally). Intrapersonal skills are phenomenological in that they involve the ways an individual knows, understands, and interprets their own experiences (e.g., interest, self-regulation, self-efficacy). Intrapersonal characteristics are often difficult to know, observe, and understand about others, these are not universal characteristics, they are traits that vary across individuals and shape who they are and how they move through the world. In other words, they are subjective. This point is important because of the risks that manifest from the subjective lens that can be characteristic of gifted underachievers. For instance, gifted underachievers can demonstrate any of these characteristics with varying intensity:

perfectionism, curiosity, inquisitiveness, a desire to solve problems, need for challenges, boredom, fear of making mistakes and failure. They are prone to be resistive if they lack interest or do not understand the relevance of a task; and experience anxiety, depression, and can withdraw or disengage easily. They are often insecure, experience high levels of self-doubt, and typically can be hyper-critical of themselves and unfairly judge themselves.

Interpersonal characteristics reflect experiences constructed through interactions with others (e.g., parents, teachers), or between an individual and an object (e.g., book, movie, picture, music) (Vygotsky, 1978). For gifted students, and more so underachievers, these experiences must involve a demonstrated show of interest and understanding for and about the gifted individual. Underachievers have a strong need for safety, a sense of belonging, and trust from others; and they need to see that others genuinely care about them beyond their giftedness. Some of the interpersonal characteristics for underachieving gifted students may include lack of trusting others, fear of rejection, feeling like they do not fit in, viewing others as having high or unrealistic expectations of them, social awkwardness and difficulty finding friends who are like them. In groups, they can be nervous and feel pressure to perform, they are uncomfortable with closeness to others and can demonstrate inflexibility in collaborations. Often, they are impulsive, impatient, critical, and judgmental of others. Interpersonal-level relationships and interactions are complex and a large part of the individual differences that bring about differentiated teaching and learning, albeit at school, home, or the work environment. All individuals bring their own unique intrapersonal strengths and limitations to the experience, therefore a "one-size-fits-all" approach may be futile.

Gifted underachievers typically often lag in their overall social and emotional development, as can be seen in the overview of the intrapersonal and interpersonal characteristics. The environment or context (e.g., home, school) further adds to the complexity of social and emotional development. Among underachieving gifted individuals, the support that they get at home and school is essential when it comes to reaching their full potential. According to Fani and Ghaemi (2011), value and importance must be placed on the person-environment fit. Attention should be given to considering the nature, intent, and quality of interactions with gifted underachievers to promote cognitive growth while addressing asynchronous social and emotional development, using intentional and directed or targeted instructional strategies and supports (i.e., scaffolds) at home and in the classroom. It is most advantageous if the home and school environment are well aligned for stability and the need for continuity of the gifted underachiever. Parent and teachers' collaborations can be carefully planned and innovative to meet areas of resistance and weakness but must be specific to where the most need is warranted (Riedl-Cross and Cross, 2015).

Classroom and home environments can be changed or adapted; and activities can be incorporated to mitigate many of the social and emotional limitations for underachieving individuals. A common problem is the misalignment of home and school environments. This can be due to the culture of the home or the lack of instructional versatility or lack of teacher training in working with gifted individuals. Regardless of the reasons, understanding the nature of the misalignment can be life-changing as it will allow the parent and the teacher to communicate, plan, and sustain collaborations. Parents should be familiar with the curriculum and the teacher's method, style, and instructional practices. Likewise, teachers should be informed about the context of the home and their patterns and practices.

Zone of Proximal Development

Vygotsky (1978) proposed that intrapersonal, interpersonal, and contextual supports would promote cognitive growth, and the concept of scaffolding can be extended to support social and emotional growth and development (e.g., Morcom, 2014). Mainly, the focus is on promoting growth, resiliency, and well-being through innovative and intentional scaffolded supports orchestrated by others or involving the individual, interactions with others, and contextual modes. The use of ZPD here is intended to identify practices aside from standardized testing and evaluation to best help gifted underachievers. As times change, some educational thinking and practices persist; Vygotsky's intention in theorizing the ZPD was to avoid psychometric-based measures of ability (e.g., IQ) in Russian schools (Fani & Ghaemi, 2011). Importantly, IQ and other psychometric or standardized measures reflect performance, but the ZPD reflects an individual's potential (Kanevsky & Geake, 2004). In the present case of SESUG, we also rely on the influence of social interactions through scaffolding. In SESUG, the goal is to provide support in the social-emotional realm from a more knowledgeable, capable, and caring individual in the life of the gifted individual. In our case, we are focused on joint accommodations between teachers in the classroom and parents in home environments (e.g., Slovák et al., 2016).

Vygotsky (1978) explains the ZPD as, "the distance between the actual developmental level as determined by independent problem solving and the level of potential development as determined through problem solving under adult guidance or in collaboration with more capable peers" (p. 86). The key point about the ZPD is for the teacher or parent to identify the target or behavior they want to impact. It is the point between what a person can already do independently and what they should be able to do independently soon. Therefore, the ZPD is directly at the point in which an individual cannot perform a task independently, but they can perform it with the assistance of more knowledgeable others, such as parents and teachers. In the case of SESUG, there are a few caveats.

First, the involvement of others can mean direct overt interaction or as subtle and covert as decision making about activities, resources, or feedback for the individual (e.g., creating an opportunity, providing a graphic organizer, written praise, or recognition, creating a space).

Second, the notion of a zone seems rigid and difficult to conceptualize from a practical standpoint. We would argue that the zone is the opportunity or space to scaffold an individual by extending the life raft (so to speak); that sets them up for success as opposed to allowing them to fail. But it must be active and intentional. It is also important to keep in mind that mistakes and failure can be rich sources of learning opportunities. However, with gifted individuals, especially underachievers, there can be social and emotional barriers that prevent typical learning opportunities when it comes to making mistakes and experiencing failure due to the perfectionistic ways in which they may think. Therefore, being mindful and knowing when to create safe spaces for mistakes and failure on small and positively influential time points during scaffolding experiences are necessary.

Third, when parents and teachers work independently or collaboratively to identify the gifted student's social and emotional ZPD and begin to contemplate the scaffolding protocol, consideration should be taken to determine the target and scaffold for the individual based on where they are now. Caution should be taken to ensure there is enough information known to decide and plan. The ZPD and the corresponding scaffold should be realistic, attainable, and the most developmentally appropriate goal or behavior for that individual; and that will be desirable to and for the gifted underachiever. The underachieving individual's active voice is important to the success of everyone involved in the scaffolding intervention. In this way, ideally the intervention will involve input from parents, teachers, and the gifted student themselves.

Scaffolding

Scaffolding is a concept in Vygotsky's (1978) Sociocultural Theory, it is a process directly or indirectly initiated by others to create an opportunity or a space that enables a gifted underachiever to solve a problem, perform a task, or achieve a goal that is outside of their current level of comfort (Wood et al., 1976). When we apply the SESUG framework to gifted underachievers, the need could be intellectual, cognitive, social, or emotional; regardless, it is a hurdle in which the scaffold is intended to meet a social and/or emotional growth area and concludes successfully with independent task completion, increased efficacy, interest, engagement, and motivation; all of which can lead to higher academic performance (Piske et al., 2017; Siegle & McCoach, 2005; Snyder & Linnenbrink-Garcia, 2013).

Coming full circle in the explanation, scaffolding can take two forms: (1) a process that involves the more socially and emotionally knowledgeable and equipped model (i.e., parents, teachers, peers); and (2) as a process of self in which the underachiever self-scaffolds using tools from collaborations or from the context (Daniels, 2001). This is like autonomous learning, except there is a scaffold in place to temporarily assist the individual. It is also important to remember that gifted individuals may also apply their own intellectual gifts to seek out self-scaffolding tools to aid in this growth (Mueller, 2009).

Autonomous learning means the scaffolded interventions emphasize personal initiative, resourcefulness, and persistence during an activity; this is characterized by behaviors such as active and engaged participation, problem-solving, focusing on goals, determination and persistence to overcome barriers (Ponton & Carr, 2000). We believe that gifted students seek autonomous learning, but they still need support and to learn from that support. Scaffolding in this way requires that the opportunity or space be one that is student-centered; and includes the student's interests, allows for student choice, satisfies their need for inquisitiveness, involves creativity (i.e., thinking outside the box), is applicable to real-world issues that are relevant and meaningful to them, and is developmentally appropriate, and within their ZPD.

In thinking about self-scaffolding (i.e., autonomous learning), we think it is critical to consider when applied to gifted underachievers for a couple of reasons. First, it combines the ideas of collaborating with others (i.e., interpersonal) and the development of one's self (i.e., intrapersonal). Gifted students may be out of balance and require balance-like interventions (i.e., things they feel in control of), they have the cognitive potential to be autonomous but are somewhat reliant on others to acquire the social and emotional scaffolds to get them back on track and stay on track.

Utilizing Scaffolding Techniques with Underachieving Gifted

Before parents and teachers explore specific intervention strategies designed to help gifted students who are deemed to be underachieving, a few factors should be considered. First, it is important to first rule out other underlying issues that may be contributing to underachievement, especially in school. In school, it may be much easier to identify the potential-performance discrepancy (i.e., underachievement) as students most likely have an established history of assessments and/or performance evaluations that have been administered as a part of regular schooling. Specifically, parents and teachers will want to ensure that the gifted student is not considered "twice-exceptional" whereby giftedness may mask some underlying form of a learning disability (Reis & McCoach, 2000) or mental health issue (Winsor & Mueller, 2020). The school counselor and school psychologist should be consulted in these cases (Winsor & Mueller, 2020).

Second, determining exact causes for underachievement can be explored through administering different instruments. For example, much research supports that gifted student underachievement can often be traced back to issues of engagement, motivation, or other *intrapersonal* factors such as self-efficacy beliefs (McCoach & Siegle, 2018). The SAAS-R (McCoach & Siegle, 2003) is an example of one such empirically validated assessment that can provide useful information in these areas.

Finally, relatedly, outcome and context should be considered. For example, gifted underachievement may reflect passive-aggressive efforts on the part of the gifted student if they feel they are being pushed unfairly in school or in a direction that does not align with their interests or values (Reis & McCoach, 2000). Context applies to home environments pertaining to diversity regarding gender, socioeconomic status, race, ethnicity, disability, religion, geography, sexuality, and language. Diversity, equity, and inclusion topics matter in the lives of gifted students regardless of whether they are high-performing or underachieving. Despite research and initiatives to change the underrepresentation of minorities in gifted programs, not much has changed over the past 20 years (Payne, 2011; Rimm, 2008; Wiley, 2020). It is simple, the less we have minority students in gifted programs, the less we know how to be successful. However, SESUG emphasizes knowing the student at the individual level, in relationship to others, and within the context that they dwell.

Implications for Practice

In the SESUG framework, we have made some interpretations and provided explanations grounded in the research literature; we now reflect on the theory and turn to practice and implementation suggestions. We are focusing on social and emotional characteristics that pose specific barriers for underachieving gifted students' intentional or unintentional thwarting of their highest potential. Under the SESUG framework, it is important to identify the social and emotional ZPD and then to differentiate the instruction to scaffold these things. In applying the SESUG framework successfully, it is important to focus on four areas: (1) developing parent-student-teacher relationships; (2) collaborating with administration when additional resources, testing and training are needed; (3) using a team approach to include counselors or school psychologists; and (4) above all, knowing the student academically and personally, and inviting them to be a part of the planning process (e.g., setting personal goals).

Role of the Teacher

Underachieving gifted students are generally disengaged from school, they report feeling bored, underchallenged, complain about mundane repetition, and fail to complete many assignments compatible with their ability level. Therefore, school engagement and efforts to promote school engagement with underachieving gifted students are important, but complex (Godor & Szymanski, 2017).

Teacher-student relationships:

- Use dynamic-innovative-creative-activities to highlight strengths and apply effective strategies to weak areas (be malleable and flexible for best results). Try these general strategies: (1) know, understand, begin with the most challenging option first; (2) compacting when they already know the material, flexibility is key; (3) using extension activities, not just more work but intentional work that aligns with their cognitive ability and scaffolds social and emotional skills; (4) independent study/reading/research; (5) passion projects; (6) project-based activities; (7) inquiry learning; and (8) use of intentional grouping, not necessarily same ability, as there are instances for leadership with mixed ability grouping (e.g., peer tutoring).
- Include structured activities that are creative and involve choice to tap into interests and include multiple developmental levels (see Figure 1.2).
- Identify the ZPD and provide opportunities to develop it but have it fit within each student's social and emotional level, and cognitive ability. Use a tool to assist level of challenge (i.e., Bloom's Taxonomy 4, 5, 6 or Webb's Depth of Knowledge 3, 4) (see Figure 1.3). The rationale for using one framework over the other may depend on the goal and the need, as they are similar but different. Gifted underachievers may not be strong in all areas, so narrow the scope between deficits and attributes. Think about activities that interest them, give them choice and control in their learning.
- Use critical thinking and problem-solving geared toward hands-on engaging activities (Figure 1.4). These are some examples that can be adapted developmentally for different ages, and for individual, paired, or small group work. Use graphic organizers, rubrics, templates, visual aids (e.g., infographics); generate a digital dictionary (e.g., to challenge them, have them include the foreign language equivalent); have them conduct interviews with a role model, leader, inventor, or entrepreneur; create a game to play with others; conduct a self-evaluation by creating a word cloud with social and emotional attributes or make it a strength/weakness word cloud; create and present a live or animated story about social and emotional barriers with solutions to overcome them; create a webpage; create a YouTube video on how to make something, or write a how-to manual; critique a public debate; identify a real-world problem and lead a class debate on it; create a journal, daily reflection, or learning log; create an interactive historical timeline;

#	Standard or Objective	Entry Level	Intermediate Level	Most Challenging Level	Social/Emotional Barriers
	Literature				
1.2					
1.3					
1.4					
1.4					
1.4					
1.5					
1.5					

FIGURE 1.2 Developmentally tiered scaffolding organizer.

Taxonomy

1. **Remember** involves being able to recall, defining, or labelling.

2. **Understand** is to summarize or classify.

3. **Apply** requires some level of implementation or to follow a procedure.

4. **Analyze**, breaks down parts of a concept for deeper analysis.

5. **Evaluate** is critiquing or making a judgement based on research.

6. **Create** is to develop something new based on all the learning.

Depth of Knowledge

1. **Level 1 (Acquired knowledge)** involves recall and reproduction. Remembering facts or defining a procedure.

2. **Level 2 (Knowledge Application)** are skills and concepts. Students use learned concepts to answer questions.

3. **Level 3 (Analysis)** involves strategic thinking. Complexity increases here and involves planning, justification, and complex reasoning. Explains how concepts and procedures can be used to provide results.

4. **Level 4 (Augmentation)** is extended thinking. This requires going beyond the standard learning and asking, how else can the learning be used in real world contexts.

FIGURE 1.3 Determining challenging level.

Source: Bloom (1956), adapted from Anderson and Krathwohl (2001), Webb (1995).

create and run an imaginary island; create a travel brochure to your favorite destination and generate a budget for the trip; critique a book or movie; create a different ending for a book or movie; collect inspirational sayings and apply them to themselves; create a public service announcement for a billboard or a commercial; write a poem or song lyrics to express how they feel when they are sad or nervous; and ideas to overcome such feelings.

■ Avoid routine or repetitive or mundane activities, individuals can disengage.

■ Talk to students about their feelings, emotions, and attitudes toward activities.

■ Allow for choices, taking control away when it is not necessary can slow down forward progress.

■ Do not close the window on future development and maturity, convey essential skills in small attainable activities.

■ Provide as many different type of activity choices as possible:
  – Visual (e.g., advertisements, murals, greeting cards, flow charts, collage, diagram, graphic organizer, photo essay, portfolio, infographics, cartoons, scrapbooks).
  – Auditory (e.g., debates, panels, editorial, interviews, music, dictation).
  – Tactile-kinesthetic (e.g., acting things out, dance, games, learning centers, role playing, drawing/coloring, simulation games, rhythmic patterns, inventions, exhibits, demonstration, collecting something).
  – Technology (e.g., slide show, website, blog, digital research or game, free applications Pinterest, podcast, animation tools, movies).

■ Optimal approach is collaboration: student-parent-teacher:
  – Communicate parent-parent, parent-child, parent-teacher, teacher-child.
  – Caution, do not allow avoidance of responsibilities. It is more about the approaches and strategies to ensure they do not make underachieving an art form!

Example of Math Scaffolding			
Standard	What is the current performance?	What supports are needed? What scaffold can I put in place?	How far can the extension be realistic?
State-##	Ready to learn about polynomials.	• Naming • Simplifying • Multiplying Provide worksheet with three levels. Have the student begin with the most challenging level, and work backwards	Multiplying polynomials.
Example of Money as an Extension Activity			
State-##	Beyond introduction to money. Move to: • Count money • Give change	• Slide template • Graphic organizer • Digital resources Provide content in all three formats, allow them to choose or have them begin with the most difficult task first	• History of bartering money. • Foreign currency • Conversion to U.S.
Example of Inventions			
State-##	Ready to learn about inventions and how they evolve from societal needs	• Teacher-Student conferencing • Peer conferencing • Scientific process instructions • Rubric/template for final project Provide discussion opportunities Determine frequency for each student	• Research societal need • Research possible solutions to the need • Explore invention prototypes • Test prototypes • Create and share

Note. Examples adapted from Winebrenner & Brulles (2012).

FIGURE 1.4 Innovative extension examples.

– Balance opportunities and experiences, it can be good to challenge them once in a while with things they may not enjoy.
– Integrate subject and creative experiences and outlets.
– Support their positive and negative expression.

Social and Emotional Scaffolding

■ Support positive and negative preferences and emotions:
■ Help them understand the benefits of winning and losing.
■ Talk through pros/cons in decision-making processes.
■ Share positive and negative stories and outcomes.

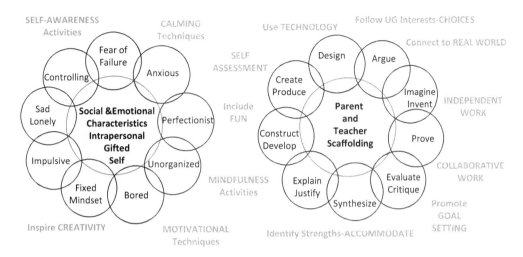

FIGURE 1.5 Scaffolding techniques for social and emotional needs.

■ Identify and use resources and experiences that demonstrate balance through assimilation and accommodation (i.e., technology supports this well).

■ Model compromising and other problem-solving skills during conflicts with others or internal struggles.

■ Engage them by making schoolwork unique, challenging, and fun to meet their strengths.

■ Make creative activities adaptable to academic work.

■ Life skills and soft skills can help them understand their comfort level and ability to be competitive and have fun.

■ Expose them to winning and losing, so they learn what motivates (i.e., intrinsic, extrinsic) them to work hard, achieve, and accomplish goals.

■ Expose them to knowing and understanding what they like and do well at versus what they do not like and do not excel at (see Figure 1.5).

Role of the Parent

Many of the ideas and practices for scaffolding from the teacher scaffolding apply to parents in the home environment and can easily be adapted for outside the classroom. However, this list applies to the home environment specifically.

■ Educate yourself about underachieving gifted students (i.e., books, websites, pamphlets, scholarly literature, others with UG children); do your research and ask questions. Being an informed advocate for your gifted child is one of the most important things you can do to help them achieve their potential!

■ Develop and sustain a strong parent-child relationship, encourage open and non-judgmental discourse.

■ Demonstrate problem-solving skills for social challenges with siblings and peers; and emotional challenges that face underachieving gifted individuals.

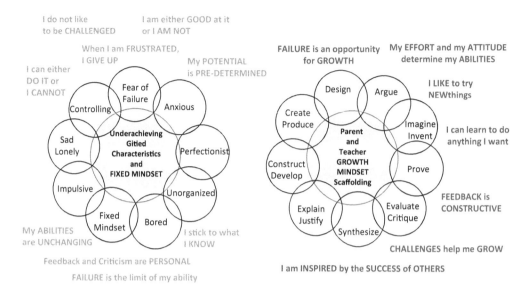

FIGURE 1.6 Factors contributing to underachievment.

- Observe your child's coping skills, be flexible when they are overwhelmed (i.e., realistic expectations should consider the situation and contexts). Encourage breathing exercises, meditation, and reflection to help with perspective-taking.

- Be conscious of the mental health of your child (e.g., depressed, anxious, suicidal). Know when to reach out for help from professionals.

- Model a growth mindset, it is not uncommon for UG individuals to possess a fixed mindset (see Figure 1.6). The mindset of a parent can directly impact their child and can influence ideas, attitudes, and behaviors (e.g., positive thinking, persistence, productivity).

- Cultivate intrinsic passions and desires, help them explore their interests through engagement in extracurricular activities. Encourage and support their passions.

- Be mindful of their chronological age, despite high achievement.

- Provide consistency in expectations and discipline within parenting and across all parents (i.e., both parents or in the case of blended families all parents and step-parents).

- Balance parental control and UG individual autonomy and independence (i.e., developmentally appropriate).

- Incorporate family rules as opposed to individual rules.

- Seek support of others more knowledgeable.

- Avoid self-doubt about your parenting skills, develop confidence that you have done several things well. When UG children observe you second-guessing yourself, this can risk introducing instability and disequilibrium into their life.

Social and Emotional Scaffolding

- Scaffold with collaborations with the teacher, provide resources and opportunities but do not do their work; it does not make you a bad parent.

- Practice acceptance, empathy, and understanding.

- Conduct regular check-ins and ask questions about their day and what they are learning. Encouraging them to rehearse what they learned is another level of knowing, understanding, and learning. They will feel worthwhile, important, and empowered.

- Model intrinsic passion, and enjoyment of doing something because it makes you feel good about yourself and makes the world a better place. Have them join you so they can see if they love it too!

- Help them set realistic goals using some of the suggestions from information provided for teachers, these are adaptable for parents and in home environments.

- Provide opportunities to interact with others that can be positive influences.

- Reflect with your UG child about what they need and what you need. Written contracts can be a good source of accountability for everyone. This is an ongoing process as your child and you change, and environments change.

- Be proud and supportive of your child's creativity and unique characteristics within reason. If you embrace and guide them, someday they will thank you; and like who they have become.

- Scaffold them with ownership, empowerment, facilitate confidence. Help them learn to be resourceful.

- Avoid routines.

Conclusion

There are many twists and turns that can emerge from the intersection of intrapersonal, interpersonal, contextual, and developmental factors (e.g., Mueller & Winsor, 2018), and it is the intersection of these both inside and outside of traditional classrooms that should be considered when examining underachievement among the gifted.

The Social and Emotional Scaffolding of the Underachieving Gifted (SESUG) framework represents the scope of where and how the literature supports (see Steenbergen-Hu et al., 2020) a trajectory of growth and development from potential to performance involving the context (i.e., home and school), interaction with others (i.e., parents, teachers, peers), and self-growth (i.e., socially, and emotionally). ZPD scaffolding for social-emotional development provides a useful and effective strategy at any point along the developmental continuum for gifted students; at any given time, there is a range of possibilities for achievement/underachievement, and much of this will depend upon the assistance given by parents and teachers.

Being successful with gifted underachievers should involve techniques and strategies that go beyond traditional norms to meet the individual where they are experiencing their resistance (i.e., contradictory to the one-size-fits-all perspective). Scaffolding practices that involve the autonomous self, interactions with others, and take into consideration diversity, individual differences, and contextual factors will provide the most effective approaches to minimizing asynchronous development by targeting developmentally appropriate practices involving gifted students' social and emotional well-being (see Mueller & Winsor, 2018). This type of collaboration with the schools is important and reflected in the SESUG framework. It is a powerful stance about the value and importance of parents and teachers who care about and work daily to help gifted students achieve to their highest potential.

REFLECTION QUESTIONS

1. Describe and discuss the intrapersonal characteristics of an underachieving gifted individual with whom you are familiar. How do these characteristics manifest in their social and emotional well-being?

2. Describe and discuss the interpersonal characteristics of an underachieving gifted individual with whom you are familiar. How do these characteristics manifest in their social and emotional well-being?

3. Explain some of the complexities of environment and its role in underachievement for gifted individuals.

4. Describe (list and explain) three potential scenarios/situations that demonstrate the complex nature of creating environments, spaces, and opportunities.

5. Explain why context matters when parents and teachers set out to scaffold the social and emotional well-being of gifted students who underachieve.

6. Contemplate the scaffolding strategies presented in this chapter. Reflect on two teacher activities/strategies or two parent activities/strategies that can promote social and emotional well-being. Cast a critical eye over each activity or strategy you selected and critique the pros and cons of the activity or strategy.

7. Different from questions 1 and 2, craft a brief vignette describing an underachieving gifted student with whom you are familiar (i.e., demographic information, interpersonal skill, intrapersonal skill, contextual/environmental factors, etc.). Develop a scaffolding plan and/or activity to address the situation you have described.

8. Think of the characteristics and manifestation of talents for gifted students from at least two different age groups that may show signs of underachievement (e.g., 2–4, 4–6, 6–10, 10–13, 14–16, 17–20). In a table, highlight their similarities and differences (compare and contrast). Explain how the scaffolding plan outlined in question 6 (or another that you have used) would be adjusted to offer strategies appropriate for each age group.

Notes

1 Mueller and Winsor (2018) labeled this the "P-E double-whammy" whereby academic environment and individual academic and developmental needs are mismatched in ways that lead to academic and social-emotional struggles for gifted students.

2 We acknowledge that our conception of applying Vygotsky's notion of the ZPD to social-emotional development goes beyond his original intention in that the ZPD is typically applied to cognitive development in individuals.

References

Anderson, L.W. and Krathwohl, D. R. (2001). *A taxonomy for learning, teaching, and assessing: A revision of Bloom's taxonomy of educational objectives.* Allyn & Bacon.

Bloom, B. S. (1956). *Taxonomy of educational objectives: The cognitive domain.* McKay Co.

Bronfenbrenner, U. (1979). *The ecology of human development: Experiments by nature and design.* Harvard University Press.

Bronfenbrenner, U. (2005). The biological theory of human development. In *Making human beings human: Bioecological perspectives on human development* (pp. 3–15). SAGE Publications.

Collins, K. H., Coleman, M. R., & Grantham, T. C. (2022). A bioecological perspective of emotional/behavioral challenges for gifted students of color: Support needed vs. Support received. *Journal of Emotional and Behavioral Disorders*, *30*(2), 86–95. https://doi.org/10.1177/10634266221076466

Covington, M. V. (1992). *Making the grade: A self-worth perspective on motivation and school reform.* Cambridge University Press.

Daniels, H. (2001) *Vygotsky and pedagogy*. Routledge/Falmer.

Dweck, C. (2006). *Mindset: The new psychology of success*. Random House.

Eccles, J. S., Midgley, C., Wigfield, A., Buchanan, C. M., Reuman, D., Flanagan, C., & MacIver, D. (1993). Development during adolescence: The impact of stage-environment fit on young adolescents' experiences in schools and in families. *American Psychologist*, *48*(2), 90–101. https://doi-org.ezproxy.memphis.edu/10.1037/0003-066X.48.2.90

Fani, T., & Ghaemi, F. (2011). Implications of Vygotsky's zone of proximal development in teacher education: ZPTD and self-scaffolding. *Procedia Social and Behavioral Sciences*, *29*, 1549–1554. https://doi.org/10.1016/j.sbspro.2011.11.396

Gagné, F. (2004). An imperative, but, alas, improbable consensus! *Roeper Review*, *27*(1), 12–14.

Gagné, F. (2012). The DMGT 2.0: From gifted inputs to talented outputs. In C. M. Callahan & H. L. Hertberg-Davis (Eds.), *Fundamentals of gifted education: Considering multiple perspectives* (pp. 56–68). Routledge.

Godor, B. P. & Szymanski, A. (2017). Sense of belonging or feeling marginalized? Using PISA 2012 to assess the state of academically gifted students. *High Ability Students*, *28*(2), 81–197. https://doi.org/10.1080/13598139.2017.1319343

Hunt, D. E. (1975). Person-environment interaction: A challenge found wanting before it was tried. *Review of Educational Research*, *45*, 209–230.

Kanevsky, L., & Geake, J. (2004). Inside the zone of proximal development: Validating a multifactor model of learning potential with gifted students and their peers. *Journal for the Education of the Gifted*, *28*(2), 182–217. https://doi.org/10.1177/016235320402800204

McCoach, D. B., & Siegle, D. (2003). The School Attitude Assessment Survey-Revised: A new instrument to identify academically able students who underachieve. *Educational and Psychological Measurement*, *63*(3), 414–429.

McCoach, D. B., & Siegle, D. (2018). Underachievers. In J. A. Plucker & C. M. Callahan (Eds.). *Critical issues and practices in gifted education: What the research says* (2nd ed.). Prufrock Press Inc.

Morcom, V. (2014). Scaffolding social and emotional learning in an elementary classroom community: A sociocultural perspective. *International Journal of Educational Research*, *67*, 18–29. https://doi.org/10.1016/j.ijer.2014.04.002

Mueller, C. E. (2009). Protective factors as barriers to depression in gifted and non-gifted adolescents. *Gifted Child Quarterly*, *53*, 3–14. https://doi.org/10.1177/0016986208326552

Mueller, C. E. & Winsor, D. L. (2018). Depression, suicide, and giftedness: Disentangling risk factors, protective factors, and implications for optimal growth. In S. I. Pfeiffer (Ed.), *Handbook of giftedness in children* (2nd ed.; pp. 255–284). Springer International Publishing. https://doi.org/10.1007/978-3-319-77004-8_15

Obergriesser, S., & Stoeger, H. (2015). The role of emotions, motivation, and learning behavior in underachievement and results of an intervention. *High Ability Studies*, *26*(1), 167–190. http://dx.doi.org/10.1080/13598139.2015.1043003

Payne, A. (2011). *Equitable access for underrepresented students in gifted education*. The George Washington University Center for Equity and Excellence in Education.

Piske, F.H.R., Collins, K.H., & Arnstein, K. (Eds.). (2022). *Servicing twice-exceptional students: Socially, emotionally, and culturally framing learning exceptionalities*. Springer Nature.

Piske, F. H. R., Stoltz, T., Guérios, E., de Camargo, D., Vestena, C. L. B., de Freitas, S. P., de Oliveira Machado Barby, A. A., & Santinello, J. (2017). The importance of teacher training for development of gifted students' creativity: Contributions of Vygotsky. *Creative Education*, *8*, 131–141. http://dx.doi.org/10.4236/ce.2017.81011

Ponton, M. K., & Carr, P. B. (2000). Understanding and promoting autonomy in self-directed learning. *Current Research in Social Psychology*, *5*(19), 271–284.

Ramos, A., Lavrijsen, J., Soenens, B., Vansteenkiste, M., Sypré, S., & Verschueren, K. (2021). Profiles of maladaptive school motivation among high-ability adolescents: A person-centered exploration of the motivational pathways to underachievement model. *Journal of Adolescence*, *88*, 146–161. https://doi-org.ezproxy.memphis.edu/10.1016/j.adolescence.2021.03.001

Reis, S. M., & McCoach, D. B. (2000). The underachievement of gifted students: What do we know and where do we go? *Gifted Child Quarterly*, *44*(3), 152–170. https://doi-org.ezproxy.memphis.edu/10.1177/001698620004400302

Riedl-Cross, J., & Cross, T. (2015). Clinical and mental health issues in the counseling the gifted individual. *Journal of Counseling & Development*, *93*, 163–172. hhttps://doi.org/10.1002/j.1556-6676.2015.00192.x

Schultz, R. A. (2010). Illuminating realities: A phenomenological view from two underachieving gifted learners. *Roeper Review*, *24*(4), 2003–2012.

Seligman, M. E. P. & Csikszentmihalyi, M. (2000). Positive psychology: An introduction. *American Psychologist*, *55*, 5–14. doi:10.1007/978-94-017-9088-8_18

Siegle, D., & McCoach, D. B. (2005). Making a difference: Motivating gifted students who are not achieving. *Teaching Exceptional Children*, *38*(1), 22–27.

Silverman, L. K. (1997). The construct of asynchronous development. *Peabody Journal of Education*, *72*(3–4), 36–58.

Silverman, L. K. (2002). Asynchronous development. In M. Neihart, S. M. Reis, N. M. Robinson, & S. M. Moon (Eds.), *The social and emotional development of gifted children: What do we know?* (pp. 31–37). Prufrock Press.

Slovák, P., Rowan, K., Frauenberger, C., Gilad-Bachrach, R., Doces, M., Smith, B., ... & Fitzpatrick, G. (2016, February). Scaffolding the scaffolding: Supporting children's social-emotional learning at home. In *Proceedings of the 19th ACM Conference on Computer-Supported Cooperative Work & Social Computing* (pp. 1751–1765). https://doi.org/10.1145/2818048.2820007

Snyder, K. E. & Linnenbrink-Garcia, L. (2013). A developmental, person-centered approach to exploring multiple motivational pathways in gifted underachievement. *Educational Psychologist*, *48*(4), 209–228. doi:10.1080/00461520.2013.835597

Snyder, K. E., & Wormington, S.V. (2020). Gifted underachievement and achievement motivation: The promise of breaking silos. *Gifted Child Quarterly*, *64*(2), 63–66. doi:10.1177/0016986220909179

Sonia, L. J., White, L. J., & Graham, S. B. (2010). Why do we know so little about the factors associated with gifted underachievement? A systematic literature review. *Educational Research Review*, *24*, 55–66. https://doi.org/10.1016/j.edurev.2018.03.001

Steenbergen-Hu, S., Olszewski-Kubilius, P., & Calvert, E. (2020). The effectiveness of current interventions to reverse the underachievement of gifted students: Findings of a meta-analysis and systematic review. *Gifted Child Quarterly*, *64*(2), 132–165. doi:10.1177/0016986220908601

Vygotsky, L. S. (1978). *Mind in society: The development of higher psychological processes*. Harvard University Press.

Webb, N. (1995). Criteria for alignment of expectations and assessments on mathematics and science education. *Research Monograph Number, 6*(1), 126–142.

Wigfield, A., Tonks, S., & Klauda, S. L. (2009). Expectancy-value theory. In K. R. Wentzel, & D. B. Miele (Eds.), *Handbook of motivation at school* (pp. 69–90). Routledge.

Wiley, K. R. (2020). The social and emotional world of gifted students: Moving beyond the label. *Psychology in Schools*, *57*, 1528–1541. doi:10.1002/pits.22340

Winebrenner, S. & Brulles, D. (2012). *Teaching gifted kids in today's classroom: Strategies and techniques every teacher can use*. Free Spirit.

Winsor, D. L., & Mueller, C. E. (2020). Depression, suicide, and the gifted student: A primer for the school psychologist. *Psychology in the Schools* (Special Issue): *Serving Gifted and Talented Students in the Schools: Opportunities for School Psychology*, *57*(10), 1627–1639. https://doi.org/10.1002/pits.22416

Wood, D. J., Bruner, J. S., & Ross, G. (1976). The role of tutoring in problem solving. *Journal of Child Psychiatry and Psychology*, *17*(2), 89–100. https://doi.org/10.1111/j.1469-7610.1976.tb00381.x

Underachievement of Gifted Learners in School

Keri M. Guilbault and Kimberly M. McCormick

Introduction

High intelligence does not always guarantee achievement or success in school. As noted in the Introduction and Chapter 1, gifted learners who persistently exhibit a severe discrepancy between their perceived potential (as measured by standardized achievement tests, tests of cognitive ability, or intelligence tests) and their actual performance (as measured by grades in school) are often referred to as underachievers. Some populations of advanced learners may be at a greater risk for underachievement in school due to additional learning differences or disabilities, linguistic or cultural differences, or the effects of poverty. These students may be forced to underachieve because the environment in which they attend school lacks appropriate funding, resources, trained teachers of the gifted, and services for advanced learners. Underachievement can have detrimental consequences for the individual and constitutes a loss of talent for society.

Underachievement affects gifted students across all socioeconomic, racial, ethnic, and geographic groups (Cavilla, 2017; Matthews & McBee, 2007). The term *underachiever* carries with it the notion that there is a relative expectation of some specific level of achievement for the individual based on their measured *potential*. In contrast, the term *overachiever* implies a student has exceeded that potential. These constructs are based on the expectations of others projected onto the individual student. One's perception of achievement or underachievement is influenced by bias, experiences, and personal beliefs of what content or goals are valuable to achieve in the first place. It is important to understand how to recognize signs of underachievement and how educators and adults in a child's life can intervene to reverse this behavior before it is too late. This chapter focuses on the literature on the social and emotional issues of the daily lives of gifted underachievers in school and practical implications for educators. As action researchers, educators and counselors may use this information to guide their work to address underachievement in their classrooms and schools.

DOI: 10.4324/9781003369578-4

Definitions of Key Terms in the Literature

Siegle (2013) stated: "Underachievement is among the most frustrating and bewildering education issues parents and educators face" (p. 1). It can be troublesome and confusing for adults when a gifted learner's high scores on tests of intelligence or ability do not result in good grades, engagement in class, or other forms of academic achievement. Educators may wonder, "How can this student be gifted with grades like this?" Classifying gifted learners as underachievers can be challenging because of the varying definitions of underachievement as well as different definitions of giftedness. To understand which students we are referring to, recent literature provides an overview of common terminology.

Gifted

There is not one universally adopted definition of *gifted*. Definitions include reference to scores on standardized tests of intelligence, academic achievement, leadership, creativity, or performance in fine or performing arts. The definition of a gifted learner may have an impact on the services an individual student receives and can potentially have the unintended consequence of keeping underachieving gifted students out of programs for the gifted.

According to the National Association for Gifted Children, "Gifted individuals are those who demonstrate outstanding levels of aptitude (defined as exceptional ability to reason and learn) or competence (documented performance or achievement in top 10% or rarer) in one or more domains" (2010). Gifted learners are found in all schools and come from all backgrounds. Another frequently used definition addresses asynchronous development often found in gifted and twice exceptional students. The Columbus Group (1991) defined giftedness as follows:

> Giftedness is asynchronous development in which advanced cognitive abilities and heightened intensity combine to create inner experiences and awareness that are qualitatively different from the norm. This asynchrony increases with higher intellectual capacity. The uniqueness of the gifted renders them particularly vulnerable and requires modifications in parenting, teaching, and counseling for them to develop optimally.

Underachievement

Underachievement has long been defined in the literature as a discrepancy between ability and achievement (Emerick, 1988; McCoach & Siegle, 2003; Reis & McCoach, 2000; Snyder et al., 2019). This may be observed through classroom performance such as poor or even average grades, and high ability or intelligence test scores. Emerick (1988) suggested several discrepancy combination models that provide helpful guidance for identification:

- high IQ score and low achievement test scores;
- high IQ score and low grades;
- high achievement test scores and low grades;
- high indicators of intellectual, creative potential and low creative productivity; or
- high indicators of potential and limited presence of appropriate opportunities for intellectual and creative development.

Overt and Covert Underachievers

Mofield and Parker Peters (2019) suggested that underachievers may be *overt* and easily recognizable to educators by their poor grades or work habits, or they may be *covert* underachievers, such as gifted students who choose not to pursue rigorous coursework. Adults must be proactive in screening for underachievement among gifted learners with covert behaviors otherwise they may slip through the cracks.

Selective Consumers

Some scholars have distinguished between underachievers and *selective consumers*, or students who perform well in subjects in which they have a particular interest, and perform poorly in other areas (Figg et al., 2012; Galbraith & Delisle, 2015). These scholars posit that selective consumers should not be viewed as underachievers. Peters (2012) offered a possible explanation for selective consumerism. According to Peters, a perceptual disconnect between content that an educator deems valuable and worthy of achievement may not align with a selective consumer's interests and motivation. As Peters (2012) stated:

> If a student in my classroom does not value what I am teaching (content) or see a reason to achieve in this particular area (relevance), then he or she is likely to underachieve regardless of my teaching style (process). This is the very heart of the expectancy-value theory (Wigfield, 1994; Wigfield & Eccles, 2000).
>
> *(p. 177)*

Twice (and Thrice) Exceptional Learners

Students with both gifts and disabilities are referred to as *twice exceptional*. Sometimes students who underachieve have an undiagnosed learning disability. If the discrepancy between performance and ability is the result of a disability, whether it is diagnosed or undiagnosed, these students are not considered to be underachievers. In identifying students as underachievers, it is therefore important to look at the root causes of the student's behavior and accomplishments, or lack thereof.

Davis and Robinson (2018) conceptualized the term *thrice exceptional* ("3e"). They define 3e students as "gifted children and youth from a cultural minority group who also have a disabling condition" (p. 278). Furthering this work and utilizing a multiculturalism lens, Collins (2021) asserted that gifted, cognitive disabilities, and cultural minority groups are all socially constructed – influenced and shaped by society, and must be addressed accordingly; she introduced a 3e model that illuminates the intersectionality of giftedness, other learning exceptionalities and cultural exceptionalities within the overarching macroculture of the larger society. She contended that whenever a student's presence within a certain environment represents a distinct culture that is not common, valued, or is in conflict with dominant social norms, then that culture also becomes an exceptionality adding to the complexity of their development. For example, Collins (2020) noted that gifted Black students with disabilities occupy a space in gifted education where non-Black teachers and peers may find it hard to understand their positionality and experiences in American society, compelling those students to "combat racial microaggression from peers, teachers, and so on, who maintain stereotypes about their disability and racial identity" (p. 5).

Collins and Johnson (2021) posit that every gifted student from a culturally under-represented group is inherently a 2e learner, and when all three exceptionalities are present, they should more accurately be referred to as 3e with appropriate accommodations and additional support services provided. In addition, Piske et al. (2022) offer a comprehensive view of 2e and 3e that extends beyond the historical cognitive discussion to include a bioecological framework that is appropriate to explore the social, emotional, and cultural contextual factors for underachievement as a consequence of lack of identification, underrepresentation, and being underserved. Thrice exceptional students require different teaching strategies to develop their gifts and talents, collaboration between family and school, and teacher competencies in addressing barriers to identification and service. Thrice exceptional learners may become selective consumers or underachieve in schools if there is a lack of understanding of cultural differences and respect for diversity. Training for educators is therefore needed on building trusting relationships with students, identifying and acknowledging bias, recognizing diverse gifted learner characteristics across cultures and backgrounds, and addressing causes of underachievement through a strengths-based approach with high expectations.

Review of the Literature

One challenge with research on gifted underachievers is the lack of consistency on how underachievement among the gifted is defined. Problems exist with the identification of gifted underachievers as well, which may impact the results of studies found in the literature (White et al., 2018). There could be many missing gifted underachievers in published research studies because they are either not identified as gifted due to their low achievement, or they may have been dismissed from gifted services once underachievement patterns set in. It is important to keep this in mind when reviewing results of relevant research.

Scholars have examined the prevalence of underachievement, causes of underachievement, sex differences, and to a lesser extent, interventions to reverse underachievement. Individual, family, and school-related factors are discussed in the literature as contributing factors to the underachievement of students who are gifted. By understanding common characteristics and causes of underachievement, educators can better identify and serve this group of at-risk students in their classrooms.

Traits and Prevalence

A wealth of research has provided insight on traits and characteristics of gifted underachievers (Matthews & McBee, 2007; McCoach & Siegle, 2003; Reis & McCoach, 2000; Seeley, 1993). Just as the gifted are not a homogeneous group, neither are underachievers. Below is a list of common signs of underachievement:

- low self-concept, low self-efficacy, or low self-esteem;
- decreased levels of motivation;
- sudden drop in grades;
- negative attitudes toward school or adults;
- lack of appropriate academic risk-taking;

- selection of less rigorous coursework;
- lack of perseverance or task commitment;
- lack of enthusiasm or interest;
- sense of social isolation or sudden withdrawal from peer groups.

Gifted underachievers may have low self-concept in contrast to their achieving gifted peers. This is especially true for academic and social self-concept (Baker et al., 1998; Mofield & Parker Peters, 2019; Ritchotte et al., 2014). It is unclear whether this lower self-concept is a result of or a precursor to underachievement. Personality differences between gifted underachievers and gifted achievers has also been noted in the literature over the last several decades. Some studies describe gifted underachievers as being more emotionally sensitive, hostile, aggressive, and less persistent than their achieving gifted peers (Rimm & Lowe, 1988; Siegle, 2013). These students may also have weaker executive functioning skills, such as organization, time management, and lack motivation (McCoach et al., 2020).

Research has consistently shown that gifted students who underachieve may be at risk for dropping out of school and a significant percentage of gifted students perform below their academic potential (Bennett-Rappell & Northcote, 2016; Seeley, 1993). Some researchers have reported that as many as 50%t of gifted learners may be underachieving or considered at risk of failing (Bennett-Rappell & Northcote, 2016). Others suggest that up to 20% of dropouts are gifted (Matthews, 2006; Matthews, 2009; Renzulli & Park, 2000; Rimm, 2008).

Studies have also revealed sex differences related to gifted underachievers. Male gifted students are significantly more likely to be identified as underachievers than their female gifted peers (Desmet et al., 2020; Desmet & Pereira, 2022; Matthews & McBee, 2007; Rubenstein et al., 2012; Siegle & McCoach, 2005). Issues with underachievement tend to emerge by late elementary school, therefore interventions must start as early as primary years of schooling.

Causes of Underachievement

Why do some gifted learners underachieve? There is a lack of consensus in the field on the root causes of underachievement of gifted learners; however, several possible contributing factors are discussed in the literature. These include interpersonal factors and social relationships, environmental factors including a lack of a challenging curriculum, psychological issues such as perfectionism, undiagnosed learning disabilities, lack of motivation, and low teacher expectations. A combination of these family, school, and interpersonal factors may lead to underachievement (Figure 2.1).

Interpersonal Factors

Several interpersonal factors are referenced in the literature including motivation, perfectionism, beliefs about the nature of one's intelligence, self-concept, and self-efficacy. A brief description of each of these factors is given in this section.

- *Motivation.* While much research exists that suggests gifted students who underachieve may do so out of boredom or lack of motivation, Snyder et al. (2013) offer an alternative reason for underachievement based on social-cognitive motivational theories. They suggest that gifted underachievers may be maladaptively motivated

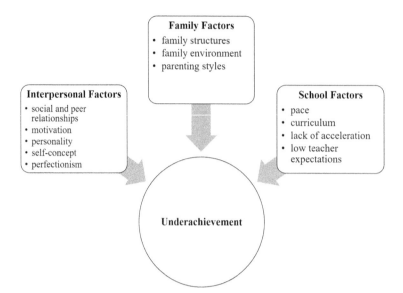

FIGURE 2.1 Causes of underachievment.

or "motivated in a way that fosters beliefs or behaviors that undermine academic achievement" (p. 231). In their 2013 study of 108 undergraduate students who had been identified as gifted during their K–12 schooling, the researchers investigated how messaging about intelligence as either mixed or malleable impacted students' implicit beliefs about their giftedness and how they interpreted their experiences with failure. Results from their study indicated that gifted students who perceived threats to their self-worth engaged in protective behaviors through different coping mechanisms including *self-handicapping*. The authors referred to this as an intentional act to self-sabotage or create an obstacle to provide an "a priori excuse or potential failure so that failure can be attributed to the handicap rather than to low ability (Berglas & Jones, 1978; Rhodewalt, 1994)" (p. 231).

■ *Perfectionism and beliefs about intelligence.* Siegle et al. (2020) explored the connection between underachievement and perfectionism, a need for cognitive challenge, and how engagement factors into learning. Their work showed positive findings for selecting interventions that connect to theories of learning such as self-regulation and achievement goal theory. Mofield and Parker Peters (2019) investigated differences between fixed and growth mindsets, types of perfectionism, and achievement attitudes among 264 gifted middle school students. For this study, the researchers used *The School Attitude Assessment Survey–Revised* (SAAS-R) (McCoach, 2000) to measure student achievement attitudes, the Mindset Assessment Profile Tool (Mindset Works, 2012) to measure students' beliefs about the malleability of intelligence, attitude toward effort, attitude toward mistakes, and belief about the importance of learning, and the Goals and Work Habits Survey (Schuler, 1994) to measure perfectionism. In this study, underachievers within their sample showed they may value a given task but did not necessarily want to put forth effort to achieve the goal. Implications for teachers included the need to address self-regulation and motivation by providing explicit guidance to underachievers so they could understand that short-term work (like homework) can be a means to a greater goal (like grades). Teachers can provide guidance on self-regulation skills, chunk assignments, help students break down tasks into smaller steps, plan for obstacles, and model strategies for coping.

■ *Self-concept.* Gifted students who underachieve are often characterized as also suffering from low academic self-concept. Underachieving gifted learners may display lower levels of self-motivation and are less goal-oriented which leads to dependence on others (teachers, peers, parents, for example) for their learning, according to Ruban and Reis (2006).

■ *Self-efficacy.* Research has revealed a positive relationship between self-efficacy and student academic performance (Robbins et al., 2004; Zientek & Thompson, 2010). Self-efficacy, or a student's belief in their ability to perform a particular activity, has been studied in relation to gifted underachievers. Students with high self-efficacy are more likely to take risks in their learning, persist with tasks, and persevere when faced with challenges (Lyman et al., 1984). Students who hold positive attitudes in self-efficacy, task meaningfulness and environmental perceptions may set more realistic goals for themselves and learn to self-regulate to accomplish those goals (Ruban & Reis, 2006). Strategies to reverse underachievement for the gifted may therefore require addressing student self-efficacy. Recent literature relates this to mindsets about the malleability of intelligence and how gifted learners perceive their own skills and how they attribute their success or failure (Rubenstein et al., 2012).

Environmental Factors

Besides interpersonal factors, there are external factors that may contribute to the development of underachievement in gifted learners. A few of these environmental factors include family dynamics or home environment and the school environment:

■ *Family.* Students can experience challenges at home and at school that may lead to underachievement. Lack of structure and stability at home and parenting styles that are authoritarian or those that are too permissive may lead to student underachievement (Garn et al., 2010). Family models and their impact on gifted learner achievement have been studied for the past four decades. Rimm and Lowe (1988) noted family structure and family environment as playing a role in development of underachieving behavior among the gifted. They stated that family environments of gifted underachievers lack structure, are more disorganized and have unclear guidelines about behavior and academic expectations. In Peterson's (2001) study of underachievers, students noted negative life influences that played a role in their behavior. This included having under-involved adults in their lives, feeling misunderstood by adults, and gaining unwelcome attention. Reversal of this underachievement resulted from developmental changes such as maturity and moving away from home after graduation. Student perceptions of events at school and home and the nature of adults' expectation and support (or lack thereof), can have an impact on the academic achievement, behaviors, and attitudes of gifted learners.

■ *School.* A lack of a challenging curriculum or accelerated content, pace that is too slow, and a lack of the use of strategies such as curriculum compacting can leave a gifted learner under-stimulated and unchallenged. Students must find tasks meaningful and valuable, or they may lack interest and motivation. As adults, we can relate to this when we think about our own work and interests. Students are no different but lack control over their environment and classroom curriculum. Too often, students are not provided choice in what they learn, how they learn, or how they show what they have learned. The student who becomes bored may act out, avoid school, or worse. The gifted student who is unable to self-advocate may develop patterns of negative behavior that contribute to a drop in grades, self-esteem, and avoidance.

■ *Low teacher expectations* can be another factor that leads to or fosters underachievement in gifted learners. This may be a particular concern for special populations of gifted students such as gifted students of color and twice-exceptional learners. Snyder et al. (2013) provide an important consideration for educators and parents:

> The types of messages students receive about intelligence related to giftedness can interact with contextual factors, including students' experiences of success and failure, to influence motivational beliefs and behaviors (academic coping mechanisms). Ultimately, these mal-adaptive behaviors likely contribute to the onset and maintenance of underachievement, as short-term selfworth benefits are out-weighed by the long-term undermining of academic achievement.
>
> *(p. 230)*

Recognizing Underachievement

One process that can help educators recognize underachievement is a functional behavioral assessment (FBA). An FBA is used to help identify problem behaviors and to determine the type and frequency of related services that may be required to address such behaviors. This is a systematic process in which data are collected through observations, interviews, and inventories to create an understanding of how events and circumstances can help or hinder an individual's behavior (Lane et al., 2007). This process allows one to understand how various components of an educational setting contribute to a student's educational difficulties. Even when behaviors look similar across different students, there could be varied reasons why these behaviors are manifested in an individual and what the antecedents of the problem behavior might be. This process can be adapted for use with gifted underachievers in school to inform positive behavior support plans.

Inventories and checklists can also be used to help identify gifted underachievers. Ford (1994) adapted an initial checklist for identifying potential underachievers from gifted programs that includes statements related to social factors, family factors, school factors/climate, and personality/individual factors. This form includes items that address environmental, cultural, and psychological issues that often exacerbate underachievement among gifted students of color. It can quickly be completed by a teacher who is familiar with a student.

The School Attitude Assessment Survey-Revised (McCoach & Siegle, 2003) is another type of inventory that can be used to help identify gifted underachievers. It measures students' perceptions of their scholastic abilities including self-concept, goal valuation, motivation, and academic self-efficacy. This self-assessment scale includes 35 questions and was developed for gifted adolescents.

Reversing Underachievement

Research studies investigating the effectiveness of specific interventions in reversing underachievement have not shown evidence of significant improvement in academic performance or grades; however, several studies report a positive impact on psychosocial outcomes (Steenbergen-Hu et al., 2020). Informed by the research, there are several steps educators can take when addressing underachievement in school:

1. Collect achievement and behavioral data.
2. Involve the gifted student in the data collection process.
3. Conduct a thorough analysis of data to consider all student needs and the antecedents that drive specific problem behaviors.
4. Develop an individualized intervention plan *with the student* based on these data.
5. Determine how student success will be evaluated and what tangible results will be used to evaluate success.

The student study team should meet frequently during the plan implementation to discuss how the student is progressing and to make any necessary adjustments. See Table 2.1 for an overview of different strategies to support underachievers in school.

When working with underachievers it is important to keep in mind that the purpose of gifted education is to develop the potential that is rooted in the individual. To reverse underachievement, educators must support the student so that their gifts and talents can develop and flourish. Educators should reflect on how an underachieving gifted student thinks and learns and then select appropriate intervention strategies. One way to think about this is to view underachievement as another learning

TABLE 2.1 Strategies to support underachievers in school

What	Why	How
Help students understand cause and effect (Siegle & McCoach, 2019)	Students need to understand that they have control when it comes to their own destinies. They have the skills and the ability to put forth the effort.	■ Work with students to help them self-reflect on their successes and failures. What is working and what is not working? ■ Offer support and time to reflect on situations that are difficult and strategize ways to change the environments or behaviors to fit student needs ■ Help break down large projects into smaller steps or tasks that can be accomplished. Students will recognize that the work is manageable and will be able to get started and see it through.
Support students as they find meaningfulness in their work and lives (Siegle, 2013)	Students need to see value and meaning not only in their overall life but in the smaller tasks that they work on each day	■ Support students' curiosity ■ Help students find value in the world around them ■ Encourage students to think beyond immediate rewards and look forward to long-term outcomes that are possible ■ Facilitate opportunities for students to collaborate with cognitive peers and role models

difference to be addressed both inside and outside of the classroom. The list below provides key tips for working with gifted underachievers:

- Identify and monitor underachieving students on an ongoing basis. Early intervention is key.
- Small steps can lead to big positive changes. An interview with a student is a great starting place.
- Set frequent meetings to check in on progress with the student.
- Be open to changing your definition of success while maintaining high expectations. Success for one student may look different than success for another.
- Be mindful of the environment both at school and home. Both contexts could be providing elements that are enormous factors in a student's underachievement.

As with any intervention, it is essential that structures are put in place sooner rather than later. Identification is the essential first step that should take place no later than middle school, if possible (Ritchotte et al., 2015). A team approach is crucial, and success is more likely when multiple personnel with various perspectives and interactions with the student take shared responsibility for the development and implementation of an intervention plan.

Achievement Orientation Model

One model for addressing gifted underachievement is the Achievement Orientation Model (AOM) (Siegle & McCoach, 2005). This model encompasses the learning theories of self-efficacy, attribution, expectancy value, and person-environment theory. It emphasizes that how an individual perceives self-efficacy, meaningfulness, and environment has a direct effect on their motivation which in turn will play a role in their ultimate academic achievement. Table 2.2 provides an overview of the AOM.

When students have positive attitudes regarding the three areas of the AOM, they can work to reach the goals that they have set for themselves. Students must have a positive viewpoint or attitude in each of their three areas. This positivity then leads to how they will choose to manage their behaviors. When one of these areas is low, it influences the student's overall motivation. An AOM-based intervention works to help gifted underachievers increase their overall learning motivation and engagement which helps improve overall school performance.

TABLE 2.2 The Achievement Orientation Model (AOM)

Components	Sample questions
Self-efficacy	Does the student think they are able to do a specific task?
Task meaningfulness	Does the student find the school task valuable or meaningful?
Perceptions of environment	How does the student view: (1) home and school events; (2) expectations that the adults in their life set and how the adults support those expectations; and (3) interaction with other students/adults?

Teacher, Counselor, and Administrator Training

Targeted professional learning for educators and other personnel is necessary to effectively identify possible gifted underachievers and implement these strategies to reverse underachievement. Unfortunately, few colleges of education provide any training for teacher candidates, school administrators, or counselors on the needs of diverse gifted learners. Given the lack of training during teacher preparation programs, it is imperative that in-service professional learning is provided for those who may work with gifted underachievers and for those who make decisions that impact their education. If there are not any trained professionals working in a school or district who can deliver this type of training, educators can pursue professional learning through organizations such as state, national, and international gifted associations. See Table 2.3 for a list of such organizations and websites.

TABLE 2.3 Professional organizations for gifted education

Organization	Website
Belin-Blank Center 2e Collaboration	https://belinblank.education.uiowa.edu/research/ini-collab.aspx
European Council on High Ability	https://echa-site.eu/
National Association for Gifted Children	https://www.nagc.org
Supporting the Emotional Needs of the Gifted	https://www.sengifted.org
World Council on Gifted and Talented Education	https://world-gifted.org/

Implications for Practice

This chapter provides background information on theories and research related to underachievement of gifted learners in school. The five recommendations displayed in Figure 2.2 will assist educators, counselors, and administrators in applying the research outlined in this chapter to address the challenges with recognizing underachievement and implementing positive changes to reverse this behavior in gifted students.

Recommendation 1: Modify the Classroom Environment

One of the first steps in effecting change with gifted underachievers is to create a shift in the classroom experience (Flint & Ritchotte, 2012). Educators can help students become autonomous learners who think and reflect deeply. This can be done by diagnosing student needs and interests and then creating motivating learning experiences based on this information. Students should be involved in the planning process and have input into what and how they are learning.

When thinking about how to modify the learning environment for a gifted underachiever, evidence supports incorporating five themes into the classroom: control, choice, challenge, complexity, and caring (Kanevsky & Keighley, 2003). Each individual factor can hinder or help motivate a learner. By putting a focus on supporting and tending to all five themes, great benefits can result.

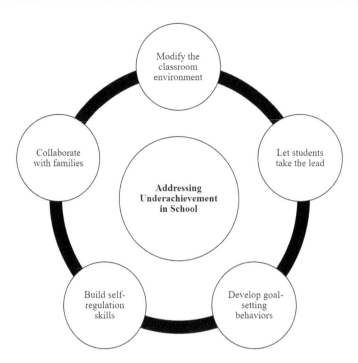

FIGURE 2.2 Five recommendations to address underachievement in school.

Recommendation 2: Let Students Take the Lead

Instructional strategies should be selected that set the stage and offer an invitation for students to enter the learning process (Tomlinson, 2002). Consider a shift to student-centered instruction that aims to develop motivated learners through a series of skills and strategies that allow them to organize new information. This is especially important when it comes to supporting selective consumer gifted underachievers. These students have a need for control, challenge, complexity, and choice. A teacher-centered classroom will not be conducive to their learning, motivation, and growth. Providing gifted underachievers with some autonomy in their learning will be more impactful (Zhang & Sternberg, 2006).

Teachers should give students the opportunity to offer and design alternative assignments so that what they are doing in school is more relevant and meaningful. Students must learn how to think like a teacher and focus on state standards and strategies in their proposed differentiated assignment. They are provided opportunities to create their own learning contracts and decide how to evaluate their work.

Recommendation 3: Develop Goal-Setting Behaviors

This recommendation addresses goal-setting theory and meaningfulness and can be one of the biggest ways to move the needle with gifted underachievers. According to goal-setting theory, a student's ability to consciously hold a goal in mind will influence their actions and impact their behavior (Morisano & Shore, 2010). Burns and Martin (2019) identified four essential guidelines to help students develop goal-setting behaviors:

1. Goals must be specific.
2. The student needs to have positive expectations about their goals.
3. The student should be ready with alternative options.
4. Take small positive steps so that motivation is heightened.

Teachers must help students identify appropriate and reasonable goals with the right level of difficulty, build their skills that relate to their goals, offer specific and constructive feedback that helps them on their journey to meeting their goals, and assist students in tracking their progress toward making their goals.

Recommendation 4: Build Self-Regulation Skills

Ridgley et al. (2020) found positive benefits for gifted underachievers when a self-regulated (SRL) microanalysis was used to assess and address the needs of struggling gifted underachievers. This approach is beneficial because it responds to the individuality of each student and can be implemented in a school setting where existing interventions are taking place. Possible data collection tools include the following:

■ Motivated Strategies and Learning Questionnaire (MSLQ)
■ Learning and Study Strategies Inventory (LASSI)
■ OnLine Motivation Questionnaire
■ Self-Regulated Learning Interview Scale (SRLIS)
■ SRL Microanalytic Assessment (Ridgley et al., 2020).

Recommendation 5: Collaborate with Families

Finally, parents and caregivers can offer important insight into how a student views their self-regulation and self-efficacy. Schools should make every effort to connect with families to gain an understanding about students and then use this information to strategize an intervention plan to work on targeting underachievement behaviors (Siegle et al., 2020). Because of the significant role that caregivers play in a student's life, they can work as models to support two important values that underlie underachievement attitudes: (1) understanding cause and effect; and (2) finding meaningfulness.

Conclusion

Underachievement of gifted learners represents a potential great loss to society. Underdeveloped talents lead to missed creative contributions and innovations. While underachievement can have pervasive effects on a student's life, what is most important to remember is that underachievement can be reversed. Adults working with gifted underachievers must first identify the root cause of the underachievement and then create an intervention plan that emphasizes and focuses on the student's strengths. Educators should include the student in setting goals, seek out mentoring and counseling resources, and collaborate with parents and caregivers to gain support and insight. Combining efforts like these will have a lasting effect on reversing underachievement in gifted students.

REFLECTION QUESTIONS

1. Covert underachievers, selective consumers, and thrice exceptional learners have a high likelihood of being overlooked. What strategies could be implemented in your classroom (or school) to support these unique learners?

2. How would you design a new approach or model for working with gifted underachievers in your school, district, or workplace?

3. According to best practices for working with gifted underachievers, what priorities do you have for your school, district, or workplace?

4. How has your understanding of underachievement in gifted students shifted after reading this chapter? Are there new details that are part of your conceptualization of underachievement? What next steps will you take with this updated viewpoint?

5. The authors noted, "Thrice exceptional learners may become selective consumers or underachieve in schools if there is a lack of understanding of cultural differences and respect for diversity." What can educators do to increase their intentionality to recognize and respect cultural differences as an asset for the purpose of adequately supporting thrice exceptional students?

Suggested Resources

Collins, K. H., Coleman, M. R., & Grantham, T. C. (2022). A bioecological perspective of emotional/behavioral challenges for gifted students of color: Support needed vs. support received. *Journal of Emotional and Behavioral Disorders*, *30*(2), 86–95. https://doi.org/10.1177/10634266221076466

Delisle, J. R. (2018). *Doing poorly on purpose: Strategies to reverse underachievement and respect student dignity.* ASCD.

Kauffman, S. B. (Ed.). (2018). *Twice exceptional: Supporting and educating bright and creative students with learning difficulties.* Oxford University Press.

National Association for Gifted Children. (2021). Parent TIP Sheets. Available at: https://www.nagc.org/resources-publications/resources-parents/parent-tip-sheets

Peterson, J9*elopment*. Free Spirit Publishing.

Piske, F. H. R. Collins, K. H., & Arnstein, K. (Eds.). (2022). *Servicing twice-exceptional students: Socially, emotionally, and culturally framing learning exceptionalities.* Springer Nature.

Rimm, S. B. (2020). Books on gifted education and parenting. Available at: http://www.sylviarimm.com/

World Council for Gifted and Talented Children (2021). Global principles for professional learning in gifted education. Available at: https://world-gifted.org/wp-content/uploads/2022/01/professional-learning-global-principles.pdf

References

Baker, J., Bridger, R., & Evans, K. (1998). Models of underachievement among gifted preadolescents: The role of personal, family, and school factors. *Gifted Child Quarterly*, *42*(1), 5–15. https://doi.org/10.1177/001698629804200102

Bennett-Rappell, H., & Northcote, M. (2016). Underachieving gifted students: Two case studies. *Issues in Educational Research*, *26*(3), 407–430.

Berglas, S., & Jones, E. E. (1978). Drug choice as a self-handicapping strategy in response to noncontingent success. *Journal of Personality and Social Psychology*, *36*(4), 405–417. https://doi.org/10.1037/0022-3514.36.4.405

Burns, E. C., & Martin, A. J. (2019). Motivational issues in gifted education: Understanding the role of students' attribution and control beliefs, self-worth protection, and growth orientation. In S. Smith (Ed.), *Handbook of giftedness and talent development in the Asia-Pacific* (Online). Springer.

Cavilla, D. (2017). Observation and analysis of three gifted underachievers in an underserved, urban high school setting. *Gifted Education International*, *33*(1), 62–75. https://doi.org/10.1177%2F0261429414568181

Collins, K. H. (2020). Talking about racism in America and in education: The reflections of gifted Black scholar and mother of a gifted Black young adult. *Parenting for High Potential*, *9*(3), 3, 5–9.

Collins, K. H. (2021). Redressing and neutralizing institutional racism and systemic biases in gifted education. In M. Fugate, W. Behrens, & C. Boswell (Eds.), *Culturally responsive practices in gifted education: Building cultural competence and serving diverse student populations* (pp. 85–104). Routledge.

Collins, K. H., & Johnson. J. (2021). Furthering a shift in the twice exceptional paradigm: Understanding the sociocultural milieu of gifted student development. *Variations²ᵉ*, *6*, 56–60.

Columbus Group. (1991, July). Unpublished transcript of the meeting of the Columbus Group. [Meeting transcript.]

Davis, J. L., & Robinson, S. A. (2018). Being 3e, a new look at culturally diverse gifted learners with exceptional conditions: An examination of the issues and solutions for educators and families. In S. B. Kauffman (Ed.), *Twice exceptional: Supporting and educating bright and creative students with learning difficulties* (pp. 278–289). Oxford University Press. https://doi.org/10.1093/oso/9780190645472.003.0017

Desmet, O., & Pereira, N. (2022). Gifted boys' perceptions of their academic underachievement. *Gifted Education International*, *38*(2), 229–255. https://doi.org/10.1177/02614294211050294

Desmet O. A., Pereira N., & Peterson J. S. (2020) Telling a tale: How underachievement develops in gifted girls. *Gifted Child Quarterly*, *64*(2) 85–99. https://doi.org/10.1177/0016986219888633

Emerick, L. J. (1988). Academic underachievement among the gifted: Students' perceptions of factors that reverse the pattern. Unpublished doctoral dissertation, University of Connecticut, Storrs.

Figg, S. D., Rogers, K. B., McCormick J., & Low, R. (2012). Differentiating low performance of the gifted learner: Achieving, underachieving, and selective consumers. *Journal of Advanced Academics*, *23*(1), 53–71. https://doi.org/10.1177%2F1932202X11430000

Flint, L. J., & Ritchotte, J. A. (2012). A commentary on "Differentiating low performance of the gifted learner: Achieving, underachieving, and selective consuming students." *Journal of Advanced Academics*, *23*(2), 168–175. https://doi.org/10.1177%2F1932202X11434641

Ford, D. Y. (1994). The recruitment and retention of African American students in gifted education programs: Implications and recommendations (RBDM9406). University of Connecticut, The National Research Center on the Gifted and Talented. Available at: https://nrcgt.uconn.edu/wpcontent/uploads/sites/953/2015/04/rbdm9406.pdf

Galbraith, J., & Delisle, J. R. (2015). *When gifted kids don't have all the answers: How to meet their social and emotional needs* (2nd ed.). Free Spirit Press.

Garn, A. C., Matthews, M. S., & Jolly, J. L. (2010). Parental influences on the academic motivation of gifted students: A self-determination theory perspective. *Gifted Child Quarterly*, *54*(4), 263–272. https://doi.org/10.1177/0016986210377657

Kanevsky, L., & Keighley, T. (2003). To produce or not to produce? Understanding boredom and the honor in underachievement. *Roeper Review*, *26*(1), 20–28. https://doi.org/10.1080/02783190309554235

Lane, K. L., Weisenbach, J. L, Phillips, A., & Wehby, J. H. (2007). Designing, implementing, and evaluating function-based interventions using a systemic, feasible approach. *Behavioral Disorders*, *32*, 122–139.

Lyman, R. D., Prentice-Dunn, S., Wilson, D. R., & Bonfilio, S. A. (1984). The effect of success or failure on self-efficacy and task persistence of conduct-disordered children. *Psychology in the Schools*, *21*, 516–519.

Matthews, M. S. (2006). Gifted students dropping out: Recent findings from a southeastern state. *Roeper Review*, *28*(4), 216–223. https://psycnet.apa.org/doi/10.1080/02783190609554367

Matthews M. S. (2009) Gifted learners who drop out: Prevalence and prevention. In L.V. Shavinina (Ed.), *International handbook on giftedness* (pp. 527–536). Springer. https://doi.org/10.1007/978-1-4020-6162-2_24

Matthews, M. S. & McBee, M.T. (2007). School factors and the underachievement of gifted students in a talent search summer program. *Gifted Child Quarterly*, *51*(2), 167–181. https://doi.org/10.1177/0016986207299473

McCoach, D. B. (2000).The School Attitude Assessment Survey-Revised (SAAS-R). Unpublished instrument.

McCoach, D. B., & Siegle, D. (2003). The School Attitude Assessment Survey-Revised: A new instrument to identify academically able students who underachieve. *Educational and Psychological Measurement*, *63*(3), 414–429. https://doi.org/10.1177/0013164403063003005

McCoach, D. B., Siegle, D., & Rubenstein, L. D. (2020). Pay attention to inattention: Exploring ADHD symptoms in a sample of underachieving gifted students. *Gifted Child Quarterly*, *64*(2), 100–116. https://doi.org/10.1177/0016986219901320

Mindset Works. (2012). Mindset assessment profile tool: Educator kit module 1 toolkit. Available at: http://achieve.lausd.net/cms/lib08/CA01000043/Centricity/Domain/173/MindsetAssessmentProfile.pdf

Mofield, E., & Parker Peters, M. (2019). Understanding underachievement: Mindset, perfectionism, and achievement attitudes among gifted students. *Journal for the Education of the Gifted*, *42*(2), 107–134. https://doi.org/10.1177%2F0162353219836737

Morisano, D., & Shore, B. M. (2010). Can personal goal setting tap the potential of the gifted underachiever? *Roeper Review*, *32*(4), 249–258. https://doi.org/10.1080/02783193.2010.508156

National Association for Gifted Children (2010).What is giftedness? Available at: http://www.nagc.org/WhatisGiftedness.aspx

Peters, S. J. (2012). Underachievers: From whose perspective? A commentary on "Differentiating low performance of the gifted learner: Achieving, underachieving, and selective consuming students." *Journal of Advanced Academics*, *23*(2), 176–179. https://doi.org/10.1177/1932202X12438718

Peterson, J. S. (2001). Successful adults who were once adolescent underachievers. *Gifted Child Quarterly*, *45*(1), 236–250. https://doi.org/10.1177%2F001698620104500402

Piske, F. H. R. Collins, K. H., & Arnstein, K. (Eds.). (2022). *Servicing twice-exceptional students: Socially, emotionally, and culturally framing learning exceptionalities*. Springer Nature.

Reis, S. M., & McCoach, D. (2000).The underachievement of gifted students: What do we know and where do we go? *Gifted Child Quarterly*, *44*(3), 152–170. https://doi.org/10.1177%2F001698620004400302

Renzulli, J., & Park, S. (2000). Gifted dropouts: The who and the why. *Gifted Child Quarterly*, *44*(4), 261–271. https://doi.org/10.1177/001698620004400407

Rhodewalt, F. (1994). Conceptions of ability, achievement goals, and individual differences in self-handicapping behavior: On the application of implicit theories. *Journal of Personality*, *62*(1), 67–85. https://doi.org/10.1111/j.1467-6494.1994.tb00795.x

Ridgley, L. M., Rubenstein, L. D., & Callan, G. L. (2020). Gifted underachievement within a self-regulated learning framework: Proposing a task-dependent model to guide early identification and intervention. *Psychology in the Schools*, *57*(9), 1365–1384. https://doi.org/10.1002/pits.22408

Rimm, S. B. (2008). *Why bright kids get poor grades and what you can do about it: A six-step program for parents and teachers*. Great Potential Press, Inc.

Rimm, S., & Lowe, B. (1988). Family environments of underachieving gifted students. *Gifted Child Quarterly*, *32*(4), 353–359.

Ritchotte, J.A., Matthews, M. S., & Flowers, C. P. (2014).The validity of the achievement-orientation model for gifted middle school students: An exploratory study. *Gifted Child Quarterly*, *58*(3), 183–198. https://psycnet.apa.org/doi/10.1177/0016986214534890

Ritchotte, J., Rubenstein, L., & Murry, F. (2015). Reversing the underachievement of gifted middle school students: Lessons from another field. *Gifted Child Today*, *38*(2), 103–113. https://doi.org/10.1177%2F1076217514568559

Robbins, S. B., Lauver, K., Le, H., Davis, D., Langley, R., & Carlstrom, A. (2004). Do psychosocial and study skill factors predict college outcomes? A meta-analysis. *Psychological Bulletin, 130*, 261–288. https://psycnet.apa.org/doi/10.1037/0033-2909.130.2.261

Ruban, L., & Reis, S. M. (2006). Patterns of self-regulation: Patterns of self-regulatory strategy use among low-achieving and high-achieving university students. *Roeper Review, 28*, 148–156. https://doi.org/10.1080/02783190609554354

Rubenstein, L. D., Siegle, D., Reis, S. M., McCoach, D. B., & Burton, M. G. (2012). A complex quest: The development and research of underachievement interventions for gifted students. *Psychology in Schools, 49*(7), 678–694. https://doi.org/10.1002/pits.21620

Schuler, P. (1994). Goals and work habits survey. Unpublished instrument, University of Connecticut, Storrs.

Seeley, K. R. (1993). Gifted students at risk. In L. K. Silverman (Ed.), *Counseling the gifted and talented* (pp. 263–276). Love Publishing.

Siegle, D. (2013). *The underachieving gifted child: Recognizing, understanding, and reversing underachievement.* Prufrock Press.

Siegle, D., Rubenstein, L. D., & McCoach, D. B. (2020). Do you know what I'm thinking? A comparison of teacher and parent perspectives of underachieving gifted students' attitudes. *Psychology in the Schools, 57*(10), 1596–1614. https://doi.org/10.1002/pits.22345

Siegle, D., & McCoach, D. B. (2005). Making a difference: Motivating gifted students who are not achieving. *Teaching Exceptional Children, 38*(1), 22–27.

Snyder, K. E., Carrig, M. M., & Linnebrink-Garcia, L. (2019). Developmental pathways in underachievement. *Applied Developmental Science.* Advance online publication. https://doi.org/10.1080/10888691.2018.1543028

Snyder, K. E., Malin, J. L., Dent, A. L., & Linenbrink-Garcia, L. (2013). The message matters: The role of implicit beliefs about giftedness and failure experiences in academic self-handicapping. *Journal of Educational Psychology, 106*(1), 230–241. https://doi.org/10.1037/a0034553

Steenbergen-Hu, S., Olszewski-Kubilius, P., & Calvert, E. (2020). The effectiveness of current interventions to reverse the underachievement of gifted students: Findings of a meta-analysis and systematic review. *Gifted Child Quarterly, 64*(2), 132–165. https://doi.org/10.1177/%2F0016986220908601

Tomlinson, C. (2002). Invitations to learn: Do students care about learning? *Educational Leadership, 60*(1), 6–10.

White, S., Graham, L., & Blaas, S. (2018). Why do we know so little about the factors associated with gifted underachievement? A systematic literature review. *Educational Research Review, 24*, 55–66. https://doi.org/10.1016/j.edurev.2018.03.001

Wigfield, A. (1994). Expectancy-value theory of achievement motivation: A developmental perspective. *Educational Psychology Review, 6*, 49–78. https://doi.org/10.1007/BF02209024

Wigfield, A., & Eccles, J. S. (2000). Expectancy-value theory of achievement motivation. *Contemporary Educational Psychology, 25*(1), 68–81. https://doi.org/10.1006/ceps.1999.1015

Zhang, L., & Sternberg, R. J. (2006). *The nature of intellectual styles.* Lawrence Erlbaum.

Zientek, L. R., & Thompson, B. (2010). Using commonality analysis to quantify contributions that self-efficacy and motivational factors make in mathematics performance. *Research in the Schools, 17*(1), 1–12.

Underachievement in the Online Environment

Using Research-Based Interventions for Underachieving Gifted Students

Kenneth J. Wright and Sally M. Reis

Introduction

Underachievement in gifted students is a source of frustration for many teachers and parents. Few experiences, for educators, are as heart-wrenching as watching a child with enormous potential begin to flounder, fall short, or simply give up on completing academic work. The causes of underachievement are complicated (Reis & McCoach, 2000) and the widespread use of online learning has added a new layer of complexity. When students began learning online, many teachers encountered deepening and serious problems with student engagement and underachievement. A report on National Public Radio (NPR) in April 2020 suggested that as many as 25% of all teens had not participated in any online schooling since the COVID-19 shutdown began (Kamenetz, 2020).

It is too early to understand the full effect of long-term online schooling for gifted students, and data on the best interventions to avoid potential damages to or benefits for this group, may be years away. However, existing models with supporting research can be adapted to the present circumstances, especially when academically gifted students are beginning to see increases in underachievement. In this chapter, we summarize the Achievement Orientation Model (AOM) which was created to explain why students underachieve and provide a framework for various types of interventions (Siegle & McCoach, 2005). Though not specifically developed for online learning, the model provides useful insights for understanding why students may be struggling and many of the potentially useful interventions can be adapted to online settings. In this chapter, methods for identifying underachievement are summarized, as are current strategies to engage students who are beginning to underachieve.

Defining and Identifying Underachievement

When an academically talented student is falling below expected levels of high academic achievement, teachers need to identify the student and take action to avoid having a short episode of underachievement turn into long-term systemic

DOI: 10.4324/9781003369578-5

underachievement (Reis & McCoach, 2000). Reis and McCoach offered a comprehensive summary of the challenges that exist in defining underachievement, and their broad definition is widely cited and explains underachievement as the discrepancy between ability and achievement. Identification of underachievement is also challenging but teacher observation is often the beginning of the process. How do teachers know that their academically talented students may be underachieving?

In a regular in-person classroom, the process of identifying students who are beginning to underachieve would typically begin when an observant teacher notices a series of changes in classroom performance. The student may, for example, begin sleeping in class, become disruptive, chronically late to class and unprepared for their academic work, or fail to complete various classroom assignments or summative tests. In an online environment, a teacher's tools need to be adapted for how to identify underachieving but high-potential students. For formerly high-performing, academically advanced students who are beginning to underachieve, teachers may ask the following questions: Does the student not log in for class? Do they always keep their camera off? Do they participate less often while doing online lessons? When their video is on, do they seem angry, depressed, easily frustrated, or overly emotional? Have they started to perform below their ability compared to former performance?

In this chapter, we discuss how the underachievement of academically talented students can be thoughtfully analyzed and potentially reversed by considering the Achievement Orientation Model (AOM) (Siegle & McCoach, 2005) and implementing the Schoolwide Enrichment Model (Reis & Renzulli, 2005; Renzulli & Reis, 1997, 2014).

Motivational Factors in Underachievement

The AOM assimilates the major causes of underachievement, including self-efficacy theory (Bandura, 1986), attribution theory (Weiner, 1986), expectancy-value theory (Eccles & Wigfield, 1995), and person-environment fit theory (Lewin, 1951). In summary, it theorizes that in order for students to be motivated, they need to (1) value the task or outcome; (2) be confident in their ability to perform the task; and (3) expect that they can be successful in their environment. When all three of these factors are present, students are more likely to be motivated and work diligently and with enjoyment. When a student is motivated, they are more likely to demonstrate effective self-regulatory behaviors, which in turn lead to higher engagement and achievement (Siegle & McCoach, 2005). When teachers review their online classes through the lens of the AOM, they may be able to begin to identify the causes for some students' underachievement.

The AOM deals primarily with motivation issues and does not include remedies for more serious underlying problems of underachievement that can be a symptom of a serious physical, emotional, or cognitive issue (Moon & Hall, 1998). If a student begins to underachieve, teachers should first contact parents/guardians to become aware of any family/home situations which may be causing underachievement. In potentially serious situations, understanding the student's circumstances in context is essential to taking appropriate action. For example, it would be unnecessary to revise the curriculum content and assemble an intervention team for a child if the problem is actually rooted in the fact that a student is unable to sleep because of a new baby in the home. Learning disabilities in high-potential students can also play a major role in underachievement and should be identified as soon as possible as such information plays a key part in crafting interventions (Reis & McCoach, 2002).

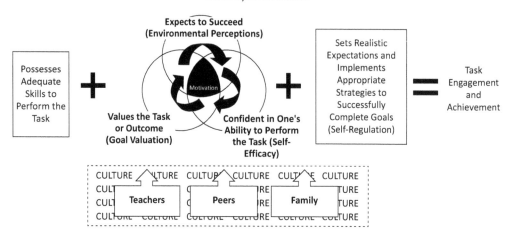

FIGURE 3.1 The Achievement Orientation Model.
Source: Siegle and McCoach (2005). Reprinted with permission of Del Siegle.

Once major problems such as those addressed above have been ruled out and it is clear the student is academically talented and that a gap exists between expectations and performance, the AOM (Siegle & McCoach, 2005) (Figure 3.1) can provide a theoretical framework for how to proceed and the SEM (Renzulli & Reis, 2014) offers educational interventions that work.

Student Valuation of the Task (Is This Worth Doing?)

When students value what they are learning, they are more likely to be engaged. Academic interests can be valuable to students in various ways, and when explaining task valuation, Siegle and McCoach (2005) suggest that students complete tasks if they enjoy them or the product completed by engaging in these academic tasks. Many academically talented students in regular classrooms have little patience for completing work they perceive as having no value. It is likely those same students, when forced to work in a home environment with little supervision and multiple distractions, will choose more entertaining and personally relevant options over their regular school assignments. The necessity for providing relevant, interesting, and personally useful curriculum to students should be applied in both online and in-person learning environments. However, students usually encounter more distractions and options at home than in traditional classrooms, and often engage in activities that they enjoy more, such as sleeping, social media, and hanging out with their friends online.

According to Siegle and McCoach (2005), teachers should focus on teaching content that is either enjoyable, useful, or preferably both. Educators can consider what they are teaching and ask, "Why would my students ever need to know this?" If no convincing reason can be found, then it is likely the students will not be engaged with that content. We might consider if the content we are teaching will prepare students for a future career. Will it help them get into college? Can we teach critical thinking skills that will help them solve complex problems? Are we introducing communication skills that can help them in their future education and work? The case needs to be made to the students about why they should pay attention. In an online environment, too many voices are competing for students' attention and if teachers do not make their case quickly, students will drift away. Some research shows that attention to an online video peaks in the first six minutes so teachers must focus on both relevance and utility at the beginning of any lesson (Geri, Winer, & Zaks, 2017).

Implications for Practice

Teachers can also use student interests to increase the entertainment value of the content they are introducing. At the beginning of the academic year, teachers can gather information about student hobbies, interests, and extracurricular activities. In one of the most compelling studies published on reversing underachievement, Baum et al. (1995) found that the completion of self-selected products based on student interests helped to reverse underachievement in 17 gifted students (ages 8–13). Gains were made by 82% of the participating students who were no longer underachieving in their schools at the end of the intervention. Using the Schoolwide Enrichment Model (SEM) (Renzulli & Reis, 2014) enables teachers to organize the introduction of enriching learning activities.

The SEM: A Successful Model for Strength-Based, Talent-Focused Education

The Schoolwide Enrichment Model (SEM) (Renzulli & Reis, 1985, 1997, 2014) is particularly appropriate for providing a strength-based, talent-focused approach for underachieving students. The SEM talent development approach provides enriched learning experiences and higher learning standards for all children, with a focus on a broad range of enrichment experiences to expose students to new ideas and skills and follow up advanced learning for academically talented children interested in further investigation. The SEM (Figure 3.2) expands Renzulli Enrichment Triad (1977) that has been implemented in thousands of schools across the country and has continued to expand internationally. The SEM integrates the Three Ring Conception of Giftedness (Renzulli, 1978), the Enrichment Triad Model (Renzulli, 1977) and has been implemented in thousands of school districts worldwide as a gifted program, enrichment program, and school-based theme approach to learning. In addition to the United States, the SEM is used in schools in China, Mexico, Chile, the Caribbean, the Dominican Republic, Grand Cayman, Puerto Rico, Argentina, Brazil, the Netherlands, Canada, the Virgin Islands, Spain, Germany, Portugal, Turkey, Bahrain, Iraq, the United Arab Emirates, Jordan, Hungary, Lebanon, Singapore, New Zealand, Indonesia, Switzerland, Croatia, South Korea, England, Japan, Peru, India, Dubai, the Philippines, and Austria (Hernandez-Torrano & Saranli, 2015; Milan et al., 2019; Renzulli, 2003; Reis & Renzulli, 2003; Sytsma, 2003).

The opportunities for enrichment approaches to learning and talent development within the context of the SEM can be used to identify and enhance interests and strengths. Teachers can use the SEM to provide exposure to areas of interest (Type I), give instruction in higher-order problem-solving, creative and critical thinking, and information processing (Type II), and also create opportunities to produce products and services so that students can pursue interests in areas of strength, Type III creative projects

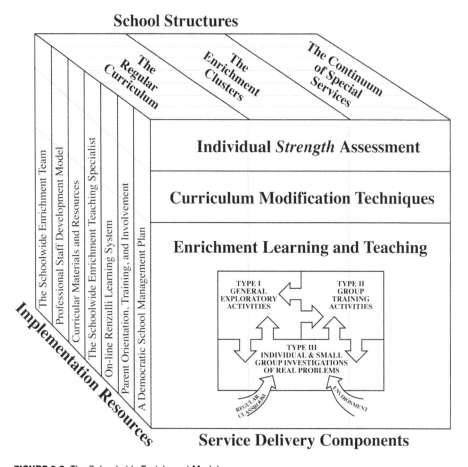

FIGURE 3.2 The Schoolwide Enrichment Model.
Source: Reprinted with permission of Joseph Renzulli.

can engage students in solving problems in advanced independent or small group work (Type III), which has been shown to positively impact students' academic, social, and emotional development (Reis & Peters, 2020). These kinds of enrichment activities are especially appropriate for underachieving learners because they provide these students access to high-level, sophisticated topics, opportunities to process information using inquiry and critical thinking, and choices to present understandings in ways that align to their strengths, interests, and talents. Other research on the use of the SEM demonstrates increased levels of student creative productivity or engagement in school (Baum et al., 2014; Brandon et al., 2021; Brigandi et al., 2018, Reis & Morales-Taylor, 2010).

Enrichment can be thoughtfully woven into the fabric of any learning experience, even during online learning, using the Enrichment Triad and the SEM. For example, Type I Enrichment can engage and stimulate students with general exploratory experiences such as guest speakers online, virtual field trips, demonstrations, and the use of tools such as Ted Talks and webinars that are designed to expose students to new and exciting topics, ideas, and fields of knowledge not ordinarily covered in the regular curriculum. For example, for students who are interested in the arts, Type I experiences can engage and stimulate engagement by enabling them to take a virtual tour of some of the greatest art museums in the world. They can watch documentaries about their favorite artists and find various how-to art tutorials to spark their curiosity.

Type II Enrichment includes instructional methods and materials purposefully designed to promote the development of thinking, feeling, research, communication, and methodological processes. Type II training, usually carried out both in classrooms and in enrichment programs, includes the development of creative thinking and problem solving, critical thinking, and affective processes; a variety of specific learning-how-to-learn skills; skills in the appropriate use of advanced-level reference materials; and written, oral, and visual communication skills. To continue with our example of the arts, Type II training can be provided in areas such as creative thinking and brainstorming as well as specific instruction in the art form in which the student has developed interests.

Type III Enrichment is the most advanced level in the Enrichment Triad Model. Although Types I and II Enrichment and curriculum compacting should be provided on a regular basis to students, the ability to revolve into Type III Enrichment depends on an individual's interests, motivation, and desire to pursue advanced-level study. Type III Enrichment is defined as investigative activities and artistic productions in which the learner assumes the role of a first-hand inquirer, thinking, feeling, and acting like a practicing professional, with involvement pursued at as advanced or professional level as possible, given the student's level of development and age. The most important feature of the model is the "flow" or connection among the experiences. Each type of enrichment is viewed as a component part of a holistic process that blends present or newly developed interests (Type I) and advanced-level thinking and research skills (Type II) with application situations based on the *modus operandi* of the first-hand inquirer (Type III). For example, students with interests and passions in the arts can pursue Type IIIs in school, spending hours drawing, painting, animating, and illustrating. For online classes there are a myriad of options involving basic household items or exclusively digital resources.

SEM Online: Renzulli Learning

Teachers who are interested in using SEM in their classroom can try a host of online resources available (www.renzullilearning.com). Renzulli Learning offers an automated, digital diagnostic assessment that creates a profile of each student's academic strengths, interests, learning styles, and preferred modes of expression. Next, a differentiation search engine examines over 50,000 enrichment activities, materials, resources, and opportunities and selects those that are appropriate for each student's profile, based on age, level of challenge, and interests. A project management tool guides students and teachers to use specifically selected resources for assigned curricular activities, independent or small group investigative projects, and a wide variety of challenging enrichment experiences. Teachers have immediate access to student profiles, browsing history, and the amount of time spent in each activity. Parents may also access their own child's profile and web activities. Students have opportunities to pursue advanced-level Type II training and Type III projects in their strength areas and areas of personal interest, using a project organization and management plan called The Wizard Project Maker. The final component in the Renzulli Learning System is an automatic compilation and storage of all student activity from steps one, two, and three into a digital version of the Total Talent Portfolio.

Field (2009) used quantitative procedures in an empirical study to investigate the effects of Renzulli Learning on oral reading fluency, reading comprehension, science achievement, and social studies achievement. Students who participated in Renzulli

Learning demonstrated significantly higher growth in reading comprehension, oral reading fluency, and social studies achievement than students who did not participate in the online program.

The first step in implementing the SEM is gathering information about students' interests, as well as the ways they like to learn and produce products. Renzulli Learning can accelerate the process for underachieving students. In this system, completing a profile enables teachers to identify students' interests and preferred product styles. If teachers do not have access to Renzulli Learning, forms are available in the book on SEM (Renzulli & Reis, 2014) and this information can easily be organized using a Google form survey. Wherever possible, teachers should try to link their regular curricular content to topics that are both interesting and relevant to students who are underachieving in school, either live or online.

Teachers should become familiar with the interests of all their students, but it is especially important to identify the interests of students who are becoming disengaged. Teachers should make attempts to find ways to connect with their students' world, and, in particular, if a student is underachieving, showing efforts to connect can make a difference. For example, during an online presentation, a student who is not paying attention can be brought back into focus with an analogy or reference to their favorite band or video game. If an unengaged student is a sports fan, the teacher can make a word problem about their favorite sports team. They can also find a news article on a topic that students will enjoy. If teachers discover that a disengaged students is really interested in Japanese animation and teachers can connect with that interest, students may be much more likely to pay attention to them. The more a student feels that the content of the online lesson is of interest, the less likely they are to disengage.

A key way for students to value the content they are learning is to enable them to choose a topic of personal interest. Of course, there should be a base level of knowledge all students receive but, wherever possible, especially for underachieving students, if teachers give some flexibility for them to choose how to express their knowledge and the content that they should explore, this can help and has helped underachieving students. The SEM (Renzulli & Reis, 2014) enables this to occur. This model can be used to provide enrichment to all students in a school and many SEM strategies can be applied in an online school format. For example, teachers can introduce students to various topics to spark their interest (Type I) by enabling them to watch videos online, visit websites, and try interactive learning games. Teachers can also guide all students through learning experiences that build on previously mastered skills. This second stage (Type II) is similar to teaching some of the creative and critical thinking skills that teachers are currently introducing in their classes.

The real potential is with the most advanced stage of the SEM in which students are encouraged to engage in some project-based experience where they pursue an strong interest or solve a real-world problem(Type III). In the SEM, Renzulli and Reis promote the value of how-to books in showing students how to take on the role of an expert but at a more junior level. When comparing the internet of 2021 with the available how-to books in print, we realize the current potential and utility of the internet far exceeds every how-to book ever written. The online resources for a Type III SEM project are expansive and beyond the scope of this chapter. However, this may be an area of real potential for engaging gifted students and the potential ability to execute Type III SEM projects online merits additional consideration, particularly if using a platform such as Renzulli Learning, with the Wizard Project Maker and hundreds of starter projects.

Curriculum Compacting to Reverse Underachievement

Another way teachers can kill student motivation is to teach content that students have already mastered. Students will not value learning experiences if they already know the material. Curriculum compacting, another core component of the SEM (Reis & Renzulli, 1992; Reis et al., 2016; Renzulli, Smith, & Reis, 1982) can be offered and provided to all academically talented students, and occasionally to other students, based on preassessments. Compacting is a widely utilized approach to differentiation of instruction that combines both enrichment and acceleration strategies (Colangelo, Assouline, & Gross, 2004). Compacting enables classroom teachers to differentiate, modify, and accelerate the regular curriculum by eliminating portions of previously mastered content. Compacting enables teachers to document required work already mastered and to replace that work with alternative, more interesting and engaging work. Research on compacting has consistently demonstrated that academically talented students can have 24–70 percent of their regular curriculum eliminated or streamlined to avoid repetition of previously mastered work, guaranteeing mastery while simultaneously substituting more appropriately challenging activities (Reis & Purcell, 1993; Reis, Westberg, et al., 1998) without any loss of achievement or drops in achievement test scores.

Teachers can implement compacting using testing software like Google forms, Survey Monkey, Qualtrics, or Mastery Connect to collect formative pre-assessments at the beginning of each unit. They can also offer advanced depth of knowledge content to students who already know the regular curricular content. Differentiation and, in particular, the use of curriculum compacting are a way in which technology provides exceptional resources. In a normal classroom it can be difficult to have the majority of the class working on one lesson with direct instruction and then a small group is sent to the side for a separate advanced curriculum. With chat rooms, breakout rooms, pre-recorded instruction videos, and the ability to push multiple assignments to different students based on pre-test scores technology, differentiation can be accomplished in a way not imagined even a decade ago. When creating advanced curriculum and using compacting, teachers need to make sure that the advanced task is not just more work but rather a more complex task that builds on their prior knowledge, and whenever possible they must enable students to pursue areas of personal interest, particularly when they have mastered the content of the regular curriculum.

Student Self-Efficacy (Do I Have What It Takes to Succeed?)

Once students are interested and engaged in the content, teachers can help students gain a sense of self-efficacy or belief they can be successful in their efforts. Students need to believe they have a reasonable chance at success (Siegle & McCoach 2005). One of the best ways students measure their ability is by past performance. However, working in an online classroom could make some students feel detached from the help they have learned to expect in school. In a normal classroom a teacher may see a student holding her pencil looking confused and as a result help to clarify the assignment. In contrast, a student who is confused in an online setting may not be so easily identified in the same way. If students have had negative experiences with online school during the COVID-19 pandemic, particularly in the early stages when both teachers and students were trying to figure out how to function in an online environment, they may have negative perceptions of online learning. For example, the student may have had some experiences online when they were lost or confused and did not do well on a subsequent exam or assignment. This may convince them that they "can't" succeed in online school. Or students may be logging in from their beds, without really paying attention. They may be listening to music or texting their friends while they are supposed to be engaged in an online class. Teachers need to give students successful and active learning experiences and support to build their confidence. Students need to feel seen and that their teacher will help them succeed. One way to build students' self-efficacy is to give specific compliments based on performance and effort. Teachers must ensure that the compliments are given for challenging tasks, as compliments about something that is easy for the students can feel belittling. Teachers should also ensure that compliments are given sincerely and in moderation, as too many compliments diffuse and lessen the value. Additional steps need to be taken to ensure appropriate online communication with students. When emailing a student a compliment, it is important to copy the parent or guardian.

Additional ways to boost students' self-efficacy in an online environment include using a progress tracker, virtual sticker chart, or showing standards-based progress. Many video games use a level-up system, experience points, or badges to show progress, and these gamification elements are intensely motivating for some students who enjoy seeing progress (Sampayo-Vargas et al., 2013). Keeping track of student progress also enables teachers to monitor another important element: level of difficulty. For example, video games and educational software frequently adjust the difficulty of the tasks based on students' performance. These adjustments are made because if a task is too easy, then students will grow bored and disengage. Video game designers also know if a task is too difficult, then students will become frustrated and quit (Deci & Ryan, 1985). Technology can enable flexible instruction options and a variety of materials to meet the needs of diverse learners. Teachers in the past had to gather books, make paper copies, and set up physical learning stations in their rooms. With online learning, teachers can create all content digitally. Initially, this may seem a difficult task but once websites, forums, pre-recorded instruction videos, tutorials, and digital resources are collected, they can be used again and again. Working in collaborative teams with other teachers and sharing resources can expedite the process significantly.

In the SEM, Type III projects not only increase students' self-efficacy, but also are correlated with other factors which may reduce underachievement. Longitudinal research on the use of the Triad Model has shown that students who completed Type III projects, both in and out of school, maintained interests and career aspirations in college and in graduate school (Delcourt, 1993; Renzulli & De Wet, 2010; Westberg, 2010). Research on the use of the Triad Model in college has also been conducted, with positive findings related to student creative productivity and engagement (Brandon et al., 2021). Starko (1988) found that students who became involved with self-selected independent studies in SEM programs initiated their own creative products both inside and outside school more often than students who did not have this opportunity. Starko also found that the number of creative Type III products completed in school was a highly significant predictor of self-efficacy.

Environmental Perceptions (Can I Be Successful *Here*?)

The third element of the AOM involves the students having students believe they can achieve in a particular environment (environmental efficacy). In a quiet classroom with monitored time, a student may be a competent reader with excellent reading comprehension. However, if that same student is asked to read at home where they are constantly interrupted by siblings, the family dog, or even parents, they may come to feel that they cannot focus or succeed in class. Unfortunately, this last variable may be the most difficult for the teacher because it is the one over which they have the least control. If a student does not have access to technology, reliable internet connections, and a quiet place to work, they may feel they are trying to learn in an environment where they cannot succeed. Sadly, in some cases, they may be correct. For certain, some teachers, counselors, parents and administrators have tried to create an environment in the home where children can be successful. Future research will show how effective these learning opportunities were. This element of a student's ability to expect to succeed in their environment may have changed drastically as the result of the COVID-19 pandemic. Some students may have a home ideal for learning with supportive parents ready to help when technology issues arise and may only need minimal help and guidance when challenges occur. In contrast, others may have no equipment, no quiet space, and no adult support at all. Again, it remains to be seen how much the home environment has affected students' education. In the interim, if teachers have students who are struggling, it may be beneficial to speak with the parents to better understand the home environment and level of support.

One component of the SEM that clearly enables students to be engaged and successful is letting them become engaged in enrichment clusters, one of the most widely known and implemented components of the SEM. Clusters are weekly enrichment opportunities that focus on students' interests and pair students with a teacher facilitator who helps each student develop a product or service in an area of personal interest. Students generally love these clusters as they are given the opportunity to choose ones they want to pursue. Clusters are held at regular blocks of time on a weekly basis, with students and teachers grouped by interest and across grade levels. The goals of enrichment clusters are higher enjoyment of enriched learning and enabling all students to apply both advanced content and process. Enrichment clusters also encourage all students to use authentic methods, content, and materials to complete products and services, as recommended in the Enrichment Triad Model. Reis, Gentry, and Maxfield (1998) investigated the impact of providing enrichment clusters to the entire population of two elementary schools and found positive effects on differentiated teaching practices. Once classroom teachers had facilitated clusters, they introduced more challenging content, as well as more authentic methodologies, advanced thinking, and problem-solving strategies in their regular classroom teaching.

Other research found that enrichment clusters can benefit performance-based identification of high potential students by broadening teachers' perceptions of students' talents and potentials when they are seen in other contexts. For example, Baum and colleagues (2014) found that using enrichment clusters in a school for twice exceptional (2e) students enabled students to become part of a social group; overcome some social, emotional, and cognitive challenges; develop ongoing mentor and professional relationships with people in talent areas; and develop expertise in areas of talent. Recently, several districts have implemented enrichment clusters online, showing that this component of the SEM can be implemented virtually.

The Important and Reciprocal Role of Self-Regulation

Research has shown that when students value the content, feel they have the skills to perform a task, and are in an environment where they can be successful, they will be motivated to put in the effort required to achieve that success. However, one critical element of the AOM lies outside the circle of three: the important factor of self-regulation. Self-regulation tends to increase when the other three factors are present, but there also appears to be a reciprocal relationship between them. Some research has shown that explicitly teaching self-regulation skills can help with motivation and achievement (Reis & Ruban, 2004). Further research needs to be conducted but it is entirely plausible that motivated and engaged students may struggle in online school in a way they would not struggle in regular school. The skills of staying organized and focused in a physical classroom may not perfectly transfer to staying organized and focused in an online classroom. Most teachers control their classroom environment, structure, pace, and limit distracting use of technology like cell phones. In contrast, in an online classroom there are a myriad of distractions on a scale some students may not be equipped to resist. Without the teacher being aware of it, they could potentially have their phone in their lap, YouTube open on another tab, and be chatting with a friend in Google chats. Students may benefit from learning self-regulation skills in this new context. Today's student needs to know how to organize files on a hard drive, Dropbox, or Google drive. Students in the past could keep a physical planner, but now may need to also learn how to work with an electronic calendar for due dates and assignments. An additional help may be the skill of learning how to manage time. In a school with bells and teachers to keep students on task, students may have never learned how to keep themself on task. With streaming videos, video games, and social media all available on the same screen as their homework some students have an extremely difficult time sticking to their work.

One strategy for underachieving students is to help them use a pomodoro timer (https://pomofocus.io/). This simple online timer is designed to help people work for uninterrupted bursts of time. The timer is set at 25 minutes work intervals and students set a goal not to visit another website, look at their phone, or do anything other than the homework assignment during that time. Students are encouraged to get as much quality work done as possible in each 25-minute session. Teachers can suggest that students who need help focusing put their phone at another table or in another room and close all computer tabs that are not needed for homework. If the homework does not require the computer, then students can be advised to set the timer on one single tab. Students can be encouraged to decide on a reward for themselves after completing a session with no distractions. For example, they might reward themself with ten minutes of a game or checking their social media feed. However, if they get to the end of the 25 minutes and they are in a highly productive mode, teachers can suggest they skip the break and just work for another 25 minutes. They should repeat these steps until the assignment is completed. This system will not work for all students, but it is essential that they each discover a workflow that is effective for them. Teachers should engage students in metacognitive discussions where they have the students express the problems with learning online and have them come up with proactive strategies to address them.

The best opportunity to reverse underachievement may be to identify students' interests and help them to engage in a Type III project in an area of intense student interest. Research on Type III suggests that students who engage in Type III Enrichment have a positive relationship between their early interests and subsequent interests and develop specific strengths, positively affecting subsequent interests (Westberg, 2010), postsecondary school plans (Hébert, 1993), career choices (Delcourt, 1993), goal valuation (Brigandi et al., 2016), environmental perceptions (Brigandi et al., 2018), levels of self-regulation (Brigandi et al., 2018; Hébert, 1993). Baum and colleagues (1995) reported that Type III enrichment was an effective approach to reverse underachievement. Brigandi et al. (2016) also found a positive connection between participation in enrichment and goal valuation. Students who engaged in Type III enrichment perceived their projects to be interesting and beneficial and believed they would contribute to their continued interest and perceptions of enjoyment in the future. Most recently, Brigandi et al. (2018) found that students who engaged in Type III enrichment benefitted from environmental supports, including exposure to challenging coursework and trusted relationships with project mentors, like-minded peers, and the gifted education teacher, which in turn positively affected their ability to self-regulate their work and self-actualize their goals.

Conclusion

In conclusion, education may have changed more in the past few years than at any other time in the last century. That change was forced due to a terrible world-wide pandemic and the full effects on student learning are still coming to light. Teachers are doing the best they can in a difficult circumstance to help students succeed, and with the AOM and the SEM, some teachers may be able to gain the theory and the tools they need to identify ways to help their high-potential students who may be underachieving both in live and in online schools. Resourceful and creative teachers, parents, and concerned adults can help to reinvent how these students learn and engage in online school.

REFLECTION QUESTIONS

1. What unique challenges do you foresee with engaging academically talented students in online learning?
2. List and describe at least five resources that you have found to be helpful in providing an engaging online curriculum. Do they need to be adapted for gifted learners? If so, to what extent (provide an example from one of the resources)?
3. What strategies are most effective in identifying the high-potential (gifted) students who are underperforming or unengaged online?
4. How can you organize students and mentors in an online format to experience Type III learning opportunities? In what ways are online options better or worse than in-person mentoring?
5. What tools and strategies may be helpful to teach academically talented students self-regulation skills so they can be successful online?
6. How might an observer recognize a student successfully utilizing self-regulation in an online environment?

References

Bandura, A. (1986). *Social foundations of thought and action: A social cognition theory.* Prentice-Hall.

Baum, S. M., Renzulli, J. S., & Hébert, T. P. (1995). Reversing underachievement: Creative productivity as a systematic intervention. *Gifted Child Quarterly, 39*(4), 224–235. https://doi .org/10.1177%2F001698629503900406

Baum, S. M., Schader, R. M., & Hébert, T. P. (2014). Through a different lens: Reflecting on a strengths-based, talent-focused approach for twice-exceptional learners. *Gifted Child Quarterly, 58*(4), 311–327. https://doi.org/10.1177/0016986214547632

Brandon, L., Reis, S. M., & McGuire, C. (2021). Perceptions of talented university students related to opportunities and autonomy for creative productivity. *Gifted Education International*. https://doi.org/10.1177%2F0261429421994335

Brigandi, C. B., Siegle, D., Weiner, J. M., Gubbins, E. J., & Little, C. A. (2016). Gifted secondary school students: The perceived relationship between enrichment and goal valuation. *Journal for the Education of the Gifted*, *39*(4), 263–287. https://doi.org/10.1177/0162353216671837

Brigandi, C. B., Weiner, J. M., Siegle, D., Gubbins, E. J., & Little, C. A. (2018). Environmental perceptions of gifted secondary school students engaged in an evidence-based enrichment practice. *Gifted Child Quarterly*, *62*(3), 289–305. https://doi.org/10.1177/0016986218758441

Colangelo, N., Assouline, S., & Gross, M. (Eds.). (2004). *A nation deceived: How schools hold back America's brightest students*. The University of Iowa.

Deci, E. L., & Ryan, R. M. (1985). *Intrinsic motivation and self-determination in human behavior*. Plenum.

Delcourt, M. A. B. (1993). Creative productivity among secondary school students: Combining energy, interest, and imagination. *Gifted Child Quarterly*, *37*(1), 23–31. https://doi.org/10.1177/001698629303700104

Eccles, J. S., & Wigfield, A. (1995). In the mind of the actor: The structure of adolescents' achievement task values and expectancy-related beliefs. *Personality and Social Psychology Bulletin*, *21*, 215–225.

Field, G. B. (2009). The effects of using Renzulli Learning on student achievement: An investigation of internet technology on reading fluency, comprehension, and social studies. *International Journal of Emerging Technology*, *4*(1), 29–39.

Geri, N., Winer, A., & Zaks, B. (2017). Challenging the six-minute myth of online video lectures: Can interactivity expand the attention span of learners? *Online Journal of Applied Knowledge Management*, *5*(1), 101–111.

Hébert, T. P. (1993). Reflections at graduation: The long-term impact of elementary school experiences in creative productivity. *Roeper Review*, *16*(1), 22–29. https://doi.org/10.1080/02783199309553529

Hernandez-Torrano, D., & Saranli, A. G. (2015). A cross-cultural perspective about the implementation and adaptation process of the Schoolwide Enrichment Model: The importance of talent development in a global world. *Gifted Education International*, *31*(3), 257–270.

Kamenetz, A. (2020, April 08). 4 in 10 U.S. teens say they haven't done online learning since schools closed. Available at: https://www.npr.org/sections/coronavirus-live-updates/2020/04/08/829618124/4-in-10-u-s-teens-say-they-havent-done-online-learning-since-schools-closed (accessed December 8, 2020).

Lewin, K. (1951). Cited in Cartwright D., & University of Michigan. Research Center for Group Dynamics (Eds.), *Field theory in social science: Selected theoretical papers* (1st ed.). Harper & Brothers.

Milan, L., Reis, S., Zanetti, M., & Renzulli, J. (2019). How Italian, European and American frameworks contribute to promoting talent development in Italian schools. *International Journal for Talent Development and Creativity*, *7*, 99–112.

Moon, S. M., & Hall, A. S. (1998). Family therapy with intellectually and creatively gifted children. *Journal of Marital and Family Therapy*, *24*, 59–80.

Reis, S. M., Gentry, M., & Maxfield, L. R. (1998). The application of enrichment clusters to teachers' classroom practices. *Journal for Education of the Gifted*, *21*(3), 310–324.

Reis, S. M., & McCoach, D. B. (2000). The underachievement of gifted students: What do we know and where do we go? *Gifted Child Quarterly*, *44*(3), 152–170. https://doi.org/10.1177/001698620004400302

Reis, S. M., & McCoach, D. B. (2002). Underachievement in gifted and talented students with special needs. *Exceptionality*, *10*(3), 113–125.

Reis, S. M., & Morales-Taylor, M. (2010). From high potential to gifted performance: Encouraging academically talented urban students. *Gifted Child Today*, *33*(4), 28–38. https://doi.org/10.1177/107621751003300408

Reis, S. M., & Peters, P. (2020). Research on the Schoolwide Enrichment Model: Four decades of insights, innovation, and evolution. *Gifted Education International*. https://doi.org/10.1177%2F0261429420963987

Reis, S. M., & Purcell, J. H. (1993). An analysis of content elimination and strategies used by elementary classroom teachers in the curriculum compacting process. *Journal for the Education of the Gifted, 16*(2), 147–170.

Reis, S. M., & Renzulli, J. S. (1992). Using curriculum compacting to challenge the above-average. *Educational Leadership, 50*(2), 51–57.

Reis, S. M., & Renzulli, J. S. (2003) Developing high potentials for innovation in young people through the Schoolwide Enrichment Model. In L.V. Shavinia (Ed.). *International handbook on innovation* (pp. 333–346). Springer.

Reis, S. M., & Renzulli, J. S. (2005). *Curriculum compacting: An easy start to differentiating for high-potential students*. Prufrock Press.

Reis, S. M., Renzulli, J. S., & Burns, D. E. (2016). *Curriculum compacting: A guide to differentiating curriculum and instruction through enrichment and acceleration* (2nd ed.). Prufrock Press.

Reis, S. M., & Ruban, L. M. (2004). Compensation strategies used by high ability students with learning disabilities. In T. M. Newman & R. J. Sternberg (Eds.), *Students with both gifts and learning disabilities: Identification, assessment, and outcomes* (pp. 155–198).

Kluwer Reis, S. M., & Westberg, K. L. (1994). The impact of staff development on teachers' ability to modify curriculum for gifted and talented students. *Gifted Child Quarterly, 38*(3), 127–135. https://doi.org/10.1177/001698629403800306

Reis, S. M., Westberg, K. L., Kulikowich, J. M., & Purcell, J. H. (1998). Curriculum compacting and achievement test scores: What does the research say? *Gifted Child Quarterly, 42*(2), 123–129. https://doi.org/10.1177/001698629804200206

Renzulli, J. S. (1977). *The Enrichment Triad Model: A guide for developing defensible program for the gifted and talented*. Creative Learning Press.

Renzulli, J. S. (1978). What makes giftedness? Re-examining a definition. *Phi Delta Kappan, 60*(3), 180–184, 261. https://doi.org/10.1177/003172171109200821

Renzulli, J. S. (2003). The Schoolwide Enrichment Model: An overview of the theoretical and organizational rationale. *Gifted Education International, 17*(1), 4–14.

Renzulli, J. S., & De Wet, C. F. (2010). Developing creative productivity in young people through the pursuit if ideal acts of learning. In R. A. Beghetto & J. C. Kaufman (Eds.), *Nurturing creativity in the classroom* (pp. 24–72). Cambridge University Press.

Renzulli, J. S., & Reis, S. M. (1985). *The Schoolwide Enrichment Model: A comprehensive plan for educational excellence*. Creative Learning Press.

Renzulli, J. S., & Reis, S. M. (1997). *The Schoolwide Enrichment Model: A how-to guide for educational excellence* (2nd ed.). Creative Learning Press.

Renzulli, J. S., & Reis, S. M. (2014). *The Schoolwide Enrichment Model: A how-to guide for educational excellence* (3rd ed.). Prufrock Press.

Renzulli, J. S., Smith, L. H., & Reis, S. M. (1982). Curriculum compacting: An essential strategy for working with gifted students. *The Elementary School Journal, 82*(3), 185–194.

Sampayo-Vargas, S., Cope, C., He, Z., & Byrne, G. (2013). The effectiveness of adaptive difficulty adjustments on students' motivation and learning in an educational computer game. *Computers & Education, 69*, 452–462. doi:10.1016/j.compedu.2013.07.004.

Siegle, D., & McCoach, D. B. (2005). Making a difference: Motivating gifted students who are not achieving. *Teaching Exceptional Children, 38*(1), 22–27. https://doi.org/10.1177/004005990503800104

Starko, A. J. (1988). Effects of the Revolving Door Identification Model on creative productivity and self-efficacy. *Gifted Child Quarterly, 32*(3), 291–297.

Weiner, B. (1986). *An attributional theory of motivation and emotion*. Springer-Verlag.

Westberg, K. L. (2010). Young creative producers: Twenty-five years later. *Gifted Education International, 26*(2–3), 261–270. https://doi.org/10.1177/026142941002600312

The Phenomenon of the (Un)Successful Gifted in Gifted Psychology Research

Ljiljana Krneta

Introduction

Attitudes toward the gifted in a social environment can be either encouraging or inhibiting for their development. In Bosnia and Herzegovina, and other countries of the region, there is no systematic support for the gifted, and the social, educational, and individual strategies in educating the gifted in the countries of the Balkans are different from those in the rest of Europe. The phenomenon of the complexity of giftedness is attracting more attention from numerous researchers. A pluralistic approach to the phenomenon of giftedness opens the way to an empirical validation of the phenomenon, but the abundance of empirical materials from both the twentieth and the twenty-first centuries provide no unambiguous results. The empirical data suggest an increasing percentage (20%t and more) of the gifted are unsuccessful (i.e., the phenomenon of underachievers in schools; Altaras, Jovanović, & Teovanović, 2012; Maksić, 2019). This chapter highlights empirical, independent research projects of Krneta, as well as some other relevant researchers. The results obtained from the relevant samples from Bosnia, Herzegovina, and Croatia may be useful to other educational systems in the region, due to the similarities between the Balkan countries. The findings reflect the social context of the countries from the region (i.e., in transition) and may be related to the education of the gifted, the brain drain, and the capacities of the (local) economy to employ the gifted and to use their creative capacities. Implications include a need to design adequate educational support for gifted students and communication in schools.

Attitudes Toward and Characteristics of the Gifted: Empirical Research

Modern approaches to research on giftedness (successful and unsuccessful, or gifted underachievers) are based on theoretical, experimental, and case studies. This chapter presents some empirical data, obtained from samples of the region (the Balkans) and using the psychometric approach.

Krneta and Krneta (2005) conducted a phenomenological study with 374 primary and secondary school students and 454 parents to explain attitudes toward giftedness,

DOI: 10.4324/9781003369578-6

the support for gifted individuals, the perception of the positionality of the gifted in social settings, and social closeness (or distance) to the gifted (i.e., the readiness of students and parents to establish various relationships with gifted individuals). Bogardus' scale for social distance was adapted and used, encompassing the following relations to someone who is gifted: (1) blood relative; (2) would be or is married to one; (3) studying together and/or sitting in close proximity (same table or desk) at school; (4) friends (spend time together in and out of school); (5) participate in excursions; and (6) distant acquaintance, i.e., to spend time after school only). Results show that social distance toward gifted individuals exists from both other students and parents, and the difference is that it is much more emphasized in other students. For other students, the highest level of closeness was established as distant acquaintances (80.75% of students) and the lowest was those who would marry (20.86%). On the other hand, parents express greater closeness and did not have pronounced distance toward them; the reported that they would engage at school (study together or sit in close proximity at school (90.31%), befriend (87.22%) and marry (72.29%). However, they expressed a certain distance in participating in an excursion (52.86%), know as blood relation (48.02%).

D. Krneta (2005, 2019) dedicated a part of his research to the complex field of giftedness, conducting 20 empirical research projects. These projects dealt with the position of the gifted in the context of social changes within the process of transition for former socialist countries and educational changes, emerging as a consequence of new social relations – social democratization caused changes and had visible implications in education; freedom of choice, expanded due to certain democratic changes in society, is a presumption of uninhibited behavior and an expression of personal dispositions, which is of crucial importance for the development and behavior of the gifted. In the educational sphere, it is manifested through changes in the system of education, the organization of classes, and the position of both students and teachers within the teaching process. An analysis of the results was carried out to identify relevant characteristics in which gifted individuals live and work, especially related to social distance toward the gifted, the quality of family interactions, perception of awards and punishments used to encourage the gifted, and the competence of students judged by the teaching faculty who work with the gifted students. It was concluded that there are a few systematic strategies in schools and in society used to encourage the gifted, and that the conditions in which the gifted individuals live and are educated are more inhibiting than encouraging. In accordance with the research results, it is claimed that this region has created a specific social environment that is unfavorable to the gifted.

Lj Krneta (2010) studied a sample (N = 1150) of primary students (676; 58.78%) and secondary (474; 41.22%) students, with 258 of them identified as gifted. The students' characteristics studied were IQ, EQ, achievement motive, self-efficacy, social and experiential characteristics (general success, gender, financial situation, place of residence). The results of the discriminative analysis show statistically significant differences between students' personality characteristics (intellectual capabilities, emotional intelligence, achievement motive, and general self-efficiency) and social-experiential features (type of school, gender, general success, place of residence, financial situation), on the one hand, and the perception of work efficiency held by teachers as "they are" and "as they should be," on the other hand.

Altaras, Teovanović, and Jovanović (2012) suggested some implications for gifted underachievers in their study, "How to recognize underachievement." They contended that underachieving gifted students are generally able to give adequate self-evaluations so they probably have an insight into their own underachievement. This conclusion supported the correlation found between objective and subjective evaluations of underachievement by Ziegler and Stoeger (2003). It is important to note that we should expect significant variations in the subjective evaluations compared to the objective indicators of underachievement. The findings of Jolić and Altaras (2014) suggested that gifted underachievers, as well as educational practice, are a reliable data source and a strong associate in recognizing the fact of underachievement. Regarding how to understand gifted underachievers, they claimed it is important to show this phenomenon as two-faced in the existing research. On one side, gifted underachievers present a problem and suffer disadvantages, especially regarding self-regulation, and partly regarding the capacity to establish warm and harmonious interpersonal relationships. The positive side of gifted underachievement reveals students who do not force themselves to do what has been predetermined they should do just for the sake of doing it.

In the research study by Krneta and Šimunić (2013) on the emotional competence of gifted students in school with a sample of 480 students (gifted, N = 52), the results indicated that compassionate communication and NVC (non-violent communication) are very well accepted by the gifted and non-gifted students. At the same time, the products of non-verbal communication and visual perception of recognizing, understanding, and regulating emotions in the gifted and other students indicate a multitude of factors of inner personal experience, related to the students' age characteristics, expressing emotionality, symbols of expressive creativity in group interaction, and richness of vocabulary.

Ristić (2015) in a study of hypersensitivity of gifted and non-gifted children, surveying a sample of 150 children aged 8–13 years, indicated statistically significant differences between the hypersensitivity of gifted and non-gifted children. The results also show that gender, age, and artistic inclinations significantly affect the academic achievement of hypersensitive gifted and non-gifted children.

Lj Krneta (2020), as outlined in *Perceived Changes in and Life Satisfaction Among the Gifted*, conducted empirical and non-experimental research on a sample of 688 secondary school students from Bosnia and Herzegovina. They were divided into two subgroups: (1) a sample of the gifted (N = 216; 31.39%), including students from secondary art schools and other secondary schools who participated in competitions at the regional, federal, or higher levels; and (2) a sample of students identified as non-gifted, including students from vocational schools and grammar schools (N = 472; 69.59%t). The sample included 346 female students and 336 male students, aged 15–18, from different locations. The research was carried out as a transversal research (i.e., the results reflect the state of the examined characteristics in the examinees for a defined period of time). The gifted and non-gifted students' subjective experiences were viewed from two aspects: their perception of the present and their vision of the future (Table 4.1). Psychology finds the terms of the perception of the present and the vision for the future as crucial in analyzing an individual's identity, so it is of a great importance to access them as an essential part of an individual's self-image or self-awareness. Therefore, it is claimed that gifted students' perception of the present and their vision for the future are relevant in their development in terms of schooling and for tasks set by themselves as relevant goals and aims to which they aspire.

Self-awareness is one aspect of the emotional-value framework, which is essential to the interpretation of performance of the gifted and non-gifted students, as indicated by "Intensity" (mainly negative 20; 2.91%; unsure 212; 30.81%; mainly positive

TABLE 4.1 Perceptions of the present among the gifted and other students in Bosnia and Herzegovina

Students	Attitude toward the present				
	Extremely negative (%)	Mostly negative (%)	Mostly positive (%)	Extremely positive (%)	Σ
Gifted	8 (3.70)	80 (37.04)	102 (47.2)	26 (12.04)	216
Other	12 (2.54)	132 (27.97)	282 (59.75)	46 (9.75)	472
Total	20 (2.91)	212 (30.81)	384 (55.81)	72 (10.47)	688

Note: Pearson's chi square 9.55196, df = 3, p = .022798.

384; 55.81%; very positive 72; 10.46%; and very negative 0). The results indicate that there are statistically significant differences in perception of the present between the gifted and non-gifted students (Chi-square = 9.55196, with three degrees of freedom, 0.05 (p = .022798)). Gifted students hold mainly positive attitudes toward the present (47.22%t compared to 59.75% non-gifted), with 37.04%, "not sure" and far fewer very positive (12.04% similar to 9.75% of the non-gifted). It seems that the gifted have a more pessimistic attitude toward the present, supporting the hypothesis that there is a difference in the perception of the present between the gifted and other students. It was evident, however, that no statistically significant differences exist in the perception of the future between gifted and non-gifted students (Table 4.2).

My research team also surveyed students' thoughts and views of the future, based on which a general attitude toward the future is determined. Using a Likert scale, eight items that relate to the students' thoughts and views on various aspects of the future were used. The items were worded as positive and negative items. As an example, for the question, "Do you look forward to the arrival of the future?," the answers were grouped on a five-point scale from "very high" to "not at all." The results show that their vision for the future is a more pronounced, accepting 175 items that pointed to the hopes and good thoughts about the future. The most acceptable items were: "Do you think about the future?"(3.71); "Is the future more important than the past?" (3.67); "How much do you believe that your future will be good?" (3.64), and "How much well-being do you expect from your future?" (3.63). The least acceptable items included: "Is the future more important than the present?" (-2.87) and "Are you looking forward to your future?" (3.19). The basic indicators of the analyzed relations between the independent variables (gender, age, and grade) and emotional intelligence are presented in Table 4.3.

TABLE 4.2 Perceptions of the future among the gifted and others in Bosnia and Herzegovina

Students	Perception of the future				
	Mostly bad (%)	Uncertain (%)	Mostly good (%)	Very good (%)	Σ
Gifted	18 (8.33)	110 (50.93)	84 (38.89)	4 (1.85)	216
Other	22 (4.66)	254 (53.81)	184 (38.98)	12 (2.54)	472
Total	40 (5.81)	364 (52.91)	268 (38.95)	16 (2.33)	688

Note: Pearson's chi square 3.97500, df = 3, p = 26419.

TABLE 4.3 Indicators of relationships between independent variables (gender, age, and class of students) and emotional intelligence

Independent variables	Emotional intelligence	Attitude toward oneself	Relations to others	Attitude toward life
Pole, gender	Pearson's chi square: 2.74597, df = 2, p = .253364	Pearson's chi square: 15.8067, df = 1, p = .000070**	Pearson's chi square: .055365, df = 1, p = .813980	Pearson's chi square: 5.39939, df = 1, p = .020150*
Age	Pearson's chi square: 91.3886, df = 12, p = .000000**	Pearson's chi square: 23.2304 df = 6, p = .000725**	Pearson's chi square: 16.4757, df = 6, p = .011430*	Pearson's chi square: 30.2402, df = 6, p = .000036**
Class	Pearson's chi square: 61.6716, df = 10, p = .000000**	Pearson's chi square: 122.849, df = 5, p = .000000**	Pearson's chi square: 27.5459 df = 5, p = .000045**	Pearson's chi square: 68.8632, df = 5, p = .000000**

Note: **significant at the 0.01 level; *significant at the 0.05 level.

Who Are the Gifted Underachievers? A Case Study (Krneta, 2017–2021)

Researching communication, giftedness, and creativity, some psychological aspects of the creative process for young and productive creators from Banja Luka are revealed. Although being very distinctive, original and completely different when expressing their creativity, it seems important to emphasize certain moments of the creative process, which significantly influenced their creative expression. The following case study (personal interviews, 2017, 2018, 2019, 2021) documents reflections of talented young people who were not formerly recognized in school for their talent, but had strong emotional support from the family and/or community programming.

From Jillian's Diary

Jillian (pseudonym) is a 7-year-old girl who could not go to school. Jillian had poor grades, and many punishments in school and home. At school, she constantly got up, distracted others, was unfocused, and did not pay attention in her classes. Her teachers were worried about her, they punished her, they scolded her, they awarded her several times when she did pay attention, but still nothing. Jillian would not stay seated or pay attention. When she returned home, her mother punished her too. One day, Jillian's mother was called to come to the school. The teachers suggested Jillian had a disorder called hyperactivity. During the discussion, a former teacher who knew her more positively asked the mother and her colleagues to follow her to the nearby classroom where Jillian was still sitting. She had turned on the radio since she had stayed alone in the classroom waiting for her mother. Jillian was observed moving up and down, right and left, moving to the music in rhythm. The teacher said, "You see? Jillian is not sick; Jillian is a dancer! I would suggest her mother take her for dance classes." Jillian was enrolled in dance, and on her first day of dance class she returned home and said to her mother: "Everyone is just like me, no one can sit there!" In 1981, after a successful dance career, Jillian established her own dance school and received an international award for her art. Jillian became a choreographer for the musicals *Cats* (1981) and *The Phantom of the Opera* (1986).

From Keri's Diary

As Keri (pseudonym) put it:

Creativity needs inspiration, motive, and the need to express yourself expressively ... by expressive fluency, we mean the ability to organize and develop ideas into appropriate systems and structures. For creativity, the moment of motive and motivation is as important for creativity as originality, fluency of ideas, creative imagination, etc. Creative personalities are people who have developed an extremely strong need to find an order where it seems it does not exist at all and who pay attention to those items that seem unclassifiable. In their need for disorder, such people have an expressed need for situations which cannot be settled by applying some already defined schemes, but which will probably have their own order. Regarding *artistic attitude*, my artistic activity takes place in the critical thinking about art and society as one unit, which inseparably exist next to each other as well as in some individual, experiential situations, referring to one wider social context. My works are not created in a vacuum, they reflect the community, influencing not only me but also all individuals of our society. My works are pervaded with the issues of political practice which undoubtedly has interwoven its roots in any and all aspects of our everyday life, the issues of art as a tool which may be used as a protective mechanism to overcome social crisis. Some of my works criticize the art institutions (the art establishment) in an ironic manner, without any clichés, on the verge of absurdity. I give comments on the social reality through other people's statements which I note down every day, everywhere and every single moment in a day and I use the selected statements to make drawings, creating a kind of X-ray of the society in which I live. I leave the elements of transgressive, narrative, and rhetorical textual to express a space for discussion. If the world of art is the world of communication between several subjects and their relationship of establishing, exchanging works, sense, meaning is art, who has the power to declare that something is art? I expect my works to wake up a new, unexpected experience, to wake up the critical awareness toward the social hypocrisy, toward the aesthetic and ideological mechanisms of power and the domination culture. Through different media I use: paintings, drawings, video art, digital collage, photos, I often use cruel jokes from everyday life, statements referring to the different types of low-ranked comedies as well as vulgar comedies, reflecting the society in its crisis and expressing them as their protective mechanism.

From Rady's Diary

As Rady (pseudonym) put it:

I learned to listen. By silencing my own being, I opened myself to the birth of something I didn't always quite understand. Sometimes it was as strange to me as if it came from someone else on whose frequency I had stumbled upon ... or it was the sobs of some long-forgotten part of me. Either way, that inner world sought to materialize by choosing different artistic media ... from my earliest memories I was preoccupied with art, but that need of mine was not met with adult approval. I was forced to retreat to a hidden corner inside me.

Rady found moments of greatest inspiration in his early childhood when expressing his creativity. When perceiving Rady's artistic creation, one may find in a special manner that true desire for freedom to create, interwoven with emotions, media, motivation, a search for unexplored aspects of soul and human existence. He claims:

> Motivation is something that leads a person through life toward quicker, easier fulfillment of their tasks and goals. If it is clearly defined and if it is being elaborated, all our work invested into something is done with much pleasure. At the beginning of life, in our childhood, our main motivation is our parents, who, more or less successfully, direct our scattered thoughts into a clear walk toward something we want. They have a very important and a bit unrewarding role to create some foundations for our future resourcefulness. In life, our motivation develops through individual values and beliefs we may acquire or reason. I have never had any idols, because I was my main motivation for 5, 10, 15, 20 years in advance, how I wanted to look, where I wanted to be, what my behavior was at the time, and how I reasoned. I believe the largest source of motivation is in thoughts ... Later on, our motivation is significantly influenced by our peers and the environment in which we live. Especially in our early years, because that is the main parameter on the basis of which we evaluate ourselves. Since my early age, I have never felt myself to be a part of my environment, a part of the pack, but it has never made me doubt myself, because of my belief that everyone has their own place under the stars, and it has motivated me to search for more and to see even more. I find most of my motivation not only in the visions I create in the future but in things I do every day for "my soul," in small victories and new lessons which life gives every day. Motivation improves our beliefs, self-confidence and self-discipline. The thing which helps me most with motivation in my professional area of life is mental housecleaning. When entering a creative process, it is important for me to have my senses open, my thoughts unburdened and free, i.e., to be confident and happy because it is the vocation I have chosen. Therefore, I like to leave all the thoughts from the outside world in front of the door before any rehearsal or show so I can commence that rehearsal openly and with self-confidence. It is an exercise and a ritual I should not neglect, so I really appreciate its role in the process.

A Holistic Approach to Addressing Underachievement in Modern Schools

Contemporary approaches to learning have some important categories for learning and development: developmental processes, quality of surrounding, communication and creativity in which the learning process includes important roles of students and teachers. The empirical research shared on the gifted and non-gifted students has contributed to the holistic approach of researching and teaching the gifted, including encouraging emotional competences in schools.

Quality education and the modern school are concepts inseparable from two complex processes: modernization and democratization of the educational system. In that sense, it is necessary to emphasize the constructivist approach that advocates the optimal development of students' personalities and emphasizes learning and development. This approach fundamentally changes the roles of students so that students no longer take a passive role (the one who listens, memorizes, reproduces), but gradually move toward an active role and participant in their educational journey.

For communication, a successful interactive role of student-teacher is achieved, and is enriched by a range of positive attitudes toward giftedness, with the student as an actor for their own development in immediate social circumstances. It is known that social circumstances, by using forms of social learning according to the model, effectively influence not only socialization and upbringing, but also overall behavior. Krneta (2014) points out that in the modern school the essence is in the perception of communication between students and teachers.

Jean Sunde Peterson and Rocha (2020) claimed that underachievers need to be part of a community of intellectual peers at a crucial time of development – especially if they struggle with internal distress or difficult situations. She suggested that struggle is not only essential to advanced development, in Dabrowskian terms, but may also be rich soil for growing creativity. Underachievers may be able to contribute unexpected perspectives and insights to discussions, and the social and emotional development of both high and low achievers can be nurtured in the process.

The Role of Emotions in the Educational Process

Emotions play an important role in the educational process, because communication with emotions encourages the balanced development of students' personalities. Complementing the impact of cognitive factors on the school performance, some conative (emotional, social, and motivational characteristics) and environmental factors also impact performance. Kretch and Crutchfield (1974) have pointed out that the term emotions refers to an excited body state which is manifested through emotional experience, emotional behavior, and physiological changes within the body. Milivojević (2008) has pointed out the integrative role of emotions using the emotion analysis method (KER). Studying the impact of emotions and emotional competency within the educational process has shown that emotions can be a motivating or inhibiting factor in the learning process. So-called *positive emotions* motivate toward completion of an activity, increase the interest for learning, influence open-mindedness, flexibility, creativity, and stimulate empathy and cooperation, harmony, and involvement within group processes. *Negative emotions* act in an inhibiting manner, blocking memories, increasing conflicts within the classroom, influencing resistance, and sabotaging communication. These negatively influence self-image and self-confidence.

Emotional Intelligence (or EQ)

The first research on emotional intelligence (or EQ) was conducted by Salovey and Mayer (1990), followed by important work by Reuven (1997), and Ciarrochi, Chan, and Caputi (2000). In understanding the EQ construct, the role of emotions (self-awareness, self-control, social-awareness, and interpersonal relations) is very important. Piske (2020) indicated that the area of giftedness covers emotional and intellectual dimensions. The intellectual aspect with its unlimited complexity is related to the emotional depth of the gifted student, just as their thinking is more complex and has more depth if compared to that of other students. Their emotions are also more complex and more intense and are experienced in different ways in the school context. Complexity is perceived through the wide range of emotions that gifted children can experience at any moment, and emotional intensity is evident from their involvement in various situations. Since gifted children show greater maturity than others in some domains, they may be at greater risk of specific types of socio-emotional difficulties if their needs are not met. These aspects may include increased awareness, anxiety, perfectionism, stress, difficulties with peer relationships, and concerns about identity and adjustment. Their teachers and families need to be attuned to the specific needs of their children and help shape a solid framework for socio-emotional health.

Emotional Competence

In my previous research (Krneta & Šimunić, 2013), I stressed the importance of emotional competence of the gifted and non-gifted students in school. The process of recognizing, understanding, and regulating emotions in a classroom is shown through a display of learning strategies (visual, auditory, kinesthetic, and digital; see also Chapter 9 in this volume) in a direct teaching process: For example, with visual learning strategy, a drawing of a human figure can be used to awaken personal emotional states; a picture with facial expressions of different emotions can be used to observe and understand emotions; and a group drawing can be used to recognize, understand and regulate one's own and someone else's emotions. A digital learning strategy involves the ability to use emotional vocabulary (e.g., the creation of "positive" and "negative" emotional terms to properly name your emotions and to regulate them).

Direct pedagogical and collaborative learning in the classroom (i.e., paired work, group work, team work, etc.) enables the expression of different forms of communication, enriched with direct activities of students and teachers. This has a strong psychological component, especially in expressing the emotions. The phrase, "Interactive learning and creativity" is used as a strategy in stimulating the emotional competence of the gifted and other students in the school. The school is seen as an action space in which both students and teachers play multiple roles. Therefore, the research by Krneta and Šimunić (2013) and Krneta (2014) in Bosnia and Herzegovina and Croatia has contributed to the development of more humane relationships in schools, enriched with the stimulation of non-violent communication and creativity.

Implications for Practice and Conclusion

How to overcome underachievement? Researchers and practitioners face many challenges when working with gifted students. In this chapter. I have shared scientific research conducted in Bosnia and Herzegovina, pointing out all the complexity of the phenomenon of giftedness that underpins achievement, or underachievement. Research has emphasized the importance of knowing what it is that intellectually moves the gifted underachievers (and the gifted students in general). I posit that there is more behind the gifted students` underachievement than the mere "lack of motivation." Motivation is the driving force that is also influenced by other factors in a student's environment; it is the experiences we live through, the connections we share, and the artistic atmosphere we create. The gifted underachievers are motivated to study, but perhaps their intellectual gifts are inadequately cultivated. For example they may feel intellectually moved toward some big goals (such as artistic expression), but it seems that they cannot find their way toward achieving that goal. In that case, they need to be specifically directed and supported.

Considering the limited studies on gifted underachievement, I recommend further research in this field. There is a need to determine the validity of different procedures used to identify the gifted underachievers (and the gifted ones in general) as well as the matter of early causes for and the occurrence of underachievement. Social influences affect the environment in Bosnia and Herzegovina, which has no strategy or systematic support for the education of gifted individuals.

REFLECTION QUESTIONS

1. Why are the social climate and context in which gifted individuals live important when addressing issues related to achievement (or underachievement)?
2. How do social perceptions by gifted students toward the present and vision for the future offer any notion of impact regarding underachievement?
3. Based on this empirical research, what would you consider to be the root causes of underachievement?
4. How do the case studies inform potential solutions regarding external factors impacting underachievement?
5. Why is a holistic approach to understanding the phenomenon of gifted underachievers important?
6. Previous chapters have mentioned self-regulation as part of learning. In this chapter we also discuss emotional intelligence (EQ). What are effective strategies to teach students self-regulation regarding their emotions?
7. This chapter notes the "two faces" of underachievement. What are they? Do you agree or disagree? Explain.

References

Altaras, A., Jovanovic, P., & Teovanovic, P. (2012). *Psihološki profil darovitih podbacivača: integracija istraživačkih nalaza [Psychological profile of gifted underachievers: a synthesis of research findings]*. Faculty for Special Education and Rehabilitation, University of Belgrade, Serbia. Available at: https://www.academia.edu/22922620/Psiholo%C5%A1ki_profil_darovitih_podbaciva%C4%8Da_integracija_istra%C5%BEiva%C4%8Dkih_nalaza_The_profile_of_gifted_underachievers_A_synthesis_of_research_findings_ (accessed April 15, 2021)/

Ciarrochi, J.V., Chan, A.Y. C., & Caputi, P. (2000). A critical evaluation of the emotional intelligence construct. *Personality and Individual Differences*, 28(3), 539–561. https://doi.org/10.1016/s0191-8869(99)00119-1

Jolić, Z. M., & Altaras, A. D. (2014). Reliability, construct and criterion-related validity of the Serbian adaptation of the trait emotional intelligence questionnaire (TEIQue). *Psihologija*, 47(2), 249–262. https://doi.org/10.2298/PSI1402249J

Kreč, D., & Kračvild, B. (1974). *Elementi psihologije*. Naučna knjiga.

Kretch, D., & Crutchfield, R. (1974). *Elements of psychology* (3rd edn). Alfred A. Knopf.

Krneta, D. (2002). *Perspektive razvoja mladih talenata u izmjenjenim ambijentalnim uslovima*. VSV, M. Palov, Vršac i Univerzitet Tibiskus, Temišvar, Zbornik radova, Međunarodni naučni skup.

Krneta, D. (2005). *Interaktivno učenje i nastava*. NUBL, Fakultet za političke i društvene nauke.

Krneta, D. (2016). *Metodičke osnove nastavnog rada-metodički priručnik za nastavnike srednje škole*. Grafid d.o.o.

Krneta, D. (2018, November 20). JS RTRS – Radio Republike Srpske, emisija Studiorum. Available at: https://lat.rtrs.tv/av/audio.php?prgid=85&fbclid=IwAR1tT4G9xQ3FTqW_Bdjz6g7jYeqR6DVtgZ-aDGzmmLiAU2ojYrttaD3WNg4

Krneta, D., & Krneta, L. (2005). Međunarodni naučni skup "Daroviti i odrasli." In *Daroviti u očima drugih [Gifted in the eyes of others]* (vol. 11, pp. 133–147). Viša škola za obrazovanje vaspitača.

Krneta, L. (2010) Paradigm of contemporary concepts of giftedness-social-emotional development of the gifted. Paper presented at International Scientific Conference, Social and Emotional Needs of Gifted and Talented, Bled, Zbornik – II MiB d.o.o.

Krneta, L. (2013). *Ličnost učenika i percepcija radne efikasnosti nastavnika*. Grafid d.o.o.

Krneta, L. (2014). Re:Thinking giftedness: Giftedness in the digital age. In *Perception in the present and the future vision of gifted and other students* (pp. 178–179). University of Ljubljana, Faculty of Education.

Krneta, L. (2016). *Nove paradigme – Holistički pristup kreativnosti djece predškolskog uzrasta*. Zbornik-Nadarjeni i talentirani predškolski otrok, Ljubljana – IX Mednarodna strukovna konferenca vzgojiteljev v vrtcah (Slovenija, Nizozemska, Velika Britanija, Bosna i Hercegovina i Češka) (pp. 18–28). Mib d.o.o.i MIB EDU.

Krneta, L. (2017). Perception of students on innovative and creative school. Book Summary, Lisbon, Summary Abstracts. I5 ICIE EXCELLENCE, INNOVATION.

Krneta, L. (2018). Research on visual observation and creativity through interactive learning- Book Summary, Paris. 16. ICIE Université Paris Descartes.

Krneta L. (2019). Perceived changes in and life satisfaction among the gifted, Ruše, keynote presentation. Mednarodna znanstveno-strukovna konferenca, Pedagoška fakulteta, Univerza v Mariboru.

Krneta, L.(2020). *Perceived changes in and life satisfaction among the gifted*. J. Hertzog (Ed).Verlag dr. Kovač-Contemporary Ascepts of Giftedness.

Krneta, L., & Šimunić, E. (2013). Metodološki problemi istraživanja darovitosti. In *Podsticanje emocionalne kompetentnosti darovitih učenika u školi [Encouraging the emotional competence of gifted students in school]* (pp. 200–214).Visoka škola strukovnih studija za vaspitače.

Maksic, S. (2019). Darovitost, edukacija darovitih, inovacije i kreativnost u obrazovanju i psihologiji. In *Doprinos istraživanja obrazovanju darovitih učenika [Contribution of research studies to gifted education]* (pp. 113–119). Grafid, doo.

Milivojević, Z. (2008). *Emocije*. Psihopolis.

Peterson, J. S., & Rocha, A. (2020). Preface. In F. H. R. Piske, T. Stoltz, & C. Costa-Lobo (Eds.), *Socio-emotional development and creativity of gifted students* (pp. 7–11). Imprensa da Universidade de Coimbra.

Piske, F. H. R. (2020). *Socio-emotional development and creativity of gifted students*. Imprensa da Universidade de Coimbra.

Reuven, B.-O. (1997). *EQ-i BarOn emotional quotient inventory: A measure of emotional intelligence*: technical manual. Multi-Health Systems.

Ristić, R. (2015) Comparing hypersensitivity of gifted and non-gifted. Paper presented at International Conference,Vršac-Arad.

Salovey, P., & Mayer, J. D. (1990). Emotional intelligence. *Imagination, Cognition and Personality, 9*(3), 185–211. https://doi.org/10.2190/dugg-p24e-52wk-6cdg

Salovey, P., Sluyter, J., & Goleman, D. (1997) *Emotional development and emotional intelligence*. Educational Implications.

Ziegler, A., & Stoeger, H. (2003). Identification of underachievement: An empirical study on the agreement among various diagnostic sources. *Gifted and Talented International, 18*(2), 87–94. https://doi.org/10.1080/15332276.2003.11673019

Practices

The Challenge and Promise of Creative Underachievers

Jennifer L. Groman

Introduction

The creative child. What picture does this paint in your mind? What are their behaviors, reactions, interests, and personality characteristics? If you are a teacher, thoughts of a child like this may delight you and inspire you to find ways to integrate creative thinking and expression into your daily lessons. It is possible, though, that thoughts of a child like this puts fear into your teacher's heart. The creative child is quirky, a daydreamer, and asks questions that are either unanswerable or take the trajectory of a lesson into far-reaching territories – far beyond the daily standard you are attempting to cover.

It is a fact: being creative increases a child's odds of dropping out of school (Kim & Hull, 2012). In their seminal work, *Cradles of Eminence*, Victor and Mildred Goertzel (1962) studied and reported trends in the childhood experiences of four hundred eminent individuals (hereafter called the Four Hundred), adding the biographies of three hundred more for the second edition (Goertzel et al., 2004). In their text, there are section titles that reference the challenge in the childhoods of these eminent individuals. Chapter 10 is titled "Dislike of School and Schoolteachers," and other subheadings include "Children Who Were Thought to Be Dull or Who Were Academic Failures" and "Creative Children as School Problems" (p. iv).

The creative individual is fascinating and often mercurial. It is through the seminal work of Goertzel and Goertzel (1962) and their extended work (Goertzel et al., 2004), that I frame the exploration of the challenges faced by creative children that may cause them to underachieve, and offer insights that might help educators improve the school experiences of creative underachievers. The chapter begins with definitions and characteristics of the creative underachieving child, and continues with various sections on the challenges of these types of children, including direct connections in the literature between creativity and underachievement, followed by a discussion of behavioral issues related to creative underachievers, the sensitivities of creative and gifted students, and issues of nonconformity. The heart of this chapter is a section on the mismatch between creative individuals and the school. The chapter concludes with suggestions and next steps for schools and teachers to ensure the promise of the creative underachiever.

DOI: 10.4324/9781003369578-8

Goertzel et al. (2004) stated that creative thinking peaks in second grade, and believed high school to be a "particularly barren period for any expression of intellectual vigor or originality" (p. 278). They asserted that college and adulthood are where individuals regain their motivation for learning for learning's sake, for intuition, and the seeking of beauty and truth.

Definitions

According to Dyrda (2000), students with Scholastic Underachievement Syndrome (SUS) simply cannot be classified into homogeneous groups, due to the striking diversity and variability in their interests and behaviors. However, underachieving students are usually defined as above the 50th percentile in terms of IQ or cognitive ability and below the 50th percentile in achievement scores (Kim & Van Tassel-Baska, 2010). Torrance (1966) found that underachieving creatively gifted individuals tend to be in the superior IQ range (118–138), and mainly in the IQ range of the 120s, rather than the very superior range (above 140) (Rimm, 2015).

For the purposes of this chapter, a definition and explanation of *creativity*, especially as it relates to underachievement, are also necessary. The relationship between creativity and intelligence is often debated. Many researchers support the threshold theory, which states that high creative potential requires a threshold IQ level of above-average intelligence, or around 120. However, a meta-analysis by Kim (2008) indicated that the relationship between creativity and intelligence may be minor, and that "the threshold theory was not supported by quantitative synthesis" (Kim & Van Tassel-Baska, 2010, p. 186), thus creativity and IQ may be perceived as independent constructs. Piirto (2004) asserted that creativity is not a separate or stand-alone thinking skill, but is domain-specific.

Creativity in individuals, then, is defined here using a foundational notion that the individuals' ideas are: (1) novel or new, and (2) appropriate to the task (Amabile, 2012; Kaufman, 2016; Kaufman & Beghetto, 2012). Kaufman and Beghetto indicated that context is important to defining creativity, and they believe creativity is leveled thus:

> Mini-c creativity can be seen in interpretations, actions, and insights (being new and task appropriate) that are novel for the individual and allow for personally meaningful connections to the world. Mini-c creativity elicits changes in understanding and impacts individuals.

Little-c or everyday creativity is creativity in a small context, and "enriches the human experience and is associated with many positive outcome variables" (Kaufman & Beghetto, 2012, p. 156). Little-c creativity impacts individuals and their zone of influence.

Pro-c level creativity is evident in expert level creators or teams of creators who have not yet attained eminence. Pro-c creativity impacts organizations, teams, and markets.

Big-C level creativity is reserved for true immortals in their field, those who achieve eminence. This type of creativity impacts culture, society, and the world, and is beyond the reach of most people.

It is important to note that mini-c and little-c creativity are very relevant to school learning cultures. It is believed that the only way to reach Pro-c and Big-C level creativity is to experience mini-c and little-c creativity in childhood and beyond, and empowering children to experience mini-c and little-c creativity prepares them for higher-level creativity interactions later. So, according to scholarly definitions, creative children are those who have new and novel ideas that are task-appropriate.

Characteristics of the Creative Thinker

Goertzel et al. (2004), in studying the lives of four hundred eminent creative individuals (the Four Hundred), found that, despite their intelligence, creativity, and potential for future eminence, three out of five of the Four Hundred had serious school problems.

It might be hypothesized that gifted children who are creative would easily fit within traditional classrooms, be welcomed and supported, and find success therein. However, that is not the case. In an article that has spread through gifted educational circles for years, Szabos (1989) compared the characteristics of a gifted child versus the bright child, that was also adapted by Kingore (2004b), as the distinction between high achiever, the gifted learner, and the creative thinker. Their chart describes the creative thinker as a daydreamer who may appear off-task, an independent, original, unconventional child who is overflowing with ideas (many of which will remain undeveloped), an intuitive individual who makes mental leaps, a child who enjoys off-the-wall humor and is unmotivated by grades, and eschews repetition for the sake of mastery. Dyrda (2000) asserted that gifted students have a great deal of creative potential, and may appear nonconforming, divergent in their thought processes, and do not meet with approval from most traditional teachers. Kim and Hull (2012) observed in the creative child a lack of inhibitions associated with self-exploration and self-expression.

In researching for this chapter, I found overwhelming evidence that traditional teachers and schools prefer students who do not exhibit the characteristics and behaviors of creative thinking, as it works against the standardized, lock-step nature of the school culture. This environment can, over time, drive the creative child into rebellion, or into hiding their creative responses and ultimately, underachievement.

Reis and McCoach (2002) noted three individual characteristics of underachieving gifted students that they saw as positive attributes. Underachieving gifted, in their viewpoint, have intense outside interests, are highly creative, and demonstrate honesty and integrity in rejecting unchallenging coursework. Types of underachievement can be seen as falling into two groups. The first are students with recurrent or chronic incongruity between their potential and their scholastic achievement. The second group consists of students whose underachievement is situational and periodic, and usually in response to temporary circumstances or problems (Dyrda, 2000; Reis & McCoach, 2002). "In the vast majority of cases the situational drops in achievement evolve with tie into chronic underachievement, making an expert and accurate diagnosis of the causes of this damaging phenomenon extremely important" (Dyrda, 2000, p. 130).

Creativity and Underachievement

I was surprised to find that there are many direct connections between achievement and creativity in the literature. Older research suggests that many gifted underachievers show potential for high levels of creativity (Whitmore, 1980). Reis and Renzulli (1982) and Torrance (1964) agree that creativity contributes to high achievement, even when paired with average or lower intelligence. According to Kim and Van Tassel-Baska (2010), "both underachieving and overachieving students might have higher creative potential than other students" (p. 190). Indeed, a number of researchers assert that gifted underachievement may be related to higher levels of creativity (Kim, 2008; Kim & Hull, 2012; Kim & Van Tassel-Baska, 2010; Rimm, 2015). Kim and Hull (2012) even posit that: "creativity can be a gift as well as a curse for some students in [the] traditional school environment, where it can lead to underachievement and even dropping out of school" (p. 174).

Kim and Hull (2012) examined creativity and its possible roles in high school dropouts. They determined that the presence of certain creative personality attributes play a role in how students temper their interactions in the school environment. "Some students may not fit well within the school system because of conflicts between their personalities and the school environment" (p. 173). These include "problems with authority, nonconformity, hostility, suspiciousness, oversensitivity, and egotism" (p. 169). Also, gifted dropouts show "negative and rebellious attitudes toward school and authority, poor peer relationship, and poor social adjustment" (p. 169), all of which relate to the presence of asynchrony, as well as a sense of resentment toward the school community due to a certain lack of support or intellectual challenge.

Behavior Challenges

Goertzel et al. (2004) noted that in the childhoods of their eminent Four Hundred, many of them engaged in activities that gained disapproval by their teachers. They explored ideas and manipulated materials, enjoyed fantasy, saw unusual uses for everyday objects, and had an energy that was misconstrued as playing rather than doing serious work tasks assigned by their teachers.

Kim and Van Tassel-Baska (2010) indicated that behavioral problems in school are common for all types of children, and are not unique to underachieving students. However, Torrance (1981) recognized a relationship between behavioral problems and creativity among underachievers. He expressed concern that teachers view creative students as difficult to manage, even punishing and discouraging creative behaviors. Thirty years later, Kim and Van Tassel-Baska (2010) confirmed this, and found that behavioral problems in underachieving high school students were related to their creativity, in that students with behavioral problems scored higher on measures of creative potential. In another study, students rated by teachers as impulsive, disruptive, and hyperactive, scored higher on tests of creative fluency (Brandau et al., 2007).

Teachers are often ill-prepared to work with gifted students, and as a result, a response to repetitive and unchallenging tasks in the classroom may be seen as misbehavior in these students (Kim, 2008; Torrance, 1962). In addition, avoiding unpleasant work and interactions with teachers (Kim, 2008), poor grades, missing assignments, general disorganization, mood swings, and intense emotions often plague the gifted underachiever (Rimm, 2015). These behaviors and teachers' dislike of them also mean that most gifted underachievers will not be selected for special classes for intellectually gifted children (Goertzel et al., 2004). Studious achievers attained the highest teacher grades among the three types of gifted high school students (social leaders, studious achievers, and creative intellectuals), while creative intellectuals attained the lowest (Kim, 2008).

In my own student teaching days, some 30-plus years ago, the most creative child in the room, whose constant movement, questioning, and delight in the world around him (even, unfortunately, an intriguing fire alarm box), made him the center of attention in one of the most mortifying experiences of my early teaching career. My cooperating teacher stood him in the middle of the room and the entire class (save one intelligent and empathetic friend) issued complaint after complaint about his behavior as he bravely bore each one. As a pre-service teacher, I learned how creative students who have not learned self-regulation can be treated in the classroom by students and teachers alike.

The intelligent and empathetic friend in this experience is also indicative of a characteristic that is often "undervalued and unnoticed when displayed by gifted children" (Goertzel et al., 2004, p. 255), which is altruism and sympathy. Often sensitivity to injustices and unfairness and the subsequent feelings of guilt cause gifted children to be scorned or ridiculed by peers.

Sensitivity and Suppression

In the peer-oriented culture of U.S. schools, children can often be afraid to think until "they learn what their classmates are thinking" (Goertzel et al., 2004, p. 278).

Kim (2008) found that when gifted students were included in programs that support and encourage creativity and giftedness, they "became highly creative" (p. 238). "If needs are not met, creative individuals may develop into underachievers" (Kim & Van Tassel-Baska, 2010, p. 85). Because creatively gifted students are apt to be kept out of gifted programming, however, they often learn to suppress their creative impulses. Peer pressures, too, can make creative children feel that their unique way of thinking and being makes them socially undesirable or weird. Sensitivity to negative feedback or fear of being laughed at for unusual attempts and responses may make creative students withdraw into fantasy, a safe place perceived as much more rewarding and accepting (Goertzel et al., 2004; Kim, 2008). They may also withdraw if things are not done their way (Rimm, 2015). Kim and Hull (2012) assert that highly creative students may "experience problems of adjustment" (p. 170) because creativity involves nonconformity, independent and innovative thinking. Torrance (1968) called highly creative children "creatively handicapped" because their creativity makes it difficult to achieve in the traditional classroom, even suggesting that a new category be added to special education for this unique group:

> An entirely different problem may manifest when highly creative children suppress their creativity and become overly conforming and obedient. They are likely to grow up with a lack of confidence in their own thinking and be overly dependent upon others in making decisions.
>
> *(Kim, 2008, p. 238)*

To fully develop, all children need safe places to explore and practice their creative ideas without judgment or fear, the creative child especially.

The Challenge of Nonconformity

I work in the university setting, instructing teachers as they work toward an endorsement in the field of gifted education. Recently, as part of an assignment submission in the creativity course, a student commented:

My daughter sometimes gets the creativity "thorn" or itch. We can usually spot this when she gets antsy or has a hard time following directions. She needs a creative outlet. Sometimes this is in the form of making something, and sometimes it comes in the form of creative or imaginative play.

(Jenkins, personal communication, May 21, 2021)

This comment put a face to – or rather, a wiggly body to – the concept of the *creative child*. There are many characteristics and behaviors of these types of children that make it difficult for them to find success in the traditional classroom.

The characteristic that revealed itself the most in the literature as a challenge to the creative child in school is behavioral manifestation of the conformity/nonconformity dichotomy. Highly creative students enjoy the risk of the unknown, and the underachieving creative child may "seem driven to be unique and determined to attract attention to that uniqueness" (Rimm, 2015, p. 4). In direct contrast to the wishes of most teachers, who prefer conforming, acquiescing students, creative students ask unusual questions, put forth innovative ideas, and prefer divergent thinking during traditional discussions and activities. Some creative children resist conformity of the traditional classroom by being rebellious or disruptive, or questioning the teacher indiscreetly (Kim & Van Tassel-Baska, 2010). Peers also tend to demand conformity to gain acceptance. The constant push-pull of the creative child's wishes for self-expression and uniqueness against the expectations of conformity creates deep unhappiness, which manifests itself in misbehavior and withdrawal. In her early work, Cramond (1974) noted that teachers, because of their desire for conformity, may even misidentify the unconventional behavior usually associated with creative children as attention deficit hyperactivity disorder. In addition, Rimm (2015) found that some achieving elementary gifted children who are not challenged in the classroom may begin to voice complaints about boring work and teachers who do not like them. As a result, older students may develop oppositionality against conventional authority.

"Highly creative students exhibit characteristics that many teachers find undesirable in traditional school environments" (Kim, 2008, p. 234). Research into specific characteristics of creative children would indicate that teachers see these children in a negative light, as problem-causers who are impulsive, subject to emotional conflict, sensitive, pessimists, withdrawn, reluctant to take on challenges, troublemakers, non-risk takers, and rebellious. Kirschenbaum (1989) found that "highly creative adolescents exhibited deeper feelings, greater original responsiveness, and fuller range of emotional expression" (as cited in Kim, 2008, p. 237).

My own statewide research of the perception of teachers regarding the characteristics of creative children shows that while teachers viewed the characteristics of creative children as positive, including originality and outside-the-box thinking, fluency, curiosity, humorous or witty, there were deeply negative characteristics, including belligerence, lacking follow-up, acting the clown, not following directions, and being a troublemaker (Groman, 2019).

Mismatch Between the Creative Individual and School

Gifted teachers, like gifted students, often have difficulties in the lock-step classroom (Goertzel et al., 2004, p. 301).

My dissertation research (Groman, 2015) explored the experiences of three teachers who had been or were currently working in gifted education, and their processes of working through existential crises as a result of the challenges of classroom teaching. What I found was that often there was a mismatch between what creative, innovative teachers believe to be best for the classroom and their students, and what the educational establishment and administration want them to do. Palmer (2007) called this "crossed purposes." They also felt as if they did not fit with some of their colleagues who embraced a more traditional teaching system. This mismatch became an underlying condition in their existential crisis.

This is important because the educational institution has remained the same for generations of students – the classroom set-up of desks and tables, the ringing bells signaling students moving in single file lines to separate and unrelated discipline-based classes. The pandemic of 2020–2021 forced public and private schools as well as institutions of higher learning to completely rethink their ways of interacting with and educating students. This shake-up of age-old ways of "doing school" could only happen in times like these.

There are many ways in which traditional schools are mismatched with gifted students, creatively gifted students, and creatively gifted, underachieving gifted students. In some ways this mismatch can be seen as a cause of or exacerbating factor in the learning lives of these students.

Kim (2008) states: "Creativity and intelligence are not mutually exclusive. Therefore, the cause of the underachievement of many gifted and talented students may be their creativity, which tends to clash with traditional school environments" (p. 234). Highly creative students in these environments often resent constraining structures, excessive rules, and the pressure for conformity (Kim, 2008). This resentment, which can be rather flagrant, pits the student against the teacher – creating a learning environment where teachers are unknowingly or knowingly extinguishing creative behaviors (Westby & Dawson, 1995). And as stated earlier, many teachers are severely underqualified to work with gifted students. Hammerschmidt (2016) stated:

> Indecisive and inconsistent training and/or a lack of training in giftedness and gifted education have been found to contribute to teachers' incorrect perceptions in the inclusive classroom. These erroneous perceptions often lead to the misidentification or misunderstanding of the gifted student, resulting in a disadvantage for teachers when they encounter students who do not fit the stereotypical or current established mode of giftedness.
>
> (p. 7)

Goertzel et al. (2004) mourned the dearth of gifted models and strategic, creative, and intelligent teaching approaches used by teachers to support gifted and talented children that reach only a small percentage of those children. For example, American author, Mary Ellen Chase, was given a fifth-grade textbook on her first day in elementary school in the 1890s. While this will seem like a positive acceleration strategy in those times, regrettably, she had to continue to use that same book for the next seven school years. Twenty-first-century teachers also experience a lack of understanding, support, and educational strategies (Alsamani, 2019; Groman, 2019, 2021).

In a classroom where the teacher does not understand the needs of the gifted and creative children, these students are usually not encouraged or given opportunities to be creative or express themselves, they do not feel as though they belong, and they are often at odds with teachers for failing to follow directions or turn in assignments on time, and for rejecting rote learning (Kim & Van Tassel-Baska, 2010). This discord "may develop into mental and emotional issues with teachers, peers, and their own self-image" (Kim, 2008, p. 235).

Creative students are sometimes described by their teachers using the descriptor of "too much," for example, the child asks too many questions, they are too independent, too impulsive, or challenge the status quo too much (Kim, 2008; Westby & Dawson, 1995). This descriptor translates into nonconformity – and school achievement is dependent on conformity (Rimm, 2015), and "creative young people are faced with paradoxical pressures – their internalized value system says to 'be creative,' [and] they translate that to mean 'don't conform'" (p. 4). Creative individuals are often faced with balancing their own creative wishes with the school's and society's pressures for conformity. Creative adults can handle these pressures, young children cannot (Goertzel et al., 2004).

In addition, many researchers find that teachers state that they like creativity and creative students, but often do not understand what creativity is or looks like (Kaufman, 2016; Kaufman & Beghetto, 2012). And while Kirschenbaum (1989) found that highly creative teachers tend to have overachieving creative students, he also determined that less creative teachers tend to have underachieving creative students.

Implication for Practice

Members of the Four Hundred appreciated teachers who let them advance at their own pace and pursue independent explorations of areas of special interest (Goertzel et al., 2004).

I am a teacher, and have been for over 30 years. It is somewhat painful to write this chapter that is so disparaging of my profession and my fellow professionals, especially with the knowledge of my own educational experience as a child. I felt completely supported as a creative being, in my home life through private lessons, summer opportunities, free time to explore my neighborhood, books, and so on. In my school life, creativity in the content areas, music, theater and the arts, was fully supported by my elementary, middle, and high school coursework and excellent instructors. It is apparent that my experience is not the norm. (See also Chapter 4 in this volume.) In addition, I hear teachers in my graduate courses describe overwhelming testing and standardization protocols, with limiting, rote teaching requirements, and complain that they have little time to practice and support creative work – in the classroom, and in their own lives.

The promise of these bright and creative children and teachers often remains largely untapped. I fear that until our schools' foundational philosophy and culture move away from lock-step instruction and standardization, only small changes at best can be made. There are supports that teachers can put in place in the meantime. The literature is teeming with suggestions and ideas to create welcoming environments for underachieving creative gifted students.

"There is an acute need for direct and frequent communication with intelligent adults. When this need is met to a reasonable degree in school, school rebellion is much lessened" (Goertzel et al., 2004, p. 249).

Delisle (2018) recommended dividing underachievers into two groups: *undera-chievers* and *non-producers*, and suggests different therapeutic approaches for each. The learning challenges and poor self-concepts of underachievers require long-term treatment through the coordinated efforts of the school, the home, and a licensed counselor. On the other hand, *non-producers* are often non-producing as a choice or rebellion. Their self-concepts are usually strong, and targeted intervention will usually improve or reverse their underachievement. Strategies for non-producers include giving them time and support to pursue topics of strong interest (Kim, 2008). A less restrictive school setting was shown to minimize underachievement in creative children (Whitmore, 1980). School environments should stress independence, choice, self-monitoring, and self-exploration, (Kim, 2008; Kim & Hull, 2012), avoid excessive competition between students, and encourage students to have pride in their own work without external rewards (Hennessey & Amabile, 2010). Torrance (1981) determined that the best predictor of future achievement is passion – or falling in love with a subject. It is also important that teachers make a conscious effort to create safe, nonthreatening environments to pursue diverse creative ideas, alternate approaches to problems, and allow making mistakes in the learning process (Kim & Hull, 2012).

Many eminent creatives experienced a "Time Out" (Goertzel et al., 2004), a period of time when their normal activities were suspended and they had time to read and study without restraint, meet new people, plan, and think. Time-out periods included illness or broken bones, but also working or living abroad. Some 10% of the Four Hundred describe a time-out period impacting their development in a significant way.

While many creative underachievers find traditional schools and teachers less than inspiring, they do find solace in tutors and mentors. They respond warmly to adults who listen to them and appreciate their special interests (Goertzel et al., 2004; Kim & Hull, 2012; Rimm, 2015), these mentors can include grandparents, family friends, and private tutors. Librarians and peer groups of intellectuals also fulfill this need, as well as school special interest groups like the debate team, theater group, school paper, and the faculty advisors of these groups.

Parents can prevent underachievement in their creative children by maintaining an allied front with one another and with the school. Parents who complain about teachers, lack of creativity in schools, or call out one family member as "the creative child" add to oppositional problems in their children (Rimm, 2015). "An early problem will be indicated if there is a different value placed on creativity by two parents" (p. 4).

Two longer-term suggestions were promising: (1) providing teachers with professional development in experiencing, recognizing, and supporting creativity in the classroom and in their own lives; and (2) teaching children self-regulation in recognizing that there are times and places for creative responses. Researchers recommend creativity training for all teachers (Kaufman & Beghetto, 2012; Kim, 2008; Kim & Van Tassel-Baska, 2010; Piirto, 2004, 2011; Storm & Storm, 2002). "Training in creativity influences teacher attitudes toward highly creative gifted students" (Kim, 2008, p. 240) and, "more subtly, teachers who model creative thought and an acceptance of differences provide a framework for self-acceptance and, most likely, a classroom environment where students are more likely to value each other's differences" (p. 240).

My own university work includes teaching a creativity course for teachers of the gifted. In a recent survey I distributed to program alumni, I found that creativity training can be extremely transformational personally and professionally for teachers (Groman, 2021). Personally, it opened them to their own creativity – not necessarily exploring creativity like painting or dance (though many continued their creative work after the course), but it allowed them to honor their own creativity, and as a result, they felt more able to see and honor the creativity of their students. Many stated that they value and understand creativity better in their students.

> Another theme of interest is that teachers appear to recognize and appreciate students who challenge the status quo, who may not always respond to authority in a positive way, and those who daydream or are disorganized. This shows an intensified openness for the nontraditional and quirky student, and understanding of the student who may not always find acceptance in school.
>
> *(Groman, 2021, p. 27)*

Torrance (1962) believed that many creative children "bring upon themselves many of their woes. Obviously, one task of education is to aid such children to become less obnoxious without sacrificing their creativity" (as cited in Goertzel et al., 2004, p. 287). The goal of guidance, Torrance (1962) believed, is to promote a healthy balance of creativity, individuality, and conformity.

Finally, an intriguing solution to the challenge of the creative child's nonconforming behavior in the traditional classroom is posited by Kaufman and Beghetto (2012). Kaufman and Beghetto offer philosophical yet practical advice to help teachers work with students to achieve balance and context to when and how they are creative. They recommend teachers instruct students in aspects of creative metacognition (CMC), to recognize the various levels of creativity (from mini-c creativity to Big-C creativity), and also to realize that creativity consists not only of novelty, but also of task appropriateness. Teachers can help children be more aware of the appropriateness of creative expression at any given time in the classroom:

> Increased awareness of the positive and negative consequences of creativity can help students decide whether to take the intellectual risks necessary to engage in and share their creative ideas, insights, and interpretations. Unless students understand both the potential benefits (e.g. developing new insights, procedures, outcomes) and potential costs (wasting one's time and effort, being laughed at, dismissed, ignored), they will not be in a position to determine whether the level of risk associated with creative expression is worth taking.
>
> *(p. 161)*

Armed with this knowledge and consistent teacher feedback on their creative strengths and limitations, children can become more self-regulated in identifying when, where, and in what ways to share their creative ideas. This type of self-regulation is a powerful tool for children throughout their school years and into adulthood.

Conclusion

I invite you to take a moment to revisit the earlier picture in your mind of the creative child. How has it shifted? Perhaps a few nontraditional or even troublesome children come to your attention now, and you are considering them with a more open heart and mind. At the very least, it is my hope that the thought of the creative child does not strike fear into your teacher's heart.

The mismatch of the creative individual and our traditional educational system puts an entire population of innovative potential at risk. If the needs of creative students are not met, they may develop into underachievers (Kim & Van Tassel-Baska, 2010). However, when creative students find themselves in an educational environment that meets their diverse needs, they can reach and exceed their potential. It is imperative that our educational culture respects a more balanced approach to standardized accountability and creative and innovative thinking. When our educational culture establishes places of learning that respect and honor originality and innovative thinking, it can recognize and realize the full promise of the creative individual.

REFLECTION QUESTIONS

1. Think of an individual who has been described (by you or someone else) as being "too" something. (For example, too sensitive, asks too many questions, too independent, too impulsive, or challenges the status quo too much.) State what that "excessiveness" behavior is and reframe it, identifying an aspect of giftedness or creativity that might offer a more appropriate description for the behavior. What insights does that excessiveness give you into that individual's needs?

2. Discuss the issue of student conformity and nonconformity and its impact on the classroom. Are there ways to teach children when conformity is expected and when nonconformity is acceptable? Are there times you can allow students to practice more divergent actions and behaviors?

3. Why do you think creatively gifted children are less likely to be identified as gifted in an academic domain?

4. Review this excerpt from Kingore's (2008) "High Achiever, Gifted Learner, Creative Thinker" article and consider the diversity of individuals whom you know and work with. Does this give you any insights into their behavior and ways of working? https://www.coloradogifted.org/wp-content/uploads/Bertie-Kingore-High-Achiever-Gifted-Creative.pdf

5. Do you think that our current understanding of giftedness, brightness, and creativity has shifted any since the publication of Szabo's (1989) or Kingore's (2008) conception of these constructs?

6. Peters (2014) asserted that the "bright" versus "gifted" debate should not be relevant in K-12 education. He stated that he finds it emblematic that

> The overall suggestion seems to be that as a teacher, educationally useful information comes from knowing if one of your students is "just bright" vs. if she is "truly" gifted. Under this, in other words, if two children are otherwise identical in their level of achievement, aptitude, creativity, etc., they should still be treated differently if one is "truly" gifted and one is "just bright."

> Do you agree or disagree with Dr. Peters? Explain. https://www.creativitypost.com/article/the_bright_vs._gifted_comparison_a_distraction_from_what_matters

Suggested Resources

Baldwin, A. Y. (2001). Understanding the challenge of creativity among African Americans. *Journal of Secondary Gifted Education*, 2(3). 121–125.

Compiled Resources about Giftedness and Creativity for Teachers and Parents. Available at: https://www.springtownisd.net/cms/lib3/TX21000442/Centricity/Domain/56/GT%20Resources.pdf

Kingore, B. (2004a). High achiever, gifted learner, creative thinker. *Understanding Our Gifted*, 15(3). 3–5.

References

Alsamani, O. A. (2019). Fostering creativity and innovation in gifted students through the eyes of gifted education educators. [Unpublished doctoral dissertation.] University of Northern Colorado. Available at: https://digscholarship.unco.edu/dissertations/573

Amabile, T. M. (2012). Componential theory of creativity. Harvard Business School, Working Paper No. 12–096. Available at: https://www.hbs.edu/ris/Publication%20Files/12-096.pdf

Brandau, H., Daghofer, F., Hollerer, L., Kaschnitz, W., Kellner, K,, Kitchmair, G., … Schlagbauer, A. (2007). The relationship between creativity, teacher ratings on behavior, age, and gender in pupils from seven to ten years. *Journal of Creative Behavior, 42*(2). 91–113. doi:10.1002/j.2162-6057.2007.tb01283.x

Cramond, B. (1974). Attention-deficit hyperactivity disorder and creativity: What is the connection? *Journal of Creative Behavior, 28*(3). 193–210. doi:10.1002/j.2162-6057.1994.tb01191.x

Delisle, J. (2018). *Doing poorly on purpose: Strategies to reverse underachievement and respect student dignity.* Free Spirit Publishing.

Dyrda, B. (2000). The process of diagnosing the underachievement syndrome in gifted and creative children. *The New Educational Review, 18*(2). 129–137.

Goertzel, V., & Goertzel, M. G. (1962). *Cradles of eminence: A provocative study of over 400 twentieth-century men and women.* Little Brown & Company.

Goertzel, V., Goertzel, M. G., Goertzel, T. G., & Hansen, A. M. W. (2004). *Cradles of eminence: Childhoods of more than 700 famous men and women* (2nd ed.). Great Potential Press.

Groman, J. L. (2015). From calling to crisis: The growth process of teachers through crisis-like incidents. [Unpublished doctoral dissertation.] University of Akron. Available at: http://rave.ohiolink.edu/etdc/view?acc_num=akron1436525010

Groman, J. L. (2019, October 20–22). The Creativity Project. Paper presented at the Ohio Association for Gifted Children Conference, Fall, 2019, Columbus, OH.

Groman, J. L. (2021). Considering the long-term transformative impact of creativity training on the work and lives of teachers. [Manuscript submitted for publication]. Doctoral Studies and Advanced Programs, Ashland University.

Hammerschmidt, M. M. (2016). Teacher perception regarding the teaching of gifted students in the traditional classroom setting. [Doctoral dissertation, Texas Tech University.] Available at: https://ttu-ir.tdl.org/

Hennessey, B. A., & Amabile, T. M. (2010). Creativity. *Annual Review of Psychology, 61,* 569–598. doi:10.1146/annurev.psych.093008.100416

Kaufman, J. C. (2016). *Creativity 101.* Springer.

Kaufman, J. C., & Beghetto, R. A. (2012). In praise of Clark Kent: Creative metacognition and the importance of teaching kids when (not) to be creative. *Roeper Review, 35*(3). 155–165. doi:10.1080/02783193.2013.799413

Kim, K. H. (2008). Underachievement and creativity: Are gifted underachievers highly creative? *Creativity Research Journal, 20*(2). 234–242. doi:10.1080/10400410802060232

Kim, K. H., & Hull, M. F. (2012). Creative personality and anticreative environment for high school dropouts. *Creativity Research Journal, 24*(2–3), 169–176.

Kim, K. H., & Van Tassel-Baska, J. (2010). The relationship between creativity and behavior problems among underachieving elementary and high school students. *Creativity Research Journal, 22*(2), 185–193. doi:10.1080/10400410802060232

Kingore, B. (2008). Differentiation: Simplified, realistic, and effective. How to challenge advanced potentials in mixed-ability classrooms. Professional Associations Publishing.

Kirschenbaum, R. J. (1989). *Understanding the creative activity of students.* Creative Learning Press.

Palmer, P. (2007). *The courage to teach: Exploring the inner landscape of a teacher's life.* John Wiley & Sons.

Peters, S. (2014, July). The bright vs. gifted comparison: A distraction from what matters. *The Creativity Post.* Available at: https://www.creativitypost.com/article/the_bright_vs._gifted_comparison_a_distraction_from_what_matters

Piirto, J. (2004). *Understanding creativity.* Great Potential Press.

Piirto, J. (2011). *Creativity for 21st century skills.* Sense Publishers.

Reis, S. M., & McCoach, D. B. (2002). Underachievement in gifted and talented students with special needs. *Exceptionality*, *10*(2). 113–125. doi:10.1207/S15327035EX1002_5

Reis, S. M., & Renzulli, J. S. (1982). A case for a broadened conception of giftedness. *Phi Delta Kappan*, *63*(9), 619–620.

Rimm, S. (2015). Creative underachievers: Marching to the beat of a different drummer. *Parenting for High Potential*, *4*(5). 6–7.

Storm, R. D., & Storm, P. S. (2002). Changing the rules: Education for creative thinking. *Journal of Creative Behavior*, *36*(3), 183–200. doi:10.1002/j.2162-6057.2002.tb01063.x

Szabos, J. (1989). Bright child, gifted learner. *Good Apple*, *34*.

Torrance, E. P. (1962). *Guiding creative talent*. Prentice-Hall.

Torrance, E. P. (1964). The Minnesota Studies of Creative Thinking: 1959–1962. In C. W. Taylor (Ed.), *Widening horizons in creativity* (pp. 125–144). John Wiley & Sons.

Torrance, E. P. (1966). *Torrance tests of creative thinking*. Scholastic Testing Services.

Torrance, E. P. (1968). Creativity and its educational implication for the gifted. *Gifted Child Today*, *12*(2). 67–78. doi:10.1177/001698626801200201

Torrance, E. P. (1981). *Thinking creatively in action and movement: Administration, scoring, and norms manual*. Scholastic Testing Services.

Westby, E. L., & Dawson, V. L. (1995). Creativity: Asset or burden in the classroom? *Creativity Research Journal*, *8*(1). 1–10. doi:10.1207/s15326934crj0801_1

Whitmore, J. R. (1980). *Giftedness, conflict, and underachievement*. Allyn and Bacon.

The Impactful Reality of Underachievement of Gifted Students

Scarred for Their Entire Life

Fernanda Hellen Ribeiro Piske and Kristina Henry Collins

Introduction

Even though it does not necessarily equate to failure in terms of grades or general task completion, underachievement and overachievement of gifted students in schools can leave these children scarred for life. The *Encyclopedia of Child Behavior and Development* suggests that underachievement occurs when a child's academic performance is below what is expected, based on the child's ability, aptitude, or intelligence (Weller-Clarke, 2011). It is also worth noting that low achievement does not necessarily mean underachievement, and many children do not operate at their full potential. In addition, underachievement can seem to be exacerbated for highly intellectual, or gifted, students. As such, one may claim that it is the label of underachievement that leaves scars rather the act of underachieving itself.

Every human being wants to feel that they contribute to something, and attach that contribution to achievement. However, an internalized sense of underachievement can leave a student feeling worthless, useless, and unworthy of their intellectual giftedness. For social and emotional well-being, it is necessary to know how to regulate such emotions and feelings. For children, this is not always easy, especially for gifted children who also have additional pressures on them to perform. For this reason, it is important to tackle the underlying factors that create underachievement or the mislabeling of students as underachievers.

One of the reasons for mislabeling gifted students is lack of teacher training. When there is a lack of training or experience by the educator to address the underlying factors or other issues labeled as underachievement, as part of the everyday learning process, it creates neglect in the proper care of these children, among other social and emotional concerns that they already feel. When there is a lack of proper identification and care, real or misperceived underachievement can certainly lead to failure for the gifted student. Any wrong beliefs about gifted students can lead to or foster failure, when those beliefs impede proper references to identify and serve these students properly.

According to Reis and McCoach (2000), Collins (2020), and Piske (2021), there are underlying, socialized, and executive functioning factors that may affect academic achievement: lack of social skills within group or team settings; super-sensitivity to

DOI: 10.4324/9781003369578-9

negative feedback; frustration with the inability to master certain academic skills; learned helplessness; lack of general motivation toward uninteresting tasks; failure to complete assignments due to perfectionism or "analysis paralysis"; lack of organizational skills; demonstration of hyper-focus or lack of concentration skills; deficiency in tasks that emphasize memory and perceptual skills; low self-esteem; and unrealistic self-expectations, among others.

Myths about Gifted Students

Myths about giftedness are another major underlying factor that can lead to underachievement. Myths about gifted students impede the identification and care of gifted students and need to be demystified. According to Peterson (2009), the empirical and clinical literature has challenged the myth that gifted students do not have unique social and emotional concerns. When the myth prevails, relevant concerns are not recognized and addressed formally or informally, proactively or reactively. The myths about the characteristics and unrealistic abilities of the gifted represent something very harmful for gifted children. In addition, missed, ignored, or mislabeled characteristics are further internalized, leaving teachers and parents even more confused about the needs of the students (Piske, 2021). Moreover, teachers and parents have unrealistic expectations about the school performance of gifted students or become hyper-focused on their gifted identities, creating a narrow image for the gifted student to see themselves. Erroneously, teachers and parents may not think that the gifted child's learning strategies need to be adapted or their social emotional development needs tending to; this is particularly so if the child does not present a behavioral challenge for the teacher or parent.

NAGC (2021) presents some myths regarding gifted students. It is a myth to think that if teachers challenge all students, then gifted children will do well in the regular classroom. The truth is that when teachers try the general "challenge all" approach, they are often unfamiliar with the needs of individual gifted students and don't know how to best serve them in the classroom. Another myth is that intellectually gifted students always feel comfortable or good in the classroom. They are not always happy, popular, and well adjusted in school. On the contrary, they may also face social situations that compromise their academic development at school. Knowing the cognitive, social, and emotional characteristics of gifted students is essential to help them identify and self-regulate their own feelings in the context of expected performance and achievement.

Another myth is that academic acceleration or grade skipping is socially harmful to gifted students. The truth is that academically gifted students often feel bored or out of place with their peers of the same age and naturally gravitate toward older students, who are more like their "intellectual peers" (NAGC, 2021). Some authors portray academic acceleration or grade skipping as something more complex, Colangelo and colleagues (2004) explain:

> Acceleration is one of the most curious phenomena in the field of education. I can think of no other issue in which there is such a gulf between what research has revealed and what most practitioners believe. The research on acceleration is so uniformly positive, the benefits of appropriate acceleration so unequivocal, that it is difficult to see how an educator could oppose it.
>
> *(p. 16)*

Piske (2021) states that acceleration is linked to the well-being of gifted students and requires qualitative investigation to know how the gifted student would feel in a classroom with new classroom colleagues. We do recognize affective bonds, which are fundamental for the gifted student to develop fully, so giving a voice to the student regarding knowing how they would feel in another classroom with older peers is very important in academic acceleration or grade skipping. Capturing a complete snapshot of the student's potential and motivation – listening to the gifted student, obtaining a perspective from the student's family, and input from the school – is essential to know whether accelerated learning will benefit the gifted student or not.

Chestnut et al. (2018) point to yet another common myth: mathematics requires raw intellectual talent or "brilliance," which misrepresents the qualifications for the skills a student must possess to succeed in related subjects that are math-heavy. This damaging myth has far-reaching consequences for the success of girls and children of ethnic minority backgrounds, who are members of an underrepresented subgroup in STEM-related subjects (science, technology, engineering, and math) and study areas. The myth that success in mathematics requires this trait is a barrier that students in these groups must overcome; women and ethnic minorities are not comparatively recommended and identified to study advanced mathematics and beyond. The authors detail the spread of this myth and explore its relationship to gender and race differences in mathematics and beyond. The authors also highlight some potential sources of this myth in children's everyday experiences and offer some strategies for debunking it.

Some people may mistakenly believe that gifted students naturally become eminent adults: to the contrary, this depends on social factors, opportunities, and stimuli. "Latent" potentials and talents can, throughout their lives, remain underdeveloped. This means that they will not always become adults performing at their expected rate of achievement, or fulfilling their sense of purpose (see also Chapter 14).

According to the Davidson Institute (2021), it is also a myth that everyone is gifted. This statement may be quite popular, however, it is not true in relationship to giftedness that is identified and nurtured in an academic setting. Renzulli (2012, 2016), in his three-ring model, stated that giftedness happens when there is an interaction between three basic groups of human characteristics: (1) above-average general and specific skills; (2) high levels of task commitment (motivation); and (3) high levels of creativity. This means that a combination of all three factors must be understood in order to also fully understand giftedness.

Consequences of and Solutions for Underachievement

Underachievement can also lead to a loss in sense of belonging in the classroom, the program, or with other gifted peers. Gifted education programs should aim to help all high-ability students achieve, and be responsive to their academic needs, their cultural values, and personal interests. Underachievement has the same effect that occurs when gifted students are not identified. It is important for educators to identify gifted students from all cultures, ethnic backgrounds, and so on. Otherwise, there will be many students who do not have the opportunity to maximize their potential due to the way programs and services are funded or due to imperfect identification practices (NAGC, 2021).

Many gifted students flourish in their community and school environment. However, some gifted children also differ in terms of emotional and moral intensity, sensitivity to expectations and feelings, perfectionism, and deep concerns about social problems. Others do not share interests with their classmates, resulting in isolation or being unfavorably labeled a "nerd." The emotions and feelings of gifted students can emerge in a variety of ways and different situations, and also are impacted by their social-emotional development that is being attended to at school and at home.

Underachievement of Gifted Students: Scarred for Their Entire Life

Underachievement of the gifted can arise from several factors, such as cognitive, psychological, emotional, and social difficulties, but it can also be linked to a personal characteristic, such as low self-motivation and low self-regulation or other reasons that, if not discovered and addressed, can scar them for their entire life.

Researchers have used different methods to explore the results on the underachievement of gifted that can contribute to understanding and the intervention for success of gifted student. Tsai and Fu (2016) carried out a case study that presents an explanatory report on the failure of three talented students studying physics at a Taiwanese university. The authors point out that the failure of the students in physics was diagnosed by the problem analysis graph of Sato's students. The authors explain that these students were asked to complete a questionnaire and follow-up interview: (1) to understand the association between their academic performance, self-concepts, and support systems, and (2) to identify the pattern of their learning behaviors. Students reported that their self-esteem was not harmed by their poor performance and that they still believed in their own potential. The study indicated that these students began to encounter academic problems during their high school years. The following learning habits resulted in their low performance: (1) lack of motivation and non-application of self-actualization in the subjects; (2) focus on memorization and mastery of skills and on the exercise of counterproductive learning strategies; and (3) lack of genuine interest in the subject.

Tsai and Fu (2016) identified that although these students had clear career goals and a generally positive self-concept, their professional development suffered from lack of execution. There are learning habits that must be re-evaluated to avoid underachievement. The performance of gifted students will depend on a healthy educational climate that promotes their well-being, among other factors. Gifted students may face difficulties in the transition from school to university, just like any other student, but they may have difficulties related to their characteristics and educational needs.

Steenbergen-Hu, Olszewski-Kubilius, and Calvert (2020) conducted a study that reviewed 14 recent empirical studies on the effectiveness of low-performing interventions on the performance outcomes and psychosocial outcomes of gifted students. The authors stated that there was no evidence that low-achieving interventions significantly improved the academic performance of gifted students ($g = 0.09$, $p = 0.387$), especially in terms of course grades. Underperformers who received interventions significantly outperformed their peers in comparisons to psychosocial outcomes ($g = 0.22$, $p = 0.001$), which consisted of a variety of measures of self-efficacy, goal assessment, environmental perceptions, self-regulation/motivation, and functioning psychosocial outcomes. Qualitative studies generally reported that low-achieving students benefited from the interventions in terms of greater motivation to learn, better self-regulation, and finding the school more meaningful. Steenbergen-Hu et al. (2020) found that the results need to be seen in the light of the relatively low quality of recent research evidence on low-performing interventions.

Desmet and colleagues (2020), in a multiple narrative investigation, examined the narratives of four gifted underachieving girls to identify aspects that appear to have contributed to the initiation, development, and resolution of academic failure. The authors found that academic performance was disrupted when participants experienced a sudden increase in curriculum demands during the transition to elementary or high school. Participants' negative self-perceptions, lack of learning skills, and negative relationships with teachers generally contributed to the maintenance of failure. The authors reported that failure began to resolve when the girls had a clear goal in mind, which for three of them was to be accepted into college. Often, the lack of acceptance causes a great deal of irreparable harm to gifted students.

McCoach and colleagues (2020) highlighted that much has been written about the relationship between giftedness and attention deficit hyperactivity disorder (ADHD), as well as the relationship between ADHD and low performance. The authors conducted a study that examined whether students who were identified as gifted underachievers were more likely to manifest symptoms of ADHD, as measured by the ADHD-IV. The authors found that more than half of gifted students met the screening criteria for ADHD, based on teacher reports, and nearly 30% of gifted students met the screening criteria for ADHD, based on parent reports. Most of these students scored high on the inattention scale. The prevalence of inattention was more than two times higher than the prevalence in the norm sample using the teacher rating scales and more than five times higher than the prevalence in the norm sample using the parent rating scales. Although parents and teachers rated students similarly on the hyperactivity scale, teachers rated students as more inattentive than parents. However, parents' high ratings of inattention negatively predicted student self-regulation, goal assessment, and self-efficacy. Self-regulation was most strongly related to inattention. We cannot know whether gifted students with high inattention have undiagnosed ADHD. McCoach and colleagues (2020) stated that the results suggest that a substantial percentage of gifted students experience attention problems at home, and that these attention problems are severe enough to merit further examination.

Fong and Kremer (2020) considered students' academic failure, defined as discrepancies between academic ability and performance, to be a widespread problem that leads to many negative consequences. Their study examined high school students' math failure, their motivational background, and its impact on future math performance, college attendance, and interest in STEM. Using data from the nationally representative Longitudinal Study of High Schools, they identified students who exhibited a math performance discrepancy between their standardized math scores in early ninth grade and their final math grade in the fall of ninth grade. They then conducted generalized structural equation modeling to identify the direct effects of mathematical motivation on math failure, along with the direct effects of math failure on future STEM and college outcomes. Informed by expectation value theory, they found that mathematical motivation, as measured by value and expectation beliefs, was significantly associated with poor performance in mathematics. Fong and Kremer (2020) also found that poor math performance was associated with a range of outcomes in the transition from high school to college, with evidence of moderation by high math ability.

According to Almukhambetova and Hernández-Torrano (2020), successful transition from high school to university is essential for the academic success of any student. For gifted people, there may be unique challenges due to their characteristics, the inability to adjust to the demands of the university environment has a negative effect on the academic performance of the gifted students, leading to failure. They identified that the learning environments of schools and universities attended by the gifted, as well as the influence of key people (parents, peers, and teachers), played a crucial role in facilitating or impeding the sense of self-determination of school graduates and, consequently, its adjustment and achievement.

Snyder and Wormington (2020) explain that academic performance has fascinated and frustrated those involved in gifted education for decades, capturing the attention of educators, researchers, and policymakers. A topic of interest in education as far back as the 1950s, low performance is often framed in terms of loss of personal and social potential. The authors explain that the study on the low income of gifted people remained quite isolated from research on motivation to achieve results over the years. The authors quoted examples, noting that researchers on motivation to perform a task, often use the term failure without due attention to how it is conceptualized and operationalized as a distinction of skill achievement. Furthermore, it is not uncommon to hear the underperformance of the gifted described as lack of motivation. The researchers point out that this reflects the oft-repeated misconceptions that all gifted students are motivated, and this motivation is static as students move through elementary and high school. Over time, the slow integration of work on failure and motivation has proved insightful. The authors report, in 2020, that what we know about underperformance in gifted populations, particularly in relation to motivation to achieve goals, has improved. But this expanded understanding also helped us to become aware of what we don't yet know. Snyder and Wormington (2020) recommend the need for interdisciplinary collaborations, diverse theoretical paradigms, innovative methodological tools, commitment to rigorous intervention projects and testing, and a passion for improving students' lives in the classroom.

This discussion about the low academic performance of gifted students, who have special educational needs, is to educate schools about the existing myth that many professionals believe that these students will perform well, which is not true, since, due to various factors, they may not develop their high skills. Bullying can also be linked to the low performance of these children, since this practice of violence can discourage them and prevent them from progressing in the educational environment.

We agree with Reis and McCoach (2000) when they state that we do not know how many students with special needs are underachieving, nor do we really know how many students with special needs have hidden talents and abilities. The authors underscore the importance of further research and investigation in this area, so that students with special needs who perform poorly in our country will receive more attention and programmatic interventions. Reis and McCoach (2000) point out that educators should explore the various reasons for high-ability students' failure if they hope to help combat failure. For these authors, it is essential to determine whether a student's failure is due to: (1) more serious physical, cognitive, or emotional problems; (2) an incompatibility between the student and their school environment; or (3) a personal characteristic, such as low self-sufficiency. lack of motivation, low self-regulation, or low self-efficacy.

Finally, Reis and McCoach (2000) emphasize that educators must develop adequate intervention strategies that address the specific area of need exhibited by students with low academic performance. The authors believe that by differentiating treatments to meet the needs of low-achieving students, we will more effectively combat the problem of school failure. Therefore, it is essential to understand where the underachievement of the gifted student comes from, only then will it be possible to understand what the student really needs in order to develop well throughout their life.

Empathy and understanding are essential for teachers to avoid underachievement of the gifted students. If there is no clarity about the need to put yourself in the place of gifted students and understand their special needs, underachievement may occur and even compromise the students' socio-emotional development.

The Socio-Emotional Development of Gifted Students

If their emotional characteristics are respected, this is the basis for each person to feel comfortable in any environment. Emotions occur in all environments and their importance is unquestionable in our lives. Laycraft and Gierus (2019) explain that emotions are composed of many different processes that are interconnected. They do not occur in isolation, but are created as a result of an event or combination of events in the external environment or in the mind. They also depend on each person's history and personality. Furthermore, an emotion is very unlikely to occur on its own, as it depends on several issues for it to emerge in different situations and contexts. Each person's emotion is consistent with the psychological adjustment they present to deal with their own feelings. (See also Chapter 4.)

The psychological adjustment of the gifted is a topic that generates controversy among researchers who take different stands. Some believe that the gifted can, in general, adapt well at school, others, in turn, argue that these students express greater vulnerability to psychological adjustment.

Sainz et al. (2020) point out that, in 1920, a research program was started to assess the fit versus the incompatibility of gifted individuals. Different authors concluded that people with very high cognitive ability were above average in almost every aspect. In this sense, it is necessary to highlight the authors who indicated that the prejudices found in relation to the emotional problems of the gifted cannot continue to be maintained. However, according to the authors, there is a second position held by researchers who argue that the gifted are at greater risk of developing adaptability problems or psychological adjustment problem than their peers because the gifted show greater vulnerability to psychological adjustment. Gifted people are thought to be at greater risk of developing social and emotional adjustment problems, particularly during adolescence and adulthood.

The interactions of the gifted with the people around them involve feelings, emotions, and affections that are expressed daily, and can create great tension. One of the reasons is that these students are not always understood or even accepted in their group, and also not by their teachers. Piske and Kane (2020) explain the importance of knowing how to deal with feelings at different times in one's life. The authors explain that among many situations experienced by gifted children at school, there are times when they can be victims of bullying, and the lack of understanding about their high abilities by the people around them can often lead to teasing.

Gifted students can experience many internal tensions and turmoil on a daily basis. Asynchronous development can also be one of the reasons for socio-emotional maladjustment. Silverman (2009) explained that asynchronous development is the hallmark of giftedness and, in a very real sense, as gifted children mature, they develop their intellect and become more imbalanced, less "normal." The more extreme their intellectual advances, the more extreme is the asynchronous development. Thus, the balance in development will exist if there is parity in intellectual, social, and emotional needs. In the early twentieth century, Hollingworth (1926) claimed that the range of intelligence considered optimal was an IQ of 125–155 and that exceptionally able students with an IQ above 160 might experience social isolation. The reason for this isolation is not due to any inherent emotional disturbance, but due to the absence of a suitable peer group to relate to. Gifted people do have a tendency to self-isolate just because they are not understood by those around them, which makes them more sensitive. The situation of isolation and tension can lead the gifted child to be more prone to emotional and social difficulties, which can further aggravate their emotional development.

Critical in finding a balance to effectively nurture healthy development is a consideration for gifted people's even more extreme cases of asynchronous development. We know that oftentimes their cognitive development is above their same-age peers, but, on the other hand, their feelings and emotions can be less mature when compared to their peers of the same chronological age, creating an even wider gap in cognitive and age development. Not only does this sometimes leave them feeling confused about how they "should" feel, but also poses a problem for teachers who expect their maturity levels to match their cognitive level.

In addition, many studies (Collins, 2018, 2020; Gross, 2016; Kane & Silverman, 2014; Peterson, 2014; Piske, 2018, 2020, 2021) have argued that gifted students can display heightened sensitivity, with a keen ability to tune into the feelings of others, which also makes them feel uncomfortable or at a lost if the feelings are associated with injustice. These perceptive children have a great ability to sympathize and worry intensely. Intense worrying can also threaten their emotional well-being as they may feel overwhelmed by the emotional intensity of those around them, and may experience stress, anxiety, and inner turmoil.

In line with this discussion of anxiety, inner turmoil, and stress, Piechowski (2014) emphasized that the gifted student can face the issue of peer acceptance. The author explained that, since we evolve as a social species, wanting to be accepted is part of our biological development. But we also grow as individuals. The tension between the need to belong and individual growth at your own rate can be a source of inner turmoil for gifted students. The pressure on these students, compounded with the intelligence-experience gap they exhibit, impacts their ability to make better decisions – or even recognize optimal choices. According to Piechowski (2014), the expectations placed on the gifted should be mitigated by the knowledge that our society has given only limited support to the education of these students. Furthermore, the author reinforces that programs aimed at these students are generally not challenging enough and, when they are, they do not have the necessary component of guidance and counseling toward socialized decision-making.

Implications for Practice

It is up to the school, teachers, managers, all professionals involved with the education of gifted students, their families and society to seek more information about the myths that permeate in gifted education, and to know what is true information. In this way, we can avoid many factors that contribute to underachievement of gifted students. In addition, understanding the social-emotional development of gifted students is as important as understanding their cognitive characteristics. Many cases of underachievement are due to a lack of understanding about the students' social, emotional, and cultural needs that further impact their educational needs in each sphere of their development. Clarifying the cognitive, social, and emotional needs of gifted students is crucial for teachers and parents to understand. Teachers need training in the area of giftedness and parents need to be enlightened about realistic expectations that they should have regarding their children's high abilities.

Conclusion

The cognitive, social, and emotional characteristics of gifted students that lead to underachievement remain misunderstood by many educators. There are still myths that maintain that gifted students should excel in every academic endeavor, and whenever they don't, this is simply them underachieving. There are those who do not acknowledge, let along address, the learning disabilities of gifted student when they co-exist. On the other hand, when students are in a position to move on when ready or compact the curriculum when they have obviously mastered the content, some educators will not extend learning with more rigorous content, also causing the students not to maximize their academic talents. The impactful reality of underachievement of gifted students can generate scars (negative implications) for their entire lives in terms of identity and talent development.

As such, we emphasize the importance of continuing education for all teachers, of continual and updated training. All students deserve to learn at a pace and level which are respectful (appropriately rigorous, challenging, and responsive to their learners' profile (see also Chapter 9). And it is the responsibility of all educators to strategically and effectively appeal to the unique needs of each student.

REFLECTION QUESTIONS

1. What are the myths about gifted student achievement that lead to their underachievement?
2. When addressing or preventing underachievement in gifted students, why is it important to understand the social-emotional development of gifted students?
3. Why is it that the mislabel of underachiever can be detrimental to gifted students?
4. What are the common underpinning or underlying factors for underachievement?
5. What would happen (or not happen) for an identified gifted student not to become an eminent adult? What might be some underlying factors for underachievement in adulthood? (See also the discussion in Chapter 14.)

References

Almukhambetova, A., & Hernández-Torrano, D. (2020). Gifted students' adjustment and underachievement in university: An exploration from the self-determination theory perspective. *Gifted Child Quarterly, 64*(2), 117–131. https://doi.org/10.1177/0016986220905525
Chestnut, E. K., Lei, R. F., Leslie, S.-J., & Cimpian, A. (2018). The myth that only brilliant people are good at math and its implications for diversity. *Education Sciences, 8*, 65. https://doi.org/10.3390/educsci8020065

Colangelo, N., Assouline S. G., & Gross M. U. M. (2004). *A nation deceived: How schools hold back America's brightest students* (vol. 1). University of Iowa.

Collins, K. H. (2018). Confronting colorblind STEM talent development: Toward a contextual model for Black student STEM identity. *Journal of Advanced Academics, 29*(2), 143–168.

Collins, K. H. (2020). Gifted and bullied: Understanding the institutionalized victimization of identified, unidentified, and underserved gifted students [manuscript accepted]. In F. H. R. Piske & K. H. Collins (Eds.), *Identifying, preventing and combating bullying in gifted education.* Information Age Publishing.

Davidson Institute (2021). *Disproving myths about gifted students.* Available at: https://www.davidsongifted.org/gifted-blog/disproving-myths-about-gifted-students/

Desmet, O. A., Pereira, N., & Peterson, J. S. (2020). Telling a tale: How underachievement develops in gifted girls. *Gifted Child Quarterly, 64*(2), 85–99. https://doi.org/10.1177/0016986219888633

Fong, C. J., & Kremer, K. P. (2020). An expectancy-value approach to math underachievement: Examining high school achievement, college attendance, and STEM interest. *Gifted Child Quarterly, 64*(2), 67–84. https://doi.org/10.1177/0016986219890599

Gross, M. U. M. (2016). Developing programs for gifted and talented students. In F. H. R. Piske, T. Stoltz, J. M. Machado, & S. Bahia (Eds.), *Altas habilidades/superdotação (AH/SD) e criatividade: Identificação e atendimento* [Giftedness and Creativity: Identification and Specialized Service] (pp. 61–75). Juruá.

Hollingworth, L. S. (1926). *Gifted children: Their nature and nurture.* Macmillan.

Kane, M., & Silverman, L. K. (2014). Fostering well-being in gifted children: Preparing for an uncertain future. In F. H. R. Piske, J. M. Machado, S. Bahia, & T. Stoltz (Eds.), *Altas habilidades/superdotação (AH/SD): Criatividade e emoção.* [Giftedness: Creativity and Emotion] (pp. 67–84). Juruá.

Laycraft, K., & Gierus, B. (2019). *Acceptance: The key to a meaningful life.* Nucleus Learning.

McCoach, D. B., Siegle, D., & Rubenstein, L. D. (2020). Pay attention to inattention: Exploring ADHD symptoms in a sample of underachieving gifted students. *Gifted Child Quarterly, 64*(2), 100–116. https://doi.org/10.1177/0016986219901320

NAGC (Nation Association for Gifted Children) (2021). Myths about gifted students. https://www.nagc.org/myths-about-gifted-students

Peterson, J. S. (2009). Myth 17: Gifted and talented individuals do not have unique social and emotional needs. *Gifted Child Quarterly, 53*(4), 280–282. https://doi.org/10.1177/0016986209346946

Peterson, J. S. (2014). Paying attention to the whole gifted child: Why, when, and how to focus on social and emotional development. In F. H. R. Piske, J. M. Machado, S. Bahia, & T. Stoltz (Eds.), *Altas habilidades/superdotação (AH/SD): Criatividade e emoção.* [Giftedness: Creativity and emotion] (pp. 45–66). Juruá.

Piechowski, M. M. (2014). Identity. In F. H. R. Piske, J. M. Machado, S. Bahia, & T. Stoltz (Eds.), *Altas habilidades/superdotação (AH/SD): Criatividade e emoção* (pp. 97–114). Juruá.

Piske, F. H. R. (2018). Altas habilidades/superdotação (AH/SD) e criatividade na escola: O olhar de Vygotsky e de Steiner. Doctoral thesis, Universidade Federal do Paraná, Curitiba/PR, Brazil.

Piske, F. H. R. (2020). The importance of socio-emotional development of gifted students. In F. H. R. Piske, T. Stoltz, A. Rocha, & C. Costa-Lobo (Eds.), *Socio-emotional development and creativity of gifted students.* Imprensa da Universidade de Coimbra.

Piske, F. H. R. (2021). *Altas habilidades/superdotação (AH/SD): Identificação, mitos e atendimento.* Juruá.

Piske, F. H. R., & Kane, M. (2020). Socio-emotional development of gifted students: Educational implications. In F. H. R. Piske, T. Stoltz, E. Guérios, D. Camargo, A. Rocha, & C. Costa-Lobo (Eds.), *Superdotados e talentosos: Educação, emoção, criatividade e potencialidades.* Juruá.

Reis, S. M., & McCoach, D. B. (2000). The underachievement of gifted students: What do we know and where do we go? *Gifted Child Quarterly, 44*, 152–170.

Renzulli, J. S. (2012). Reexamining the role of gifted education and talent development for the 21st century: A four-part theoretical approach. *Gifted Child Quarterly, 56*(3), 150–159. https://doi.org/10.1177/0016986212444901

Renzulli, J. S. (2016). The role of blended knowledge in the development of creative productive giftedness. *International Journal for Talent Development and Creativity*, 4(1), 13–24.

Sainz, M., Ferrando, M., Prieto, L., & Ruiz-Melero, M. J. (2020). Competencias socioemocionales y alta habilidad: Superdotados y talentos. In F. H. R. Piske, T. Stoltz, E. Guérios, D. Camargo, A. Rocha, & C. Costa-Lobo (Eds.), *Superdotados e talentosos: Educação, emoção, criatividade e potencialidades*. Juruá.

Silverman, L. K. (2009). Searching for asynchrony: A new perspective on twice-exceptional children. In B. MacFarlane & T. Stambaugh (Eds.), *Leading change in gifted education: The festschrift of Dr. Joyce Van Tassel-Baska* (pp. 169–181). Prufrock Press.

Snyder, K. E., & Wormington, S. V. (2020). Gifted underachievement and achievement motivation: The promise of breaking silos. *Gifted Child Quarterly*, 64(2), 63–66. https://doi.org/10.1177/0016986220909179

Steenbergen-Hu, S., Olszewski-Kubilius, P., & Calvert, E. (2020). The effectiveness of current interventions to reverse the underachievement of gifted students: Findings of a meta-analysis and systematic review. *Gifted Child Quarterly*, 64(2), 132–165. https://doi.org/10.1177/0016986220908601

Tsai, K., & Fu, G. (2016). Underachievement in gifted students: A case study of three college physics students in Taiwan. *Universal Journal of Educational Research*, 4, 688–695.

Weller-Clarke, A. (2011). Underachievement. In S. Goldstein & J. A. Naglieri (Eds.), *Encyclopedia of child behavior and development*. Springer. https://doi.org/10.1007/978-0-387-79061-9_2984

Addressing Underachievement Connected to Home-School Cultural Discontinuity

Extending Practices of Parent Engagement that Fosters STEM Talent Development among Gifted Black Students

Kristina Henry Collins and Cheryl Fields-Smith

I spent the majority of my most memorable childhood moments sitting at the kitchen table in a small two-bedroom home with my mom and step-dad, playing board games, solving logic puzzles, reading recipes and "how to" manuals, problem-solving home-based issues, dissecting auto-mechanic diagrams, and discussing current "state of the home" affairs. It was these parent-engaged STEM experiences that later influenced and fostered intrinsic motivation for my STEM interest, STEM academic success, and STEM talent development in school. By the time I was 3 years old, my mom and my step-dad had taught me to play chess. In the middle of the table, held up by the salt and pepper shaker, we kept a small notebook of high scores and winners of board and card game competitions such as Taboo®, Scattergories®, Yahtzee®, Scrabble®, Dominoes®, spades, rummy, and bid whiz, just to name a few. I would sit and watch my mom complete a crossword puzzle book in one sitting or play solitaire for hours. At least once a month, we proudly glued paper to the back of a 1000-piece puzzle that we had completed and hung for art throughout the house. My mom would write down recipes on index cards and require me to mathematically adjust measurements of listed ingredients to fit the desired servings for that day.

By age 10, I could take a technical instructional manual of any kind, make sense of the complicated diagrams, and effectively communicate those instructions to anyone wanting to build something. I had done it so many times, assisting my step-dad in the yard as he built and/or rebuilt many cars from frame to functional. My step-dad also kept these huge atlas and maps that intrigued me and kept my attention for hours; I recognized, early on, the patterns for the numbering system for all major highways and mile markers that ran north to south and east to west. If there was something that needed to be fixed around the house and we didn't have the right tools or couldn't afford to bring in a professional to fix it, we substituted and/or engineered tools. We did not often eat together as a family

DOI: 10.4324/9781003369578-10

at the kitchen table, but the kitchen table was my educational playground where many hours of family-based and culturally relevant, critical thinking skill development were the central themes of every activity.

Introduction

At first thought, the idea of a young girl and her parents[1] sitting around the kitchen table playing games presents itself as nothing more than typical family time for any American household. However, the vignette above and others throughout this chapter provide a personal testimony of day-to-day practices of Black parental engagement that fosters STEM identity and serves as an additive to the realm of culturally responsive STEM talent development as defined by and experienced within the home.

Negative Impact of Home-School Cultural Discontinuity on Student Achievement

There are many challenges faced by Black families as they attempt to engage and collaborate with the school on behalf of their children. Coined by Irvine (1991), a lack of cultural synchronization refers to the misalignment between White teacher and Black families' values and ways of being as well as differences in expectations related to parental roles in children's learning. It is under these conditions of home-school discontinuity that the deficit perspective of Black parental engagement was defined and continues to be viewed by today's educational system. In addition to the deficit thinking about their level of engagement, Black families also battle the stereotypes about who they are ethnically. This, the authors contend, is not adequately addressed in the research, especially as it pertains to potential causes for underachievement by gifted Black students. Cooper (2007) studied the advocacy roles of 14 Black mothers through detailed interviews. These mothers of low-income or working-class status discussed what Cooper refers to as "motherwork," "an important act of cultural resistance and empowerment" (p. 491) as well as their educational views, their choice of school, and experiences. Her findings revealed a prevalent stereotype that portrayed Black mothers as uncaring, angry, and combative in their interactions with school officials who therefore were of the mindset that "African-American parents are more of a deficit to their children's educational development than an asset" (p. 492). This mindset creates a roadblock for mutually respected home-school partnerships and calls into question Black parents' practices for student learning at home and their views on school achievement.

Perceiving culturally different families as incapable or not willing to contribute to the development of their child's education creates exclusionary practices within the school that also lead to unwelcoming and unequal involvement of these families (Abrams & Gibbs, 2002; Cooper, 2009). This further alienates parents and marginalizes their value as a source of academic and talent development. Subsequently, schools and research maintain a focus on the parents' attendance, or the lack thereof, and not the positive influences of their cultural presence in their children's educational development. Grave impacts can develop from these cultural misunderstandings and exclusionary practices that not only stifle family-school relationships, but also negatively affect Black students' academic achievement (Hill, 2011).

Rejecting the deficit-based framework of Black parental engagement allows researchers to systematically reveal the cultural capital that Black parents bring to the educational table as well as breaking down the structural constraints that bind them. Just as parents who are more familiar with the discourse of the school are more likely to be involved at the school, so will educators who familiarize themselves with the customs, learning style, and behaviors of the home. Likewise, they will be better equipped to implement complementary culturally responsive structures within the school.

Authors' Positionality and Conceptual Framework

Together, the authors boast backgrounds and extensive experiences as a career STEM practitioner, STEM educator, family engagement expert, and social science researchers. They are uniquely positioned to bring a cultural perspective and scientific skillset to explore family roles in cultivating STEM talent and development in Black students, where racialized understanding of empowerment, identity, and survival are critical. Positing the importance of evaluating social and political contexts of underachievement in terms of diversity, equity, and inclusion (DEI), the authors share the personal testimony of Hope (a pseudonym), as anecdotal evidence affirmed by theories of ecological parental engagement and culture as practice, to reveal traps for underachievement and missed opportunities to maximize cultural capital and student potential.

Hope, a Black female, grew up in the southeastern part of the United States. She excelled exceptionally in school on a dual-diploma AP track, was not identified as gifted, and her family's financial status would be defined as low socio-economic, based on the federal income definition. Additional vignettes used throughout the chapter also support the presentation of Collins' (2018b) Black Parents' STEM Engagement (BPSE) Model, which demonstrates a construct for Black parental engagement that fosters Black children's STEM identity. Extending Bronfenbrenner's (1977) view of ecology, the Ecologies of Parent Engagement model (EPE) (Barton et al., 2004) offers a framework that goes beyond the cultural context of parental involvement. It includes the beliefs and actions of everyday social behavior, or practices of parental engagement. These beliefs and actions influence the decisions of what and why parents do what they do; this is comparable to what Coolahan et al. (2002) defined as parenting behaviors and styles. Barton et al. (2004) contended that parental engagement is a mediation process between space and capital with the community/home-based space as one of those spaces. Barton's terminology of space and capital were drawn from Pierre Bourdieu's (1977) *Culture as Practice* framework (Barton et al., 2004; Prasad, 2005) and *Funds of Knowledge* framework (Amaro-Jiménez & Semingson, 2011; Moll, Amanti, Neff, & González, 1992; Tan & Barton, 2010; Wright, 2011). And to Barton's own credit, she confirmed that it "has been difficult to construct an account of parental involvement grounded in everyday practice that goes beyond a laundry list of things that good parents do for their children's education" (Barton et al., 2004). The EPE model, however, does confirm that the values, as evident in their cultural capital, of family engagement practices among non-White families are present and different; the voice of the community, or socialized domain, is inherently included within the model. That voice is detailed in the parenting styles and practices implemented that yield successful student achievement as a direct result of those everyday beliefs and behavior within the community/home-based space. Lowe and Dotterer (2013) echoed the EPE model, noting that parenting practices are best understood within their socialized domain.

The BPSE model provides a much-needed cultural context to understanding how Black families can and do engage in STEM talent development outside of schools. The authors utilize historical context, a critical literature review, and the highlighted vignettes as elements within a critical race methodology (Delgado & Stefancic, 2012) to show how educational system problematizes traditional parent involvement concepts, specifically as they relate to STEM and gifted education for Black students. The findings demonstrate a value and potential for the BPSE model to inform research on Black family engagement in STEM identity and talent development, especially for gifted and talented Black students who have shown significant academic success and interest in STEM.

Defining Black Students' STEM Identity and STEM Talent Development

The BPSE construct and its theoretical framework introduce a contextual examination of culture as practice to effectively foster STEM identity and self-concepts for Black students who have shown significant interest or gifts in areas of STEM. This introduction offers a foundation by which to explore Black parents' role in STEM talent development, for the purpose of increasing Black students' achievement and persistence in STEM disciplines. Absent a contextual definition of Black students' STEM identity or self-concept, the first author explored major Black students' identity theories and frameworks; conducted a critical analysis of empirical studies that examined STEM issues among Black students at each of the P-12 educational levels; and synthesized the findings to inform the conceptualization of Black student STEM identity and the operationalization of STEM talent development (Collins, 2018a).

Ford (2010), in her work related to culturally and linguistically diverse (CLD) gifted children, asserted: "the need to focus more assertively and proactively on students' culture—their values, beliefs, habits, customs, and traditions—may be greater now than ever before" (p. 50) in order to acknowledge, respect, and otherwise affirm their cultural identities (Ford, 2004). She went on to proclaim: "at its essence, the learning environment is about relationships, communication, and expectations—focusing specifically on students' sense of membership and belonging" (Ford, 2010, p. 51). In addition, Ford noted that parents create experiences to nurture their gifted children's cultural identities and social/emotional well-being, which are basic needs that must be met in order for any student to reach their [STEM] potential (Ford, 2004). Moreover, Maxwell (2004) claimed that in order "to develop adequate explanations of educational interventions, we need to use research methods that investigate contexts and processes that generate phenomena and outcomes" (p. 7). Halgunseth (2009) noted: "the two most influential environments in which young children develop are their homes and their early childhood education program" (p. 56). Thus, examinations of community and home-based spaces would be warranted to evaluate effective STEM identity and talent development.

As such, for the purpose of this chapter, Black students' STEM identity refers to the gender-based, racial identity (Collins, 2018a; see also Ford, 2013; Henfield, 2012; Leonard, Walker, Cloud, & Joseph, 2017; Whiting, 2006, 2009) that is central to one's positive self-perception of STEM talent (competence, ability, value, interest, and sense of belonging) within the STEM domain. STEM talent development is defined as the filters and catalysts (Kronborg, 2010) that positively nurture academic potential

(Ford, 2004; Halgunseth, 2009; Horn, 2015) and influence one's motivation to learn and further develop talent in the STEM domain (Collins, 2018a). With that position, the authors of this chapter were taken back to that kitchen table with a new question: What connections exist between Black parents' engagement practices and Black students' STEM identity and talent development?

Connecting Black Parents' Engagement to Effective STEM Identity and Talent Development

It was a well-understood rule, "nothing but A's in this house" as my mom explicitly voiced her expectations based on her beliefs and perception of my talents and intellectual ability. She would constantly tell me that I was really smart. Ironically and perhaps commonly so, however, I never saw myself as a mathematician or scientist, just smart and good at solving math and science problems.

Hope's mother offered no formal guidance as it related to academic pathways or career selection. She did, however, set very high standards and consistently communicated high expectations regarding Hope's academic achievement to be demonstrated by high grades. While high expectations and an authoritarian approach[2] by parents have been cited as a potential source for underachievement, this was not the case for Hope. Without the regard of intellectually gifted and no high expectation to achieve by the school, the high expectation by Hope's mother based on perceived abilities and exhibited inquisitive nature at home offered the social-emotional support needed to nurture Hope's intrinsic motivation. Like Hope's mom, many Black families' practices and style of parenting represent responsiveness to their culture, what they value, and their goals for their children.

As the primary caretakers, parents are, by default, the child's first and earliest teachers, formally and informally; they are by far the most accessible link to connect classroom learning to students' personal real-world experiences, values, and interests. Parent involvement has been researched and confirmed through various testimonies of administrators and educators alike as highly associated with high student academic outcomes (Latunde & Clark-Louque, 2016). The belief that effective parental involvement has a significant influence on student achievement and career selection is evident through the numerous educational policy mandates regarding parent involvement, which require schools to implement plans for parental involvement at different levels of school operation and support (Fields-Smith, 2005; Mendez, 2010). Most notably, the federal government has continually enacted educational programs such as Project Head Start in 1967 (Mendez, 2010), public policies within the "No Child Left Behind" Act of 2003, and the "Race to the Top" (McGuinn, 2012), as initiatives to operationalize parent engagement and hold schools accountable for it.

The authors show the connection between Black parents' STEM engagement and Black students' STEM talent development through a documented, historical context for Black parental engagement and a critical analysis of the literature and empirical research of STEM achievement. This is complemented by anecdotal evidence which serves as a good way to scrutinize disparities (Sullivan, 2015) and help introduce new concepts or define immeasurable ones (Sazanavets, 2019), and is highlighted through the lived experiences of Hope, as a Black STEM student, and the parent of gifted Black STEM students.

Postulating Parental Engagement

While all stakeholders might agree on the benefits of parent involvement, most still struggle with appropriate and effective parent-as-partner involvement that will maximize student achievement in the child's educational experiences (Alexander et al., 2017; Halgunseth, 2009; Han & Love, 2015). Parental involvement and parent engagement have been the terms traditionally employed in the research literature. The phrase parent involvement signifies a home-school relationship focused almost exclusively on supporting or reinforcing school-based conceptions of children's learning. Thus, the term parent involvement tends to refer to traditional roles such as volunteering in the classroom, attending school conferences and performances, and supporting school fundraisers. In their seminal research, Barton, Drake, Perez, St. Louis, and George (2004) chose to replace the term parent involvement with parent engagement to extend its conceptualization beyond what parents do to also include the motivations and strategies related to parents' decisions to participate in their children's education. This distinction represented a major shift in parental involvement research from a narrow focus based solely on activities families do that reinforce or support school learning and instead, to acknowledge that families make decisions to participate in their children's learning well beyond the school, including in the home and in the community. The expansion of conceptualizations of parental engagement is critical because, inevitably, some ways that parents choose to be involved will reside outside of the school and therefore, will likely be invisible to school staff. Like Barton et al. (2004), we assert that effective parental engagement occurs everywhere learning takes place for the student, and parents make decisions to engage in their children's learning, which are worthy of further study for their impact on student achievement.

Based on the meanings established in the research, the authors contend the following: (1) parent involvement has been grounded in a framework and perspective of the school's needs, expectations, and goals for children learning; (2) practices of parental engagement by the school should acknowledge the cultural values/knowledge that parents offer; and (3) parental engagement, as a distinct extension of parent involvement, offers a more comprehensive view of what parents do and why and can function somewhat independently of school. In other words, parental engagement is not dependent on the educational system's acceptance or acknowledgment of its existence. This important distinction in defining parental engagement creates an opportunity also to rethink parental roles and influence in academic and talent development processes within, and outside of, educational structures.

Historical Context of Black Parental Engagement

To understand the dynamics and strength of Black parenting as they relate to engagement in the schooling of their children, it is essential to consider the historical and cultural context of successful parent engagement prior to desegregation. As a caveat to the culture, style, and successful practices of engagement during that time, this contextual consideration informs the cultural values and strengths of contemporary, parent engagement practices of today.

> When my mom speaks of her time in school, she fondly remembers her gym teacher that not only taught her health and wellness, but acted as a mentor and staple in the community. She compares going to school in the segregated South to attending a historically Black college and university (HBCU) today in terms

of a sense of community-parenting and commitment to teaching students how to navigate in society. She noted that even though there were many things they lacked in terms of textbooks, technology, and other resources, they made up for in developing strong sense of self, purpose, and value in the community. She further proclaimed that much of this pride and purpose was lost when schools were desegregated in exchange for better resources and facilities; Blacks seemed to always use a "white ruler" to measure their own worth. As a mother, she was grateful for the education that I received in a desegregated school system. However, as a grandmother, she feels that our society, or at least my home community, has returned to those segregated, neighborhood schools but this time without the pride and value for community for the Black families. She contributes this to the mismanagement of desegregation and posited that we were stripped of our identity and pride; our talents are longer ours until they have been validated by the white norm.

Before *Brown vs. the Board of Education* (1954), all of the stakeholders within the Black segregated formal schooling environment – the educators, the principal, the bus drivers – resided in the same neighborhoods, worshipped in the same churches, and served in the same close-knit communities where the children lived (Siddle Walker, 1996). Siddle Walker (1996) documented this critical, but indirect role of Black parents during segregation as a position of trusting that their Black teachers and principals had their children's best interests at heart. Black parents' rare appearance inside the school during this period reflected this trust and parents' high regard and reverence for the teaching and learning that took place there. However, Siddle Walker's (1996) "Their Highest Potential" also demonstrated the significant levels of support and sacrifice Black parents and even childless members of the segregated Black community made to ensure children could learn even when their local Boards of Education implemented roadblocks to their schooling. Massive resistance to the education of Blacks in integrated public schools in the South continued even after the passing of *Brown vs. the Board of Education*.

Indeed, during integration, some Black families chose to send their children to integrated public schools under much duress and outright hatred in the context of white massive resistance - famously depicted by the experiences of the Little Rock Nine.[3] Yet, even during this time, Black parents had alternative options to educate their children. For example, Cecelski (1994) documented the ways in which a Black community in Hyde Park, North Carolina, fought to keep their Black segregated school open in resistance to integration. Moreover, rather than subject their children to oppressive learning environments during the highly contested implementation of integration, some Black families turned to Catholic schools to educate their children (Irvine & Foster, 1996). Interestingly, Catholic social teachings affirmed the parent's role as the primary educator and therefore, supported positive home-school relationship building (Lore, Wang, & Buckley, 2016). As a result of the massive resistance directed toward circumventing integration and African-American families' diverse responses, public schools in the South did not become fully integrated until the 1970s, which is less than 50 years ago (Morris, 2009).

Perry, Steele, and Hilliard (2003) dynamically demonstrated the importance of considering the relative newness of integrated public schools when interpreting the achievement of Black children in the US. Yet, today, schools have returned to segregation under de facto circumstances with influences from neoliberalism and gentrification, which has resulted in the isolation of Black and Latino students in poverty, particularly in urban communities (Brown, 2016). Re-segregated, or racially isolated, schools have tended also to be under-resourced (Semuels, 2016). Thus, scholars such as Milner (2015) have called for a reframing of the Black-White achievement gap from a focus on test score differences to an interpretation of the gap as an educational opportunity gap. Milner explained:

> I believe a focus on an achievement gap places too much blame and emphasis on students themselves as individuals and not enough attention on why gaps and disparities are commonplace in schools across the country. Opportunity, on the other hand, forces us to think about how systems, processes, and institutions are overtly and covertly designed to maintain the status quo and sustain depressingly complicated disparities in education. (p. 8)

Contemporary Context of Black Parental Engagement

Oftentimes, and regardless of, economic status or educational background, Black parents are viewed as disconnected and even unconcerned about the educational process of their children (Fields-Smith, 2005; Joseph, Hailu, & Boston, 2017; Leonard, Walker, Cloud, & Joseph, 2017). This judgment is more often than not based on an approach that values a "tally" of the number of school visits, the number of volunteer organizations in which the parent is engaged, monetary donations, and other activities that contribute to the success of the school (Bowers & Griffin, 2011). This standard of judgment comes from the influences of White, middle-class perspectives of a parental involvement that oftentimes marginalizes families who have other cultural values (Casanova, 1996; Fields-Smith, 2007) and subsequently, approach family engagement of those cultures as a deficit that needs to be improved or changed (Halgunseth, 2009). For example, the Head Start program, designed to buffer the impact of poverty on pre-school children, was initiated to offer comprehensive services to families and promote child learning based on the critical role that parents play in child development. At a core of the Head Start program, The Companion Curriculum (TCC) was used as a preventive intervention to increase parent involvement and the teacher-parent relationship. However, its premise for parent involvement was centered on parents' presence in actual school activities and parents supporting and/or extending school-initiated endeavors and values (Mendez, 2010). Such in-school presence is not always possible for parents who work long hours on extraordinarily laborious jobs.

Reconciling the Historical and Contemporary Contexts of Black Parental Engagement

> As parents, my husband and I make sure that our two sons (ages 12 and 19) who have both been identified as gifted with strong interest in STEM as well, are first grounded in a strong sense of who they are as Black men and members of a marginalized race. We make sure that we know what is being taught at school and fill any perceived void of African-American contribution and cultural perspective. We have conversations with them about survival, success, and significance outside of the home. Noting their multiple interests and potentiality to include

STEM, sports, and music, we make sure that they understand the impact of STEM skill development and STEM talent development as a way to secure their future career choice and sustained quality of life. To complement and. in certain cases, make up for the shortcomings of their formal educational opportunities, I have implemented my own STEM skill development independent of state's standards and school expectations in terms of scope, sequence, and standard of excellence.

In a racialized society, Black parents understand that it is their children's racial identity that is central and that through this they have already experienced and will experience all other things, including discrimination, racism, stereotyping, stereotype threat, imposter syndrome, and the like. as they attempt to find their own fit in American society. As such, gifted Black students' high ability level, proven academic success, and their STEM skill and identity development are still second to their racial identity. Having experienced it personally, Hope's husband knows there will be those who value, promote and/or encourage their sons' athletic and artistic skill development over their academic skill development. Consequently, they and parents like them do not always trust that the public or private schools which their children attend will sufficiently address their children's learning with these major considerations or from their cultural perspective.

During the pre-*Brown* era, Black parents' deferment to schoolteachers and principals exemplified a level of trust between home and school that remains highly desirable today. In contrast to today's schools, Black students attending segregated Black schools were taught by a 100% Black teaching staff from their community, who maintained a mutual trust in the judgment of parents related to their own children's ability as well as the parents' ability to support their children at home. Casanova (1996) recognized that trust was as an essential element of the home and school relationship; parents trusted that teachers had the best interest of their children at the forefront of what they did, so parents left educators to do their jobs. Fields-Smith (2005) stressed that with the positions and relationships that educators had in the community, trust and empowerment were bestowed upon them that allowed parents to maintain a direct role that was not as active within the building and decision making of the schooling of the child; parents would often come in contact with the same school professional in an informal, community setting, therefore, there was little or no need for parents to have a presence at school. Parents trusted that school leaders and teachers had their children's best interests at heart and therefore, Black parents in segregated schools tended to revere and defer to teachers. Entering into the school was unheard of out of respect for the work of schooling (Siddle Walker, 1996).

Grantham and Collins (2013) noted that Black parents who are engaged in the academic development of their children refuse to stand by and let their children "fail or face attacks unnecessarily and unjustly" and defined bystander teachers as those who "watch Black students' ability atrophy" (p. 4). They asserted that Black parents who choose to homeschool have different reasons that those of White parents. Similarly, we posit that Black parents who also actively engage in STEM identity and talent development at home and community-based activities find it a priority as well to ensure the quality of education is also culturally responsive. We further predict that this will remain the case unless Black parents gain a sense of trust in educators and the formal educational system to prioritize their children's interest.

Black Parents' Successful Engagement

We now discuss the social and cultural factors affecting Black parents' successful engagement in their child's STEM identity and talent development.

Navigating Boundaries of Social Dominant Practices

Even though one might argue that trust is an important element in any relationship, and not unique to Black parental engagement, its relevance within the context of the civil rights movement and desegregation makes trust a cultural value and foundation that has been absent in the post-*Brown* era. With mandated desegregation, mistrust existed resulting from environmental factors such as unfamiliarity, intolerance, and unfair judgment that encompassed a lack of cultural synchronization between the expected educational relationships of White teachers and Black parents that now simultaneously exist alongside that of White teachers-White parents relationships (Irvine, 1991; Milner, 2010). After the desegregation of schools, most Black children and parents not only found themselves adapting to a new culture, but had done so without the benefit of those social exchange relationships that they once had with school officials that also served them in their respective communities (Fields-Smith, 2005). As a result, Black parents had to try to maneuver through an educational system that did not value or even consider the historical foundation of their relationships to the school or the successes of their parent engagement practices, style, and cultural structure. The same practices of engagement that worked so well for them to support student achievement now functioned in very different dynamics. Furthermore, the reinforcement of a social dominant practice and tradition disenfranchised many Black parents, making their efforts for academic development of their students invisible and not valued.

Negative Characterization of Black Parental Engagement in Schools

Today, many middle-class, Black parents may be found making their presence known and are involved more directly in the school environment. However, those that do, may not necessarily view themselves as equal partners in the decision-making process; nor do they see their influence considered in the formal process of educating their children (Fields-Smith & Neuharth-Pritchett, 2009). Their involvement may not be seen as a positive or productive element:

> Even in my quest to be engaged as a parent in school as an equal partner in the educational process of my sons, I face resistance especially by those educators and administrators who think that my presence and active engagement somehow question their competence. I experience the negative characterization of my parenting style even though my sons have shown success well beyond that of their peers. When the school officials are not aware of my background and expertise, I have been met with the presumption of illiteracy, poverty, and "angry Black woman syndrome." Furthermore, rarely have any of my sons' teachers tried to utilize my skillset as a STEM educator or parent-as-partner to assist in the classroom.

Many Black parents will confess that the relationship they have with school personnel is often confrontational, grounded in mistrust and a perception of competition for control to ensure that their children are provided an equal chance and equity in education (Casanova, 1996; Fields-Smith, 2005). Cooper (2007, 2009), suggested that these negative characterizations exist because of school personnel's tendency to stereotype Black parents as angry and uninvolved. As the author explained, since our beliefs frequently guide our actions, Black parents often experience bias and disenfranchisement when trying to engage in their children's learning. Cooper specifically focused on the experiences of Black mothers in schools. The role of Black fathers has rarely been considered in family engagement literature, which perpetuates the misconception of the absent Black father within Black families. Focused on cultural notions of care and framing Black moms' engagement as justice-seeking, Cooper admonished parental involvement research for its lack of acknowledgment of the issues of power-sharing and cultural differences that exist in Black parents' home-to-school relationships. Further, Cooper poignantly described the contentious context which Black families must navigate in order to assume a partnership role in their children's schooling. She stated: "Traditional school-based models of parent involvement rarely account for the many ways that low-income and working-class Black parents participate in their children's education and display educational care. These traditional models, instead, privilege white, middle-class behavior norms" (p. 381). This focus on White, middle-class norms has led to ignorance regarding the legacy of care as it has been manifested and still exists among the Black community.

Indirect School Engagement

On the other hand, a contemporary Black parent whose presence is not felt in the school does not necessarily mean they are absent in their engagement of the child's educational process. Moreover, that lack of presence can also be linked to school staff's tendency to limit their consideration for what effective family engagement looks like and to ignore what Black families do outside of school to contribute to children's motivation and education. Evidence of indirect school engagement, on the part of the Black parent, can be measured on the level of engagement that the student exhibits in school. Studies with Black adolescents have confirmed work that linked Black family cohesion and Black parental monitoring (parenting style or emotional climate of parent-child relationship) to increased motivation and school engagement of minority students. Monitoring was measured by "practices that include positive parenting, discipline effectiveness, avoidance of discipline, and extent of parental involvement in the child's life" and includes awareness of the child's social and educational status as well as setting and enforcing boundaries, expectations, and rules (Annunziata, Hogue, Faw, & Liddle, 2006; Hofferth, 2003; Lowe & Dotterer, 2013).

> To my recollection, my parents and my closest friends' parents never volunteered at the school. As a matter of fact, my parents never came to the school except for mandated parent conferences, awards programs, and graduation. For the most part, my step-dad left the concerns of formal schooling to my mom. My mom often reminded me that it was not necessary, and in my best interest that she never "had" to come to the school (typically teachers only communicated with parents if there was a problem). She stressed expected behavior and taught me to advocate for myself in terms of getting what I needed from teachers to learn. If I ever felt like my teachers were unfair or did not afford me opportunities to learn, then I would let my mom know and at most, she would send in a note to that teacher.

The only other communication I remembered was on the back of the report cards we received where teachers would always note how smart they thought I was followed by how I talked too much in class. My mom would always respond with the same "we are proud of her and will talk to her about her excessive talking in class.""Talk to" always translated into punishment/restriction and a butt whipping that I better not talk about with my teachers. Subsequently when my excessive talking in class did not decrease, teachers would respond with "I guess your mom didn't talk with you" and give me additional work in an attempt to keep me quiet.

Collins (2017) encouraged parents to work closely with the school, but to take primary responsibility for the talent development of their children, noting an effective scaffolding approach to complement the formal education process with authentic ways to explore the child's talents and interests. She asserted that parents who effectively nurture the dual identities of their children, including but not limited to closely monitoring the school curriculum/courses and child development from diverse sources, afford children an opportunity to maximize their gifts and talents.

It Takes a Village Mentality

In their book, Grantham et al. (2013) addressed Black parenting issues within an "it takes a village" perspective noting a common belief among Black parents that they do not raise their children alone:

As a parent and advocate for my own children, I have become a voice for other gifted, Black students and their families; my background in STEM, gifted programming, and curriculum & development positions me to effectively advocate for equity and quality in education that benefit my children and other children that look like them regardless of socio-economic class, cultural capital, and/ or influence. Oftentimes, I take on the role of parent-partner for other parents who feel defeated and lost in the fight to maintain equity for their child in terms of information, access, and accommodations. Appreciating and giving value to the role that I play in their lives, many of my students and other children in the community affectionately refer to me as "mama."

Fictive kinships, such as "play-aunts," "play-mothers," etc.. are very inherent within the Black community and play a significant role in Black child self-identity (Chatters et al., 1994; Nelson, 2013, 2014). This leads to significant parental-type engagement by extended family and community members (Pearson et al., 1990). While this mindset contains benefits in child-rearing support, it can present challenges for the parent if there exist conflicts in expectations between the home and the school (Mendez, 2010).

Multidimensional Cultural Attributes

The authors contend that one must consider the multidimensional attributes of parenting that influence the activities that parents choose to engage in. It is critically important to understand the cultural attributes and style of parental engagement in child development. Black parenting practices are embedded in and influenced by a unique style of parenting and cultural traditions that consequently influence a child's interest and development, all of which are closely connected to one's experiences and value systems that are grounded in cultural dynamics.

[BT]Distinct among leaders in the research of multidimensional and contextual Black family engagement is John Fantuzzo. Many of the studies by Fantuzzo and his colleagues validated Black family engagement within the context of the cultural structures in the home and community (Fantuzzo et al., 2004). This research perspective allowed for identification of unique attributes in Black parenting style and practices that were not viewed as deficits in intellectual value in comparison to White, middle-class parenting styles and practices. Their empirical research with urban, low-income, Head Start parents (Coolahan et al., 2002) and urban, low-income parents of kindergarten students revealed a multidimensional perspective of Black parent behaviors and styles. The work of Fantuzzo and his colleagues distinguishes Black family involvement dimensions from the Black parent-child relationship. Black family involvement dimensions that positively affect student learning include "home-based involvement, school-based involvement; and home-school conferencing" (McWayne et al., 2004). Accordingly, Black parental engagement is the style and goal-directed, behavior, or activities (supportive home learning environment), direct school contact of Black parents practiced within the cultural context of child.

Operationalizing and Extending the BPSE Construct for Classroom Instruction

A critical review of the literature has revealed gaps in the research that addresses a contextual examination of Black parental engagement practices that effectively foster STEM identity and self-concepts for Black students who have shown significant interest, gifts, and success in STEM disciplines. An exhaustive analysis of documented research revealed a failure to significantly include contextual consideration of Black parental engagement that specifically fosters STEM identity, development, or achievement, and, when it does, it is typically from a deficit or school-support perspective. However, collectively examined, commonalities and themes such as common STEM perceptions, parental beliefs, parental actions, parental expectations, student experiences, and so on emerged. There exists an overarching cultural structure that impacts the parental value of STEM which consequently guides parental engagement and significantly influences their child's STEM self-concept. It is through this analysis, along with the historical perspective of Black parenting style and engagement that a cultural, contextual perspective on the BPSE construct is introduced and operationalized. The theoretical, multi-dimensional construct of BPSE includes: (1) specific, goal-directed STEM practices – those specific behaviors (beliefs and actions) that foster the student STEM competence and interest; (2) style of parenting – the emotional climate in which parenting behaviors, or activities are expressed; and (3) cultural structure of parenting – the environmental and ethnic, contextual perspective of the parent-child interaction. The BPSE construct is situated within a theoretical domain of the community/home-based space as illustrated in Figure 7.1.

Solidified by the cultural capital and resources of the home and community, BPSE exposes the multidimensional attributes in Black parenting style and practices that foster STEM talent development. However, when a lack of sociocultural synchronizations (cultural discontinuity) is present, boundaries are created. These boundaries negatively impact the transferability of BPSE and the STEM skills that are being

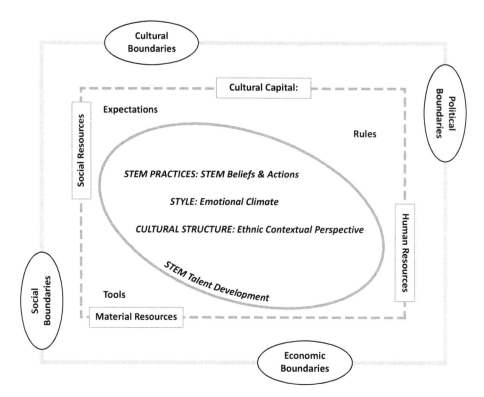

FIGURE 7.1 Theoretical domain for Black Parent STEM Engagement.

developed. Barton's and Bourdieu's work offers a fitting example of the complex analysis of "relations between lifestyle, life chances, and material resources" (Prasad, 2005, p. 9) by which to examine BPSE more validly.

Derived from social positioning, Bourdieu (1977) extended the concept of human capital to include cultural capital, social capital, economic capital, and symbolic capital (Prasad, 2005) that is grounded in the existence of social practice. An individual implicitly acquires habitus, or culture as practice, as a system of dispositions through the culture in which he or she lives; the habitus constantly adapts to "produce practices that are appropriate in their context" (Prasad, 2005, p. 8). Even though habitus is formed implicitly, it can be transformed through a reflection on action, or socio-analysis over time that can evoke awareness of disposition and lead to a specification of techniques and practices that is deliberate. Different types of environmental boundaries border the home and community: social, cultural, political, economic, etc. (Barton et al., 2004; Prasad, 2005). Substantiated for the field of STEM, Archer et al. (2012) affirmed that the extent to which science identity is internalized can be fostered by families though cultural, economic, and social capital is structured by social inequalities. It is through the critical analysis of these works that the theoretical domain of BPSE is offered.

■ *BPSE boundaries.*Vygotsky and other constructivists contend that all knowledge is socially constructed (Gergen, 1997;Vygotsky, 1978). Therefore, social boundaries refer to the unequal power that people have in defining what constitutes knowledge. The value of that knowledge is determined, in part, by how well information fits into the current, accepted community of practice (cultural boundaries), while political boundaries are the systematic processes and issues that affect the meaning of knowledge. Financial situations and power (economic boundaries), however, can affect the social negotiation, or communication methods of that knowledge.

- *BPSE cultural capital and infrastructure.* Within these spaces are the underlying structures of everyday STEM practices such as expectations, rules, and tools (habitus; Bourdieu, 1977) that shape STEM activities in their scope, focus, and purpose (the game; Bourdieu, 1977). The STEM practices are used to steer the student toward goals that the culture values and are bounded by the (cultural) capital or resources (human, social, material, etc.) that individuals (players; Bourdieu, 1977) bring to that space. Human resources are the people in that space who act as more knowledgeable others (MKO; Vygotsky, 1978). Accepting that all knowledge is socially constructed and culture creates cognition (Gergen, 1997; Phillips, 1997), social resources include commonly held, everyday practices and interactions used to communicate knowledge, or ways of thinking and doing. Material resources are marked by the multiple representations of the knowledge. We confer that identified and sometimes intertwined boundaries are important to consider because they determine if knowledge is internal, general, and transferable or bound to the time and place in which it was constructed.

- *Culture as practice at work.* Critical to Black students' STEM self-concept and talent development, parents must nurture a love for STEM subjects and expose students to STEM careers and programs that support the STEM disciplines in which they have shown interest or emerging talent (Ing, 2014; McGee & Spencer, 2015). Similarly, as a source of successful identity development and borrowing from the concept of strong, athletic identity development, Beamon (2010) reported, "sports sociologists have noted family, including parents and siblings, is the earliest and most influential socializing agent into sports participation" (p. 297). And, while there may be controversial opinions and negative effects related to such Black athletic social patterns, especially for those elite athletes, it cannot be denied that there is an overwhelming presence in skill development and successful participation in athletics that could inform strategies for the same within STEM skill and talent development that begin with a positive STEM self-concept in Black students.

The BPSE Construct at Work in the Community

As noted above, the village mentality contributes to significant parental-type engagement by extended family and community members as well. As an example of what that might look for STEM identity and talent development, a recreational coach (human resource) from a local community center (material resource) who takes on the role of mentor or father-figure may incorporate STEM practices through the use of the game of basketball (social resource) to foster STEM skill development in basic math, geometry skills, statistics, etc. and/or pique STEM interest in careers such as sports analyst, sports medicine and kinesiology, design engineers (flooring, balls, scoreboards, etc.) as part of his coaching techniques (style). As iterated in Figure 7.1, embedded in this practice and style is the impact of the cultural structure that values extended family relationships and shared mentoring, or the "it takes a village" mentality. All of these underlying elements explain the "what and why" of the recreational coach actions (Fields-Smith & Neuharth-Pritchett, 2009; Grantham et al., 2013; Mendez, 2010; Pearson et al., 1990). In addition, it may be possible that the coach is strategically navigating within the social, cultural, political, and/or economic boundaries that elevate the attractiveness and importance of sports in that community. Referring to disenfranchised groups, Torrance stated:

> We can point with some degree of success in the identification and cultivation of talent among disadvantaged groups in instrumental and vocal music, dancing, dramatics, visual art, and athletics … these are kinds of talents that are valued among disadvantaged cultures in the United States.
>
> *(1969, p. 73)*

Implications for Practice

My teachers had no idea of the rich STEM-related activities happening within my home and community. For example, I didn't extend my home-based exposure to auto mechanics through the school's auto-shop, the male-dominated class presented as a choice for students who did not plan to go to college, but wanted to learn a vocation. I had no formal educational opportunities to explicitly connect or directly highlight my STEM skillsets in such a way that I found valuable in contributing my perceived STEM assets and further developing my STEM identity. I went on to college and majored in engineering only because my AP calculus teacher told me I should. She declared that I, as a Black female, could carve out my own path and future in the engineering field, noting the scarcity of both Blacks and females in the field. Aspiring to be a first-generation college student in my family, I didn't know anything about college or engineering. My teacher offered no additional information about engineering options, but constantly talked about what university she attended with pride. So, I applied, was accepted, and attended that same university. The only other university that I even considered, but knew we couldn't afford, was the private HBCU (Historically Black College and University) that my cousin went to the year before. I declared a major in electrical engineering only because "electrical" was the most familiar term of all of the engineering options listed based on my experience at home often time trying to fix things around the house, including the TV, radio, hot plate, etc. I did go on to earn a bachelor's degree in engineering and worked in the field for six years while serving in the military. In my early adult years, I never saw anyone that looked like me portrayed as a scientist or engineer to even offer a reflective identity or possibility of that concept for me. I did not persist in a specific STEM career field past early adulthood, I have remained a STEM educator. Reflectively speaking, I have maintained a high STEM identity that I have used to also positively influence my own children's' STEM identity and talent development.

While the STEM skills were transferable, the discontinuity between the teaching approach and the value of those skills created a compendium of "hidden talents" that were not nurtured at school for Hope, as an unidentified gifted, Black student. The complex interplay between Black parental STEM engagement and other extraneous variables needs to be addressed by further research. One way to separate the complexity of potential influences is to specifically investigate ways that Black parents engage in STEM practices that have positively affected Black students' STEM identity. Gifted, Black students who are showing academic success and high interest and/or talent in STEM are an optimal population with which to do this.

Conclusion

A critical review of the literature has revealed gaps in the research that addresses a contextual examination of underachievement and marginalizes the impact of home-school discontinuity. Black parents' STEM engagement practices that effectively foster STEM identity and self-concepts for Black students, who have shown significant interest, gifts, and success in STEM disciplines, should be adopted in school-based STEM learning. Through an introduction of a conceptual definition of BPSE, the authors offer a foundation through which to explore Black parents' role in STEM talent development for the purpose of increasing/maintaining Black students' interest and achievement in STEM disciplines. The authors contend that research on Black parents' STEM engagement that fosters student STEM talent development is also necessary for the purpose of building contextual, cultural STEM practices into the institutionalized structures of education that are meant to do so. Singer et al. (2005) recognized that STEM development through experiential activities could ensure an integrated, comprehensive, and affective curriculum that leads to stronger self-concepts and scholarly identities. Agreeing with them, we conclude that a critical examination of and further research on Black parents' STEM engagement in developing strong STEM self-concept and achievement in their children for the purpose of identifying key components are worthwhile. These components, or cultural schemas, of BPSE can be further examined to determine if those schemas can be applied and built into educational structures. Additionally, questions such as, do gifted Black students who develop a culturally influenced STEM identity understand STEM concepts more deeply than those who just do well in school-based STEM subjects as a manifestation of their academic gifts, can be explored.

REFLECTION QUESTIONS

1. Based on this chapter, what are the major take-aways and mind-shifts regarding Black parents' engagement that all educators need to recognize?

2. There is a saying: "Behind the school stands the parent, and behind the home, the teacher." What does this mean in the context of school-home collaboration?

3. The authors noted that the research has "revealed a failure to significantly include contextual consideration for Black parental engagement that specifically fosters STEM identity, development, or achievement, and when it does, it is typically from a deficit or school-support perspective." Generally speaking, to what extent are you aware of some of the cultural values of Black families in your community? Describe them.

4. What are some specific ways schools/teachers can work with families to ensure cultural continuity (interest, values, ways of knowing and teaching) in the education of gifted Black students?

5. You have been asked to develop a F.U.N. (family unit night) Time at the school's next Gifted Orientation Program. The program aims to educate parents on how to identify characteristic of giftedness at home and to educate teachers on how to translate contextualized manifestations of talent and potential into an academic setting. Maximizing this as an opportunity for teachers, parents, and students to act as partners in nurturing STEM talent in gifted students, what activities would you include in a 2-hr program? Present activities in a table with the rationale, and amount of time spent on the activity.

Notes

1 Throughout this chapter, we use the term parent or parental to include biological as well as non-biological guardians of children, such as adoptive parents, foster parents, and grandparents.
2 Using Baumrind's original classification scheme and those derived from it, Asian-American and African-American parents tend to be more likely to be classified as authoritarian than European-Americans. Researchers have speculated that this may be due to problems in measurement, which tend to be culturally grounded in European-American behavioral norms, differences in the cultural meaning of discipline, as well as differences in neighborhoods and peer groups. In general, stricter parenting has greater benefits in high-risk environments or when consequences of perceived adverse actions are greater and become high-stake, which is the case for African-Americans historically in America.
3 See Beals (2007).

References

Abrams, L., & Gibbs, J. (2002). Disrupting the logic of home-school relations: Parent involvement strategies and practices of inclusion and exclusion. *Urban Education, 37*(3), 384–407.

Alexander, J. J., Cox, R. B., Behnke, A., & Larzelere, R. E. (2017). Is all parental "noninvolvement" equal? Barriers to involvement and their relationship to Latino academic achievement. *Hispanic Journal of Behavioral Sciences, 39*(2), 169–179.

Amaro-Jiménez, C., & Semingson, P. (2011). Tapping into the funds of knowledge of culturally and linguistically diverse students and families. *The Magazine of the National Association for Bilingual Education (NABE), 33*(5), 5–8.

Annunziata, D., Hogue, A., Faw, L., & Liddle, H. (2006). Family functioning and school success in at-risk, inner-city adolescents. *Journal of Youth and Adolescence, 35*(1), 105–113. https://doi.org/10.1007/s10964-005-9016-3

Archer, L., DeWitt, J., Osborne, J., Dillon, J., Willis, B., & Wong, B. (2012). Science aspirations, capital, and family habitus: How families shape children's engagement and identification with science. *American Educational Research Journal, 49*(5), 881–908.

Barton, A., Drake, C., Perez, J., St. Louis, K., & George, M. (2004). Ecologies of parental engagement in urban education. *Educational Researcher, 3*(4), 3–12.

Beals, M. (2007). *Warriors don't cry: A searing memoir of the battle to integrate Little Rock's Central High School*. Simon Pulse.

Beamon, K. (2010). Are sports overemphasized in the socialization process of African American males? A qualitative analysis of former collegiate athletes' perception of sport socialization. *Journal of Black Studies, 41*(2). 281–300.

Bourdieu, P. (1977). *Outline of a theory of practice*. Cambridge University Press.

Bowers, H., & Griffin, D. (2011). Can the Epstein model of parental involvement work in a high-minority, high-poverty elementary school? A case study. *Professional School Counseling, 15*(2), 77–87.

Bronfenbrenner, U. (1977). Toward an experimental ecology of human development. *American Psychologist, 32*, 513–531. http://dx.doi.org/10 .1037/0003-066X.32.7.513

Brown, E. (2016). On the anniversary of *Brown V. Board*, new evidence the public schools are resegregating. *Washington Post* (May 17, 2016). Available at: https://www.washingtonpost.com/news/education/wp/2016/05/17/on-the-anniversary-of-brown-v-board-new-evidence-that-u-s-schools-are-resegregating/?utm_term=.ecd369ae3523

Casanova, U. (1996). Parent involvement: A call for prudence. *Educational Researcher, 25*(8), 30–32, 46.

Cecelski, D. (1994). *Along Freedom Road: Hyde County, North Carolina, and the fate of Black schools in the South*. The University of North Carolina Press.

Chatters, L. M., Taylor, R. J., & Jayakody, R. (1994). Fictive kinship relations in Black extended families. *Journal of Comparative Family Studies, 25*(3). 297–312.

Collins, K. H. (2017). From identification to Ivy League: Nurturing multiple interests and multi-potentiality in gifted students. *Parenting for High Potential, 6*(4), 19–22.

Collins, K. H. (2018a). Confronting color-blind STEM talent development: Toward a contextual model for Black student STEM identity. *Journal for Advanced Academics, 29*(2), 143–168. https://doi.org/10.1177/1932202X18757958

Collins, K. H. (2018b, April). The Multidimensional Structure of Black Parent Engagement in STEM: Introduction of the Black Parent–STEM Engagement Questionnaire (BP-SEQ) Instrument. Paper presented at American Education Research Association (AERA) Annual Convention, New York

Coolahan, K., McWayne, C., Fantuzzo, J., & Grimm, S. (2002). Validation of a multidimensional assessment of parenting styles for low-income African-American families with pre-school children. *Early Childhood Research Quarterly, 17,* 356–373.

Cooper, C. W. (2007). School choice as 'motherwork': Valuing African-American women's educational advocacy and resistance. *International Journal of Qualitative Studies in Education, 20*(5), 491–512.

Cooper, C. W. (2009). Parent involvement, African American mothers, and the politics of educational care. *Equity & Excellence in Education, 42*(4), 379–394.

Delgado, R., & Stefancic, J. (2012). *Critical race theory : An introduction* (2nd ed.). New York University Press.

Fantuzzo, J., McWayne, C., & Perry, M. (2004). Multiple dimensions of family involvement and their relations to behavioral and learning competencies for urban, low-income children. *School Psychology, 33*(4), 467–480.

Fields-Smith, C. (2005). African American parents before and after *Brown. Journal of Curriculum and Supervision, 20* (2), 129–135.

Fields-Smith, C. (2007). Social class and African-American parental involvement. In J. A. Van Galen & G. W. Noblit (Eds.), *Late to class: Social class and schooling in the new economy* (pp. 167–202). State University of New York Press.

Fields-Smith, C., & Neuharth-Pritchett, S. (2009). Families as decision-makers: When researchers and advocates work together. *Childhood Education, 85*(4), 237–242. doi:10.1080/00094056.2009.10523087

Ford, D. Y. (2004). A challenge for culturally diverse families of gifted children: Forced choices between affiliation or achievement. *Gifted Child Today, 27*(3), 26–29.

Ford, D. Y. (2010). Culturally responsive classrooms: Affirming culturally different gifted students. *Gifted Child Today, 33*(1), 50–53.

Ford, D.Y. (2013). Black females: Blacked out and whited out. Available at: http://www.drdonnayford.com/#!black-females/c1zop

Gergen, K. (1997). Constructing constructivism: Pedagogical potentials. *Issues in Education: Contributions from Educational Psychology, 3,* 195–202.

Grantham, T., & Collins, K. H. (2013). Upstander parents choosing to homeschool gifted, Black students. *Parenting for High Potential, 2*(8), 4–9.

Grantham, T., Trotman Scott, M., & Harmon, D. (Eds.). (2013). *Young, triumphant, and Black: Overcoming the tyranny of segregated minds in desegregated schools.* Prufrock Press, Inc.

Halgunseth, L. (2009). Family engagement, diverse families, and an integrated review of the literature. *Young Children, 64*(5), 56–58.

Han, Y., & Love, J. (2015). Stages of immigrant parent involvement–survivors to leaders: Meeting immigrant parents on their own terms is the optimal way to foster parent engagement and thus student achievement. *Phi Delta Kappan, 97*(4), 21.

Henfield, M. (2012). Masculinity identity development and its relevance to supporting talented. *Gifted Child Today, 35*(3). 179–186.

Hill, N. E. (2011). Undermining partnerships between African American families and schools: Legacies of discrimination and inequalities. In N. E. Hill, T. L. Mann, & H. E. Fitzgerald (Eds.), *African American children and mental health,* Vols. 1 and 2: *Development and context, prevention and social policy* (pp. 199–230). Praeger/ABC-CLIO.

Hofferth, S. (2003). Race/ethnic differences in father involvement in two-parent families: Culture, context, or economy? *Journal of Family Issues*, *24*(2), 185–216.

Horn, C.V. (2015). Young scholars: A talent development model for finding and nurturing potential in underserved populations. *Gifted Child Today*, *38*(1), 19–31.

Ing, M. (2014). Can parents influence children's mathematics achievement and persistence in STEM careers? *Journal of Career Development*, *41*(2), 87–103.

Irvine, J. J. (1991). *Black students and school failure: Policies, practices, and prescriptions*. Greenwood Publishing Inc.

Irvine, J. J., & Foster, M. (1996). *Growing up African American in Catholic schools*. Teachers College Press.

Joseph, N. M., Hailu, M., & Boston, D. (2017). Black women's and girls' persistence in the P–20 mathematics pipeline: Two decades of children, youth, and adult education research. *Review of Research in Education*, *41*(1), 203. doi:10.3102/0091732X16689045.

Kronborg, L. (2010). What contributes to talent development in eminent women? *Gifted and Talented International*, *25*(2), 11–27.

Latunde, Y. Y, & Clark-Louque, A. (2016). Untapped resources: Black parent engagement that contributes to learning. *Journal of Negro Education*, *85*(1), 72–81.

Leonard, J., Walker, E. N., Cloud, V. R., & Joseph, N. M. (2017). Mathematics literacy, identity resilience, and opportunity sixty years since *Brown v. Board*: Counter-narratives of a five-generation family. In J. Ballenger, B. Polnick, & B. Irby (Eds.), *Women of color in STEM: Navigating the workforce* (pp. 79–107). IAP, Information Age Publishing.

Lore, M., Wang, A., & Buckley, M. (2016). Effectiveness of a parent-child home numeracy intervention on urban Catholic school first grade students. *Journal of Catholic Education*, *19*(3), 142–165. doi:10.15365/joce.1903082016.

Lowe, K., & Dotterer, A. (2013). Parental monitoring, parental warmth, and minority youths' academic outcomes: Exploring the integrative model of parenting. *Journal of Youth Adolescence*, *42*(9), 1413–1425.

Maxwell, J. (2004). Causal explanation, qualitative research, and scientific inquiry in education. *Educational Researcher*, *33*(2), 3–11.

Mendez, J. (2010). How can parents get involved in preschool? Barriers and engagement in education by ethnic minority parents of children attending Head Start. *Cultural Diversity and Ethnic Minority Psychology*, *16*(1), 26–36.

Milner, H. R. (2010). *Start where you are, but don't stay there: Understanding diversity, opportunity gaps, and teaching in today's classrooms*. Harvard Education Press.

Milner, H. R. (2015). *Rac(e)ing to class : Confronting poverty and race in schools and classrooms*. Harvard Education Press.

Moll, L., Amanti, C., Neff, D., & González, N. (1992). Funds of knowledge for teaching: Using a qualitative approach to connect homes and classrooms. *Theory into Practice*, *31*(2), 132–141.

Morris, J. (2009). *Troubling the waters: Fulfilling the promise of quality public school for Black children*. Teachers College Press.

McGee, E., & Spencer, M. B. (2015). Black parents as advocates, motivators, and teachers of mathematics. *Journal of Negro Education*, *84*, 473–490.

McGuinn, P. (2012). Stimulating reform: Race to the top, competitive grants and the Obama education agenda. *Educational Policy*, *26*(1), 136–159.

McWayne, C., Hampton, V., Fantuzzo, J., Cohen, M., & Sekino, Y. (2004). A multivariate examination of parent involvement and the social and academic competences of urban kindergarten children. *Psychology in the Schools*, *41*(3), 363–377.

Nelson, M. (2013). Fictive kin, families we choose, and voluntary kin: What does the discourse tell us? *Journal of Family Theory & Review*, *5*(4), 259–281.

Nelson, M. (2014). Whither fictive kin? Or, what's in a name? *Journal of Family Issues*, *35*(2), 201–222.

Pearson, J., Hunter, A., Ensminger, M., & Kellam, S. (1990). Black grandmothers in multigenerational households: Diversity in family structure and parenting involvement in the Woodlawn community. *Child Development*, *61*(2), 434–442.

Perry, T., Steele, C., & Hilliard, A.G. (2003). *Young, gifted, and Black: Promoting high achievement among African-American students*. Beacon Press.

Phillips, D. (1997). How, why, what, when and where: Perspectives on constructivism and education. *Issues in Education: Contributions from Educational Psychology, 3*, 151–194.

Prasad, P. (2005). *Crafting qualitative research: Working in the postpositivist traditions.* Sharpe.

Sazanavets, F. (2019, August 19). Anecdotal evidence is often the best evidence. *Scientific Programmer.* Available at: https://scientificprogrammer.net/2019/08/14/anecdotal-evidence-is-often-the -best-evidence/

Semuels, A. (2016). Good school, rich school; bad school, poor school: The inequality at the heart of America's school system. *The Atlantic* (August 25, 2016). Available at: https://www.theatlantic .com/business/archive/2016/08/property-taxes-and-unequal-schools/497333/

Siddle Walker, V. (1996). *Their highest potential: An African American school community in the segregated South.* University of North Carolina Press.

Singer, S. R., Hilton, M. L., & Schweingruber, H. A. (Eds.). (2005). *America's lab report: Investigations in high school science.* National Academies Press.

Sullivan, J. (2015). Anecdotes as evidence: Proving public contracting discrimination in a strict scrutiny world. *Engage, 16*(2), 16–22. Available at: https://fedsoc.org/commentary/ publications/anecdotes-as-evidence-proving-public-contracting-discrimination-in-a-strict -scrutiny-world

Tan, E., & Barton, A. (2010). Transforming science learning and student participation in sixth grade science: A case study of a low-income, urban, racial minority classroom. *Equity & Excellence in Education, 43*(1), 38–55.

Torrance, E. P. (1969). Creative positives of disadvantaged children and youth. *Gifted Child Quarterly, 13*(2), 71–81.

Vygotsky, L. S. (1978). *Mind in society: The development of higher psychological processes.* Harvard University Press.

Whiting, G. W. (2006). From at risk to at promise: Developing scholar identities among Black males. *Journal of Secondary Gifted Education, 17*, 222–229.

Whiting, G. W. (2009). Gifted Black males: Understanding and decreasing barriers to achievement and identity. *Roeper Review, 31*, 224–233.

Wright, B. L. (2011). Valuing the "everyday'" practices of African American students in K-12 and their engagement in STEM learning: A position. *The Journal of Negro Education, 80*(1), 5–11.

Reversing Gifted Underachievement in Kazakhstan

Teachers' Perception, Experiences, and Practices

Zauresh Manabayeva and Daniel Hernández-Torrano

Introduction

One of the most common misconceptions about gifted students is that because they typically demonstrate characteristics such as superior cognitive capacity, retention of large quantities of information, advanced comprehension, varied interests, and high curiosity, they do not face challenges and do not require any support at school (Clark, 2008; Renzulli, 2012). Moon (2009) disputes this myth by stating that often a mismatch between the educational environment in the form of content and curriculum and the ability of a gifted student leads to boredom and demotivation. As a result, a gifted student whose potential was not disclosed is often found to be underachieving.

Reversing Gifted Underachievement: Teachers' Perceptions, Factors, and Strategies

Although there is no common definition of gifted underachievement, Reis and McCoach (2000) propose three categories of gifted underachievers. The first portrays gifted underachievement as the discrepancy between ability and achievement; the second depicts underachievement as the mismatch of anticipated and substantial achievements, and the third category describes underachievement as a failure of individuals to self-realize their potential. Schultz (2005) also identified three categories of underachievement. These included: (1) a mismatch between existing potential and actual potential; (2) a disparity between expected potential and actual achievement; and (3) a failure to develop potential.

Scholars rely on these three conceptualizations of gifted underachievement, but the first definition seems more widespread in the literature. For example, Reis and McCoach (2000) defined underachievement as a temporal disparity between a student's actual capacity and accomplishment accompanied by disengaged behavior. The authors believe that underachieving students show a great difference between their performance

DOI: 10.4324/9781003369578-11

results in cognitive tests and their actual performance, which is shown to teachers and revealed in their grades. In this regard, Schultz (2005) found that almost 50% of students with high thinking capacity are underachieving according to this definition. More recent studies suggest that 15–40% of gifted students perform academically lower than their potential allows (Figg et al., 2012). Moreover, dropouts among those identified as gifted are increasing, puzzling educators all over the world (Montgomery, 2009).

Despite increasing research on gifted underachievers in the last few decades, studies addressing and reversing gifted underachievement remain limited (Reis & McCoach, 2000). Therefore, this study aims at examining teachers' understanding and practices with gifted underachievers in a specialized school for gifted students in Southern Kazakhstan. More specifically, this study aims to answer the following research questions:

1. What characteristics define gifted underachievers in the opinion of Kazakhstani teachers?
2. What factors contribute to the underachievement of gifted students in the eyes of these teachers?
3. What strategies do these teachers use in the classroom to reverse the pattern of gifted underachievement?

The education of gifted students in Kazakhstan has a long tradition and has been strongly influenced by the particularities of the education system during the Soviet era (Yakavets, 2014). The Soviet education system focused mainly on three domains of learning: math, sport, and arts. These domains were typically developed in special schools with their own recruitment criteria and clubs that would provide additional educational opportunities, usually after school time (Grigorenko, 2017). Working with gifted children was generally aimed at preparing children for academic Olympiads (Yakovets, 2014) and attracting more gifted students in order to increase the number of scientists and engineers in technology. Competitions within other countries in the Soviet Union and with the West were a further incentive (Grigorenko, 2017).

Specialized schools for high-ability students in math and science and preparation to succeed in academic Olympiads are still the main approaches for the education of gifted students in the current Kazakhstani education system (Hernández-Torrano et al., 2019; OECD, 2014). However, a project has recently been launched to create a network of selective schools for gifted and talented students as an attempt to adjust to the fast-developing global market requirement and increase the quality of education in the country. The network of gifted schools became an experimental platform to change the way education for the gifted is delivered in the country by developing a curriculum in collaboration with international experts and translating its experience throughout the country (Yakovets, 2014, p. 523). Today the network implements several programs, including physic-mathematical (FM), chemical-biological (CB) directions, and an international baccalaureate (IB) program, developed in cooperation with a strategic partner: the International Examination Council of the University of Cambridge. These schools have advantages over other mainstream schools regarding autonomy in finance, resources, developing, and implementing their programs. In order to be enrolled in these schools, learners 12–13 years old should pass the Johns Hopkins Center Talented Youth (CTY) tests on logical thinking, math, and three main languages in Kazakhstan: Kazakh, Russian, and English. Enrolled students get an opportunity to learn deeper STEM-related subjects (mathematics, biology, physics, and chemistry) compared to mainstream schools (OECD, 2015, p. 95), in addition to advanced opportunities to learn language skills and critical thinking skills.

Despite their brief history, these schools are considered to be top performing within the country and internationally, and each individual student is under the close supervision of experienced teachers. However, there is evidence that even such selected gifted students are not always academically successful in all academic subjects. Thus, some students might underachieve in some specific subjects, while achieving in others (Almukhambetova & Hernández-Torrano, 2020). International practice shows that even gifted learners in such selective schools for gifted and talented students can struggle academically and are often under threat of dropout. Considering that these schools are considered a model for other schools around the country and that the experiences in these schools are expected to be transferred to other schools nationally, teacher perceptions, experiences, and practices with gifted underachievers in this context are worth being explored.

Methods

The Sample

The population of the study was teachers from a selective school for gifted and talented students in Southern Kazakhstan. The study implemented maximum variation sampling procedures to recruit a diverse sample of teachers with experience interacting with gifted underachievers in English, Math, Biology, Chemistry, and Physics in the selective school (Creswell, 2014). The participant sample included teachers who had experience in preparing 10th-grade and 12th-grade students for the Cambridge International Exam since this was one of the high-stakes tests students in this school encountered. Eight teachers were involved in the study: two English teachers (one female and one male), two Chemistry teachers (one female and one male), two Physics teachers (one female and one male), one Math teacher (a female), and one Biology teacher (a male). All of them have dealt with gifted underachievers in the past.

Data Collection Tools

Semi-structured one-on-one interviews were used as the main data collection tool in this study. The interview contained open-ended questions since they are useful in retrieving answers from the participants that were not influenced by any viewpoints of the researcher or prior research findings (Glesne, 2011). Also, a semi-structured interview was used in this study since the open-ended questions would allow the participants to answer them in various ways, generating new ideas and concepts to further build an understanding of the central phenomenon (i.e., gifted underachievement) (Creswell, 2014). The questions of the interviews were directed to obtain data on the nature of gifted underachievement and factors to reverse the pattern of underachieving students. All participants provided written consent to participate in the study prior to the commencement of the interviews.

Data Procedures and Analysis

Content analysis was used to analyze the collected qualitative data following the six steps proposed by Creswell (2014). First, after collecting the data, the authors transcribed the field notes and read them carefully to identify the research statements (Miles et al., 2014). Second, the transcripts were translated into English verbatim since the interviews were conducted in Russian. Third, the authors organized the text into relevant categories according to research questions. Fourth, the authors highlighted the core ideas and organized them in a matrix table. Fifth, similar ideas in the text to develop statements of the findings were highlighted. Sixth, the authors read and analyzed the highlighted ideas to identify the final statements to uncover the research findings. Overall, the qualitative data analysis brought an in-depth understanding of the nature of gifted underachievement and helped to explore the factors hindering the pattern of gifted underachievement at the research site. To ensure the confidentiality of the data, the names of teachers were coded as T1, T2, and up to T8, according to the overall number of interviewees.

Results and Discussion

The data analysis revealed three major categories aligned with the research questions: (1) the characteristics of gifted underachieving students; (2) major factors contributing to their underachievement; and (3) common classroom strategies used to reverse patterns of underachievement.

Characteristics of Gifted Underachievers

The data analysis revealed three main profiles of gifted underachievers according to teachers' beliefs, characterized by (1) low socio-emotional skills; (2) different abilities and interests; and (3) physiological peculiarities.

Gifted Underachievement as Low Socio-Emotional Skills

The first group of gifted underachievers was described as those having low socio-emotional skills, preferring their own company, and avoiding group work. The issues teachers noticed with such students was that they put their own interests above their academic life and tended to be unfocused in the class, being engaged with non-academic activities (e.g. drawing, looking out the window, reading a book). This makes them silent and invisible from the rest of the class, as well as from their teachers. Teachers believe it is important to focus on this gap to avoid late identification of gifted underachieving students and provide timely support to help those students to focus on their academic life. These characteristics strongly align with the description by Montgomery (2009), who depicted gifted underachievers as those who refuse to work and lack concentration, show avoidance goals, subvert group work, and have a poor attitude to school. Figg et al. (2012) labeled students as "selective consumers" who put their own passions and interests over grades and results.

A sharp contrast to students with low socio-emotional skills were the gifted underachievers represented as self-confident. These students, according to teachers, are mature enough to realize their own potential and are not afraid to express their opinion against the majority belief. Such self-confidence and self-reliance might cause misunderstanding and conflict between gifted students and their peers and teachers. In this direction, researchers have suggested that such kinds of stress resulting from conflicts and misunderstandings are more likely to impact on the academic attainment of gifted students (Desmet et al., 2020; Schultz, 2005).

Gifted Underachievement as Different in Their Abilities

Teachers in this study believe that gifted underachievers might be good at critical thinking, good at abstract thinking, have a good sense of ethics, and other specific peculiarities that make them different from the rest of the class. Correspondingly, Heyder et al. (2018) suggest teachers and instructors acknowledge those abilities and peculiarities of gifted underachievers since neglecting their diverse abilities can be one of the factors contributing to gifted underachievement. Therefore, it seems essential that teachers recognize the natural potential and skills of gifted underachievers and put enough effort into incorporating those skills into learning. Yet, it also came out that students can over-rely on their quick study skills during classes and be completely unprepared for high-stakes tests at school. These kinds of students have good thinking predispositions, which allow them to grasp and understand class materials very well. However, they mostly lack the perseverance to review materials they learned during classes so that they can show their whole potential during tests. Richotte et al. (2015) confirmed that gifted underachievers of this type could face academic difficulties just because they do not have enough perseverance, and highlighted the importance of fostering learning skills in managing their own learning.

Gifted Underachievers Have Physiological Peculiarities

Teachers in this study also recognized gifted underachievers as those who experience physiological issues in expressing their thoughts and dealing with health issues in their academic life. Teachers realize the importance of teacher support for such students who might require additional time for task accomplishment due to students' physiological difficulties. Walker and Shore (2011) referred to such children as "twice exceptional" and asserted they can still show outstanding abilities in complex subjects like Math and STEM. However, if the "twice-exceptional" peculiarities of gifted students are not accounted for, it can result in their underachievement (Hands, 2009). On the other hand, gifted underachievers might show some specific learning preferences. This case was supported by the example of Figg et al. (2012) who also highlighted the importance of identifying the learning preferences of gifted underachievers since students might skip the class of the construct and teaching mode that does not correspond to the student's learning profiles.

Factors Contributing to Gifted Underachievement

The findings of this study suggest that, according to teachers, gifted underachievement is a result of several factors at the student, curriculum, and environmental levels.

Factors Contributing to Gifted Underachievement at the Student Level

At the student level, the unipotentiality of gifted underachievers and lack of learning goals are the main factors that contribute to gifted underachievement, according to teachers. An example of a student with unipotentiality could be a student who is very competent in math but struggles in the English language because they find it difficult to properly express ideas or opinions verbally. Likewise, teachers also emphasized that students' subject choice, which is mostly based on their natural predisposition for a subject, often causes difficulty for teachers in raising students' interest in other subjects. Although McCoach and Siegle (2003) considered the domain-specific nature of gifted students as a factor in underachievement, a recent study by Fong and Kremer (2020) challenges this theory, asserting that subject-specific predisposition, on the contrary, gives teachers clarity on what subject students should explicitly be supported in to reverse gifted underachievement.

The inability of gifted underachievers to set goals is another main factor in feeding gifted underachievement. Almost all the participants in the current study confirmed a negative footprint of not setting goals by students in their academic achievement, life career pathway, and overall academic commitment. Similarly, another teacher highlighted that gifted underachievers usually struggle to set academic goals. While McCoach and Siegle (2003) support the importance of teachers' role in helping gifted underachievers to set learning goals, Mofield et al. (2016) and Richotte et al. (2015) argue against, emphasizing that setting goals will still be ineffective if students have not enough level of motivation and commitment.

Factors Contributing to Gifted Underachievement at the Curriculum Level

The particularities of the curriculum of the specialized school for gifted and talented students also emerged as a critical factor of gifted underachievement, according to teachers. Highly demanding curriculum requirements caused burnout and decreased motivation, especially for newly admitted students, who were accepted into the selective middle school after they finished 6th grade in mainstream secondary schools. It is important to consider the different backgrounds of students at this stage, as well as the curriculum content and intensity of school life that students are accustomed to in their prior schools, where the curriculum was less demanding. Therefore, newly gifted admitted 7th-grade students, who have transitioned into a completely new environment with higher learning demands and a highly competitive environment, meet stricter rules and higher level of tasks. As a result, students are often exposed to stress and anxiety, which directly cause demotivation and underachievement. Richotte et al. (2015) confirm this finding and explain that school curricula with complex levels of content might be difficult to handle for middle school students who still lack perseverance and self-regulation of their own learning.

Environmental Factors: Parents' Influence on Gifted Underachievement

According to teachers' perceptions, it is highly likely students will underachieve when their school commitment and interests do not fit their parents' expectations. Sometimes this disconnect can have a long-term negative effect on students' academic life from middle school up to high school. In the same way, high school students also experienced pressure from their parents when choosing a major subject directly related to the student's future careers. As a result, some students demonstrate low motivation when studying a subject that does not correspond to their interests. Reis an McCoach (2000) explained this gap as an internal factor that might result from a contradictory parenting style where over-restriction by one parent would be constantly followed by overprotection by another. Our findings align with those of Schultz (2005) and Landis and Reschly (2013), who suggested that parents might not have enough skills and knowledge to provide enough support in schooling. Therefore, schools can play an essential role in explaining and clarifying for parents their children's true commitment and how to effectively direct their children's interest into a successful future career.

Environmental Factors: Teachers' Influence on Gifted Underachievement

Alongside this, teachers can serve as precursors of gifted underachievement in at least three ways. First, a lack of effort from teachers to increase the motivation of students may contribute to gifted underachievement. Koca (2018) indicated the importance of teachers as contributors to increased motivation by communicating students' academic competence and nurturing their social skills. This was confirmed by the findings of the study, where extrinsic motivation addressed by teachers in the form of verbal praise and actions could motivate and increase students' commitment to a subject. Teachers asserted that they could contribute strongly to increasing students' self-efficacy and academic competence. As argued by Montgomery (2009), gifted underachievers are vulnerable to having lower self-esteem, which leads them to false beliefs about their self-efficacy in their academic life.

Second, negative teacher-student relationships are another key factor contributing to gifted underachievement, based on the findings of this study. The importance of positive student-teacher relationships on gifted underachievers' academic success has been highlighted in previous studies (e.g., Desmet et al., 2020; Koca, 2018). Correspondingly, most teachers responded that the student's attitude to a subject mostly lies in their relationship with the teacher instructing that subject. This is consistent with previous literature in other contexts, which suggests that negative teacher-student relationships should be considered a crucial factor contributing to gifted underachievement. For example, in the study of three gifted underachieving girls by Desmet et al. (2020), almost all participants pointed to the importance of having a positive relationship with their teachers. This was one of the first research efforts to demonstrate the vulnerability of gifted students to their relationship with teachers when students' commitment and motivation depended on the attitude their teachers showed toward them.

Third, teachers indicated that their busy workload is another factor that makes them ineffective in identifying underachievement and reversing it. The teachers encounter some challenges related to spending sufficient time developing quality lessons, preparing lesson materials, writing reports, and conducting action research and lesson study sessions to improve their teaching practice. As a result of such a busy workload, teachers admitted missing timely identification of gifted underachievers, as well as late identification when the student is at the stage of being under threat of dropout. Although teachers realize the importance of their role in successfully reversing gifted underachieving students, they also admit they cannot always physically dedicate time to grounded support of gifted underachievers. Although there is no direct research addressing the correlation of teachers' workload with the students' underachievement, the negative effect of heavy teacher workloads on students' academic achievement has been observed in previous studies (e.g., Kimani et al., 2013). Moreover, these findings can be explained by the insights of the teachers about the special needs gifted underachievers require (Davidson, 2012), which is reasonable due to the myth that gifted learners do not encounter learning difficulties and do not need support from their teachers due to their high learning capacity (Clark, 2008; Renzulli, 2012).

Interventions to Reverse Gifted Underachievement

The intervention patterns identified in this study involve a complex approach where teachers emphasize the emotional and cognitive aspects of their students. Weiner

(1982) concluded that interventions aimed at academic and behavioral enhancement should always be based on complex approaches, which include not only the improvement of cognitive aspects but also the rewarding and emotional consideration of gifted underachievers. As a result, two main intervention strategies were commonly suggested by the teachers: (1) building teacher-student relationships based on trust; and (2) an individual and a differentiated teaching approach.

Positive Teacher-Student Relationship

The perception of the overwhelming majority was that a positive teacher-student relationship is the most helpful and effective way to reverse underachievement. Teachers believe any interaction to reverse underachievement should start with building healthy relationships with students. This finding is important since all participants claimed that having a positive relationship with their students allows them to motivate students and set future learning goals. Hence, any interaction may have only limited effect until teachers have built a trustworthy relationship with their students. This finding appears to be consistent with Moon and Brighton's (2008) study, which considers teachers as the most influential agents interacting with students daily. Teachers can identify underachievement, boost students' motivation, and effectively engage learners in the learning process. Additionally, Cavilla (2017) argues that positive teacher-student relationships are a prerequisite for successful academic intervention. Teachers are aware of students' learning styles and interests and, as a result, this allows them to develop relevant instructional environments for those gifted underachievers. Similarly Schultz (2002) identified that healthy teacher-student relationships promote self-confidence and motivation in students since students feel they are important and valued. Schultz (2002) also argues this kind of approach strongly impacts on the development of the cognitive, interpersonal, and social skills of students.

Individual and Differentiated Approach

The second learning strategy that emerged from the analysis was differentiated instruction of gifted underachievers. Teachers disclosed their preference for implementing differentiated instructions due to two main reasons. First, the unique nature of gifted underachieving requires unique (i.e., differentiated) instructions. Therefore teachers should develop tasks that address students' learning needs, preferences, and interests. Second, differentiated instructions allow teachers to consider timing and task scale as a result of providing equal opportunity for students. This appears to be consistent with previous studies in this context, which suggests that individualized approaches to underachieving students facilitate learning when addressing the interests and learning goals of students (e.g., Maddox, 2014). Additionally, Bennett-Rappell and Northcote (2016) identified that differentiated instructions were essential when gifted underachievers required modifying time and the volume of work for them, and the results of such implementation were successful. At the same time, one teacher indicated the difficulty of preparing differentiated instructions due to the large amount of additional work and time it requires. Although Van Tassel-Baska and Stambaugh (2005) did not indicate the teacher's workload, they pointed to the importance of appropriate implementation of differentiated approaches while working, especially with gifted students.

Implications for Practice

The findings have the following implications. First, by reading through the characteristics explored in this study, teachers can better understand the nature of the gifted underachieving students they have in their classes. Second, teachers can self-reflect on some gifted underachieving students in their classes and on the practices they have been applying to reverse them after reading the explored factors and reversing approaches presented in this study. Moreover, based on the findings presented in this study, teachers can better understand the importance of motivation and support provided by teachers for students' academic commitment. Collectively, this study has the potential to bridge the gap of reversing patterns for gifted underachievers.

School principals should consider the findings of this study to review the approaches used for newly admitted students during their transition from mainstream secondary schools into selective schools and consider providing additional support in acquiring new curriculum demands in a less stressful way for students. Accordingly, school administrations might include some professional development opportunities on the reversing approaches for gifted underachievers in workshops and other professional development sessions conducted among teachers to improve their practice.

Policy-makers can also consider the findings of this study to update the overall approach to the identification and education of gifted students in Kazakhstan and other similar contexts. Traditional approaches to the education of gifted students, which include demanding curricula and participation in academic Olympiads, should be complemented with opportunities for diverse gifted students to manifest their talents in multiple areas of knowledge in less academic areas, such as music, sports, and the arts.

Conclusion

The aim of this qualitative study was to explore teachers' understanding and practices with gifted underachievers as well as identify the factors that contribute to gifted underachievement and the reversing patterns teachers apply in their everyday practice.

The findings of this study suggest that teachers can recognize common characteristics to identify gifted underachievers, even though none of the teachers provided a precise definition of gifted underachieving students. A conclusion to be drawn from these findings is that gifted underachievers represent in teachers' eyes a diverse group of students with different characteristics and behavior. In this regard, gifted underachievers are vulnerable socially and physiologically due to the natural peculiarities of their behavior and personality, who, therefore, demand more academic support from teachers than other gifted students.

Another major finding of this study was that gifted underachievement might arise due to factors at the student, curriculum, and environmental levels. Overall, this suggests that gifted underachieving students are sensitive to both internal and external factors and, therefore, require corresponding support at every level from peers, parents, and teachers. A related conclusion is that, to avoid gifted underachievement or timely reverse underachievement, teachers need to conduct a complex analysis to be able to timely identify and provide support for their gifted learners. A common practice to reverse underachievement in this study included a complex approach where teachers emphasize the emotional and cognitive aspects of their students. The perception of the overwhelming majority was that a positive teacher-student relationship is the most helpful and effective way to reverse underachievement. Teachers believe any interaction to reverse underachievement should start with building healthy relationships with students. A differentiated instruction of gifted underachievers was also commonly addressed to reverse gifted underachievement and the most effective approach to support these gifted students.

Limitations of the Study

The results of the study should be interpreted in light of several limitations. First, the limitation is the research site, which is a specialized school for selected gifted students. Therefore, teachers' experience of gifted underachievement may not reflect those in other specialized and non-specialized secondary schools. Second, the number of participants in this study was limited, and the participants themselves were purposefully selected. Third, the research gap in the context of gifted underachievement practices in Kazakhstan might not have been completely disclosed due to the chosen research design. The research has involved only teachers' voices, while mixed research with quantitative would have probably provided a broader picture involving other stakeholders as well. Nevertheless, the present study highlights the importance of supporting and encouraging the learning of gifted underachievers, mainly by their teachers, and provides several suggestions on how to tackle and reverse gifted underachievement in Kazakhstan, Central Asia, and beyond.

REFLECTION QUESTIONS

1. According to this study, how did Kazakhstan teachers conceptualize gifted underachievement? How does this definition compare to other definitions and/or descriptions for underachievement?

2. The findings of this study revealed three common characteristics of gifted underachievement recognized by Kazakhstan teachers: low socio-emotional skills, different abilities and interests, and physiological peculiarities. What personal and external factors contribute to these characteristics? What actions or activities by the gifted students might you recognize as indicators of these characteristics?

3. How can a demanding school curriculum promote gifted underachievement ? What are examples of gifted student responses to it?

4. What role does the environment (e.g., teacher, parents, school culture, policies; instructional practices, peers, etc.) play in gifted underachievement at school?

5. Revisiting the suggested strategies that Kazakhstan teachers offer to reverse gifted underachievement, do you think they will work in America's gifted education culture? How do they compare (similarities and differences) to what you have initiated or observed?

Acknowledgment

This chapter is adapted from Z. Manabayeva (2020). Reversing gifted underachievement in Kazakhstan: Teachers' perception, experiences, and practices. Master's thesis, Nazarbayev University. Available at: https://nur.nu.edu.kz/handle/123456789/4895

References

Almukhambetova, A., & Hernández-Torrano, D. (2020). Gifted students' adjustment and underachievement in university: An exploration from the self-determination theory perspective. *Gifted Child Quarterly, 64*, 117–131. https://doi.org/10.1177/0016986220905525

Bennett-Rappell, H., & Northcote, M. (2016). Underachieving gifted students: Two case studies. *Issues in Educational Research, 26*(3), 407–430. https://search.informit.org/doi/10.3316/aeipt .213800

Cavilla, (2017).

Clark, B. (2008). *Growing up gifted: Developing the potential of children at school and at home* (7th ed.). Pearson.

Creswell, J. W. (2014). *Educational research: Planning, conducting and evaluating quantitative and qualitative research* (4th ed.). Pearson.

Davidson, J. E. (2012). Is giftedness truly a gift? *Gifted Education International, 28*(3), 252–266. https://doi.org/10.1177/0261429411435051

Desmet, O. A., Pereira, N., & Peterson, J. S. (2020). Telling a tale: How underachievement develops in gifted girls. *Gifted Child Quarterly, 64*(2), 85–99. https://doi.org/10.1177/00169862198886

Figg, S. D., Rogers, K. B., McCormick, J., & Low, R. (2012). Differentiating low performance of the gifted learner: Achieving, underachieving, and selective consuming students. *Journal of Advanced Academics, 23*(1), 53–71. https://doi.org/10.1177/1932202X11430000

Fong, C. J., & Kremer, K. P. (2020). An expectancy-value approach to math underachievement: Examining high school achievement, college attendance, and STEM interest. *Gifted Child Quarterly, 64*(2), 67–84. https://doi.org/10.1177/00169862198905

Glesne, C. (2011). *Becoming qualitative researchers: An introduction* (4th ed.). Pearson.

Grigorenko, E. L. (2017). Gifted education in Russia: Developing, threshold, or developed. *Cogent Education, 4*, 1–12. https://doi.org/10.1080/2331186X.2017.1364898.x

Hands, R. E. (2009). The phenomenon of underachievement: Listening to the voice of a twice-exceptional adolescent. Doctoral dissertation, University of Massachusetts Amherst, Available at: https://scholarworks.umass.edu/dissertations/AAI3372264

Hernández-Torrano, D., Tursunbayeva, X., & Almukhambetova, A. (2019). Teachers' conceptions about giftedness and gifted education: An international perspective. In M. A. Zanetti, G. Gualdi, & M. Cascianelli (Eds.). *Understanding giftedness: A guide for parents and educators.* Routledge.

Heyder, A., Bergold, S., & Steinmayr, R. (2018). Teachers' knowledge about intellectual giftedness: A first look at levels and correlates. *Psychology Learning & Teaching, 17*(1), 27–44. https://doi .org/10.1177/1475725717725493

Kimani, G. N., Kara, A. M., & Njagi, L. W. (2013). Teacher factors influencing students' academic achievement in secondary schools in Nyandarua county, Kenya. *International Journal of Education and Research, 1*, 1–14.

Koca, F. (2018). Motivation to learn and teacher-student relationship. *Journal of International Education and Leadership, 6*, 1–20. https://doi.org/10.1177/1475725717725493

Landis, R. N., & Reschly, A. L. (2013). Reexamining gifted underachievement and dropout through the lens of student engagement. *Journal for the Education of the Gifted, 36*, 220–249. https://doi .org/10.1177/0162353213480864

Maddox, M. (2014). Exploring teachers' experiences of working with gifted students who underachieve. Doctoral dissertation, Walden University. Available at: https://www.proquest.com/docview/1501974339?pq-origsite=gscholar&fromopenview=true

McCoach, D. B., & Siegle, D. (2003). The School Attitude Assessment Survey-rRvised: A new instrument to identify academically able students who underachieve. *Educational and Psychological Measurement*, *63*, 414–429. https://doi.org/10.1177/0013164403063003005

Miles, M. B., Huberman, A. M., & Saldaña, J. (2014). *Qualitative data analysis: A methods sourcebook*. Sage.

Mofield, E., Parker Peters, M., & Chakraborti-Ghosh, S. (2016). Perfectionism, coping, and underachievement in gifted adolescents: Avoidance vs. approach orientations. *Education Sciences*, *6*(3), 21. https://doi.org/10.3390/educsci6030021

Montgomery, D. (Ed.). (2009). *Able, gifted and talented underachievers*. John Wiley & Sons.

Moon, T. (2009).

Moon, T., & Brighton, C. (2008). Primary teachers' conceptions of giftedness. *Journal for the Education of the Gifted*, *31*(4), 447–480. https://doi.org/10.4219/jeg-2008-793

OECD. (2014). Reviews of national policies for education: Secondary education in Kazakhstan. OECD Publishing. Available at: http://dx.doi.org/10.1787/9789264205208-en

OECD. (2015).

OECD & The World Bank. (2015). *OECD reviews of school resources: Kazakhstan 2015*. OECD Publishing. https://doi.org/10.1787/9789264245891-en

Reis, S. M., & McCoach, D. B. (2000). The underachievement of gifted students: What do we know and where do we go? *Gifted Child Quarterly*, *44*(3), 152–170. https://doi.org/10.1177/001698620004400302

Renzulli, J. S. (2012). Reexamining the role of gifted education and talent development for the 21st century: A four-part theoretical approach. *Gifted Child Quarterly*, *56*(3), 150–159. https://doi.org/10.1177/0016986212444901

Schultz, B. H. (2005). Defining underachievement in gifted students. *Group*, *28*(2), 46–50.

Schultz, R. A. (2002). Understanding giftedness and underachievement: At the edge of possibility. *Gifted Child Quarterly*, *46*, 193–208. https://doi.org/10.1177/001698620204600304

Van Tassel-Baska, J., & Stambaugh, T. (2005). Challenges and possibilities for serving gifted learners in the regular classroom. *Theory into Practice*, *44*, 211–217. http://dx.doi.org/10.1207/s15430421tip4403_5

Walker, C. L., & Shore, B. M. (2011). Theory of mind and giftedness: New connections. *Journal for the Education of the Gifted*, *34*, 644–668. https://doi.org/10.1177/016235321103400406

Weiner, I. B. (1982).

Weiner, I. B. (1992). *Psychological disturbance in adolescence* (2nd ed.). John Wiley and Sons.

Yakavets, N. (2014). Reforming society through education for gifted children: The case of Kazakhstan, *Research Papers in Education*, *29*, 513–533. https://doi.org/10.1080/02671522.2013.825311

Understanding and Utilizing Learner Profiles to Combat Apathy and Incurious Behaviors in the Classroom

Vanessa Velasquez and Kristina Henry Collins

Introduction

A very important factor in characterizing student performance as underachievement is time. A prognosis of underachievement must be based on a consistent pattern of performance behavior over an extended period of time. Two common topics that ensue when discussing these patterns of performance behavior are motivation and potential. It is not uncommon for teachers and parents to proclaim that a student is not motivated or not living up to their potential. Motivation can be expressed as a product of expectation and value. Potential is often defined as latent qualities or abilities that may be developed and lead to future success or usefulness. However, effective teachers design instruction that motivates and individualizes engagement to maximize potential.

When teaching children, it is important to focus on the needs of each child in the classroom. Differentiated instruction (Tomlinson, 1999) still remains one of the most popular and effective strategies used to individualize instruction, address developmental enrichment, and enhance the curriculum for advanced and gifted students. As such, it also serves as an ideal teaching strategy to address underachievement of gifted students. Differentiation is proactively adjusting teaching and learning to meet kids where they are. Teaching from the principle of meeting kids where they are compels educators to acknowledge student performance on a continuum that serves as a baseline for appropriate and personal development. This changes from day to day and week to week, depending on the students' needs. Contrary to a polarized scale that simply labels a child as underachieving or overachieving, when it has been determined by observing a student's performance over a significant period of time, this also allows educators to formatively assess and focus on proactive measures of adapting behaviors such as apathy and incurious behaviors in real time to prevent a diagnosis of underachievement weeks and/or months later.

Differentiated Instruction and Learning

Differentiated instruction is part of a response to intervention (RtI) model; it is a teacher's response to learners' needs. In differentiated instruction, the teacher draws on strategies

DOI: 10.4324/9781003369578-12

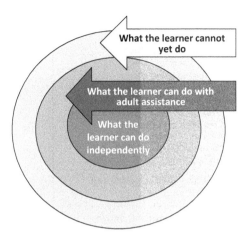

FIGURE 9.1 Vygotsky's zone of proximal development.

that help focus on individual students, small groups of students, and the whole class. Because grouping is fluid, goal readiness, development and progress monitoring (zone of proximal development;Vygotsky, 1987) are necessary, which consequently nurtures and fosters independent and lifelong learners. See Figure 9.1.

Progress monitoring includes systematic observations and ongoing diagnostic assessment to monitor student progress frequently, and to adjust teaching or lessons to help students move forward successfully in their learning. This includes pre-assessing students to determine if they have already mastered skills and concepts.

Learners' Profile

Students come from different backgrounds and each child has their own way of learning and processing information. Differentiated learning includes the way students engage with the curriculum via differentiated content, process, or products based on a response to the learners' profile. A learner's profile encompasses indicators about the student's academic readiness, personal interests, and cultural values. In addition to framing our discussion with a shared understanding for differentiation, differentiated instruction and differentiated learning, Figure 9.2 provides a description of a shared understanding. of other important student traits related to the learners' profile.

Social Emotional Learning (SEL) has to do with how students feel about themselves, their work, and the classroom as a whole. Social and emotional learning should not be approached as an intervention or separate from cognitive development.We are responsible as educators for educating the whole child – that includes head, heart, and hands – for developing their minds (head), what they hold dear to their hearts (interests, values, and passion), and their personal goals (hands; what they want to do). Tapping into the *affective domain* is the gateway to helping each student become more fully engaged and successful in learning.

Academic readiness refers to a student's knowledge, understanding, and skill related to a particular sequence of learning. It is most commonly determined by an evaluation of student performance on particular formative and summative assessments. Interest refers to those topics or pursuits that evoke curiosity and passion in a learner. Cultural values refer to what a student finds desirable, important, or "right"; they are the shared

Student Traits	Shared Understanding/Definitions
Learners' Profile	...refers to how students ~~learn~~ "make meaning" best. These include influences such as preferred learning style/ memory, intelligence, interest, culture, gender, etc.
SEL Profile (Affective Domain)	...has to do with how students feel about themselves, their work, and the classroom as a whole; gateway to helping each student become more fully engaged and successful in learning.
Readiness	...refers to a student's knowledge, understanding, and skill related to a particular sequence of learning.
Interest	...refers to those topics or pursuits that evoke curiosity and passion in a learner.
Cultural Values	...refer to what a student find desirable, important, and/or "right"; the shared beliefs, customs, language, knowledge, roles, technology, history, etc. within their culture.

FIGURE 9.2 Student traits related to learners' profile.

beliefs, customs, language, knowledge, roles, technology, history, etc. within a culture. Socialization and cultural experiences often influence approaches to knowledge, also known as cognitive diversity. Cultural capital (unique strengths) can be used as a tool for learning and to facilitate academic performance. At the same time, educators cannot allow generalizations about a group of people to lead to naive stereotyping about individuals within that group. Knowing each student, especially his or her culture, is essential preparation for facilitating, structuring, and validating successful learning for each and every student. Success for the diverse populations that schools serve calls for continual re-examination of educators' assumptions, expectations, and biases. We maintain that it is at the intersection of academic readiness, cultural values, and personal interest that a more realistic representation of a student's potential or motivation lies (Figure 9.3).

Based on this, to what extent a student is engaged depends on to what extent what they are learning includes each of these elements. To the contrary, to what extent a student shows apathy or incurious behaviors depends on to what extent each of these are lacking or absent. In addition, indicators refer to what influences students' "making

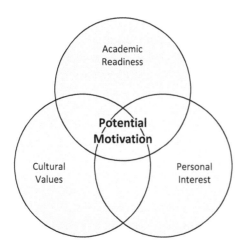

FIGURE 9.3 Potential and motivation as an intersection of readiness, interest, and values.

meaning" process as they are engaged. An example of that influence is preferred learning style.

Preferred Learning Styles and Multiple Intelligence Integration Theories

A major indicator that educators have reported considering when differentiating instruction based on learners' profile is preferred learning style. However, there is much debate about preferred learning styles. Some scholars claim that there is no research to validate the existence or benefit for achievement based on preferred learning styles (Furey, 2020) while others have categorized three preferred learning styles (Akkoyunlu & Soylu, 2008; Anderson, 2016). The three most commonly referenced learning styles are explained here. Table 9.1 offers examples of everyday tasks and responses to show how learners from these categories might approach the task at hand:

- *visual (spatial)*: learner prefers using pictures, images, and spatial perceptions;
- *aural (auditory-musical)*: learner favors using sounds and music;
- *physical (kinesthetic)*: learner favors using body, hands, and tactile sense.

TABLE 9.1 Commonly preferred learning style approach to example everyday tasks

Scenario/tasks	Visual (spatial)	Aural (auditory-musical)	Physical (kinesthetic)
Want to learn something new	Watch a video online	Ask someone to explain how to do it	Figure it out by trying to do it
Using a navigational app	Follow the map view	Listen to the directions	Rotate and adjust the app; do not use—keep walking/driving and figure it out using landmarks
Recall how to spell a word	Write it down and see if it looks right. (symbolic visual)	Spell it out loud to hear if sounds right	Trace the letters in the air (finger spell)
Memorize a phone number	Write it down. (symbolic visual)	Keep saying it out loud over and over again	Practice "dialing" out the numbers
Study/working distractions	People walking by	Loud noises	An uncomfortable chair
Remember most when meet someone new	Their face	Their name	What they did
Pick, given a choice of three listed prizes	A poster	An mp3 download	A game or sports ball
When purchasing a new product	Read reviews online	Ask a friend or salesperson to explain the features	Try or test it
Pick, given a choice of three listed outings	A movie	A concert	An amusement park
Practice for a presentation	Flash cards	Record yourself and listen to it over and over	Practice delivering the presentation, doing and saying it out loud

Educators may find that some students might respond similarly in more than one preferred learning style category. Language (vernacular, dialect, jargon; informal language; alliterations) and gender also play a role in students' preferred learning style. Students' creative use of language can enhance the acquisition, storage, retention, recall, and use of new information as well as meanings of words and phrases, especially colloquial expressions. Like culture, socialized gender roles influence the approach to knowledge acquisition. Same gender and opposite gender interaction and engagement influence students' own goals, needs, and approach to learning. It is also important to note that learners tend to prefer different learning strategies that are appropriate to the material, to the task, and to their own goals, needs, and stage of learning according to individual differences. So responses may vary in different settings, different subjects, and different activities, which support differentiated instruction and learning.

Some theorists include a fourth preferred learning style: verbal (linguistic), also referred to as reading/writing (Brady, 2013; Rolfe & Cheek, 2012). Learners who prefer this style prefer using words. Learning styles and multiple intelligences theory integration (Eissa & Mostafa, 2013; Sener & Cokcaliskan, 2018) asserts it is the existence of multiple intelligences that influences preferences with learning:

- *logical (mathematical)*: learners prefer using logic, reasoning, and systems;
- *social (interpersonal)*: learners favor learning in groups or with other people;
- *solitary (intrapersonal)*: learner prefer to work alone and to be a self-reader.

Sensory Memory Modes

Then there are other scholars who claim learning styles are more appropriately referred to as sensory memory modes (Davis, 2007; Metivier, 2022; Sprenger, 2003). Sensory memory comes from the five senses, also called sensory registers, and refers to the short-term memories that are being stored while that particular sense is being stimulated. Of the five sensory registers, iconic, echoic, and haptic are closely aligned to preferred learning styles and multiple intelligences. In teaching and learning, sensory memory modes are the meaningful ways learners retain and organize sensory memories to foster long-term memory:

- *iconic memory*: learner better retains information that is gathered through sight;
- *echoic memory*: learner better retains information gathered through auditory stimuli;
- *haptic memory*: learner better retains information acquired through touch;
- *olfactory memory*: learner associates information and/or experiences with smell; olfactory memory also helps you identify tastes because molecules from the food you chew go into your nose;
- *gustatory memory*: learner associates information and/or experiences with taste.

If there is no solid evidence that supports the consideration of preferred learning styles to positively impact student achievement, then why should we discuss them? We should discuss preferred learning styles because successful learners tend to use learning strategies that are appropriate to the material, to the task, and to their own goals, needs, and stage of learning according to individual differences. This is important when differentiating instruction, and why it is beneficial for educators to learn how to observe and respond appropriately to them.

Preferred Learning Strategies and Memory (PLS/M)

For the purposes of this chapter we use our synthesized adaptation of the highlighted theories to offer a learning strategy within differentiated instruction. Exchanging the term style for strategy, we introduce preferred learning strategies and sensory memories (PLS/M). Table 9.2 shows how each of the theories is integrated into this consolidated theory.

Training and encouraging students to utilize all of the PLS/Ms foster multiple ways of knowing, sharing, and performing for effective and efficient learning.

Learning Channels

As noted earlier in the chapter, successful learners tend to use learning strategies that are appropriate to the material, to the task, and to their own goals, needs, and stage of learning, according to individual differences. As such, recognizing student cues and behavior that align with the different PLS/M is an important skill for educators to possess. Table 9.3 illuminates potential student PLS/M cues within four different types of learning or engagement settings: passive listener, non-engagement student, an active engagement student, and formal testing. Table 9.4 highlights appropriate teacher responses and tools to general student behavior as indicators for identifying which PLS/M theory is being used for learning.

Learning channels and observation strategies used to identify a student's PLS/M behavior provide guidance for what the educator can look for in order to determine the appropriate differentiated instruction. Educators can use differentiated responsive strategies to support and foster different modes of learning and meaning-making.

TABLE 9.2 Preferred Learning Strategies and Memory (PLS/M)

Preferred Learning Strategy and Memory	Preferred learning styles	Multiple intelligence	Sensory memory mode
Learner prefers using pictures, images, and spatial perceptions, and retains information through sight	Visual (spatial)	Logical (mathematical)	Iconic memory
Learner favors using sounds and music, and retains information through listening	Aural (auditory-musical)	Social (interpersonal)	Echoic memory
Learner prefers using words and symbols, and systematically retains information	Verbal (linguistic) (reading/writing)	Logical and solitary (intrapersonal)	Iconic and echoic memory
Learner favors using body, hands, and tactile sense, and retains information through touch	Physical (kinesthetic)	Social (interpersonal)	Haptic memory

TABLE 9.3 Student PLS/M behavior in various learning channels

Learning Setting	Description	Visual PLS/M Cues	Auditory PLS/M Cues	Reading/Writing PLS/M Cues	Kinesthetic PLS/M Cues
Passive Listening	*Whole group learning; lecture-based teaching setting*	Constant student-to-bulletin/display eye contact and focus.	Constant student-to-teacher eye contact and focus; focuses on speakers mouth. Student listens without much eye contact except when speaking	Constant note-taking without consistent eye contact or focus on display; adds additional annotates already written information.	Constant and perhaps, pronounced repetitive body movement and change in seating position during lecture
Non-Engagement	*Non-participating student in a small group classroom setting or informal environment*	Student gazes around the room looking at visuals and other 3D objects; Draws/doodles on lesson materials or creates their own visual aids.	Student positions ear toward speaker or sound with head lowered or raised toward ceiling; looks to others to explain information. Student pays attention to and notices distant sounds.	Student takes individual notes in addition to others provided; Reads and works ahead of group.; spends additional or extra time color-coding information.	Student may not talk or write anything down; exhibits slight repetitive body movement.
Active Engagement	*Student that is actively contributing in a small group classroom setting or informal environment*	Student uses/draws graphics and visuals to convey, explain, and understand information.	Student reads aloud to convey, explain, and understand information; talks through a problem when engaging with group. Rhythmically recites and/or repeats information given.	Student volunteers to take notes, organize, and maintain records for group; researches and/or offers additional information.	Student constantly touches, grabs, and holds any manipulatives; prematurely engage with tools of start activity prior to completely reading directions. Moves, fidgets, and/or changes body positioning while working.
Formal Testing	*Testing environment; Individualized learning and responding*	Student adds additional graphics to existing visuals; draws and translates questions and prompts into representative visuals/graphics to help answer questions.	Student quietly mumbles questions and prompts to herself; chooses audio aids when available.	Student add memorized notes and/or verbal aids on test; writes down ideas. Student takes longer to test with tendency to read/re-read all words on the page.	Student may standing or kneel in chair when testing; will initiate his or her own breaks or pause during testing.

TABLE 9.4 Observing responding students' behavior within PLS/M

PLS/M	Student behavior	Appropriate teacher's response	Responsive learning tools (examples)
Visual	Observes the room for any visuals that are present Pays attention to detail Easily confused when teacher is talking if there are no visual aids present Exhibits an elaborate imagination	Integrate drawing while teaching Offer complementing diagrams and various types of visual aids with written notes Use sentence stems	Charts and graphic organizers Strategic use of bulletin boards in classroom Diagrams of step-by-step instruction Use of outlines
Auditory	Watches presenter/ speaker exclusively when talking Avoids constant eye contact with presenter and/or holds head down when taking notes Reads and "thinks" out loud Avid storyteller	Audio-record lectures Speak clearly and loudly Use lapel microphone during class Integrate various sound effects throughout lesson Allow for whole class reading of the text whenever possible	Podcasts Multimedia presentations Pre-recordings of directions and lessons
Reading/writing (verbal)	Very organized and detailed note-taking Journal-style and narrative-style writing even in more technical classes	Provide detailed, written instructions Integrated student note-taking guides as part of lessons	Composition books Reflection journals Dictionaries and other reference books
Kinesthetic	Constantly moving Constantly touching and engaging with objects and peers in the class When talking, student will use hand movements	Introduce "texturized" and tactile learning into the lesson Use outdoor learning spaces when available Give breaks to allow movement	Manipulatives Student-immersion learning (using body to explain/explore concepts)

Implications for Practice

Generally speaking, the school, program, or teacher should provide an array of learning opportunities for students PK–12 when addressing underachievement in gifted/talented (G/T) students. Integrating the learners' profile – academic readiness, cultural values, and personal interest – plays a major role in understanding what motivates students to perform academically. Provisions to improve services and achievement of G/T students should also be included in the district and campus improvement plans. As part of the plan, development coordinators should document promising practices currently implemented, the challenges noted, and the skillsets and training needed for teachers to implement and address underachievement with confidence. Culturally responsive programs and educators should include, inform, and assist families with informal and complementary opportunities to maximize learning. Provision of in-school, and when possible, out-of-school options relevant to the student's area of strength should be available during the school year. Additional options specific to the classroom and curriculum should include (Collins et al., 2022):

1. Instructional and organizational structures that enable identified underachieving students to work together as a whole group, to work with other students in small groups, and to work independently.
2. A continuum of learning experiences that leads to the development of advanced-level products and performances.
3. Opportunities to accelerate in areas of strength and strengthen areas of struggle.

Classroom Structure

The physical organization of the classroom matters. A well-organized classroom structure supports different modes of learning so that it is likely that more students will learn effectively and efficiently.

Figure 9.4 displays an example of how a student-centered classroom may be structured to foster an environment that maximizes student potential by (1) nurturing independent and collaborative learning, and (2) promoting student partnership and accountability for their own learning process. It promotes an environment that is conducive to differentiated learning and preferred learning strategies and sensory memory (PLS/M). For this structure, educators would take time at the beginning of the academic year to set the tone for independent learning that is nurtured through a zone of proximal development and differentiated instruction. Stations are established around the perimeter of the room to use space, and allow the use of various resources already in the room, such as bulletin boards, whiteboards, interactive boards, and so on. While learning stations are numbered in Figure 9.4, they are designed to be integrated into the instructional workshop in any order. Students may rotate through multiple learning stations within a given curriculum unit, all activities and engagements are varied in complexity and responsive to the learners' profile. Organization of station assignments can be handled in several ways. As an example, the teacher can utilize pocket charts labeled with the different stations with assignments inserted in the folders; the teacher would group kids according to their needs and places a card with the group members' names in the appropriate pocket before the students arrive. This could also be accomplished with a peg board and key tags, a folder holder, or just by writing groups' memberships on the board.

Other Promising Practices Responsive to Learner Profiles

Differentiated instruction and learning can be implemented as part of an universal design for learning (UDL). It is optimal for integrating a multitude of approaches to include those that are commonly used as part of a multi-tiered system of supports for all students (see also UDL and CR-MTSS in Chapter 10).

Precision Teaching

Diagnostic and prescriptive teaching strategies are intended for students who have difficulty learning without support (Sprick, 2019). The development of a prescriptive teaching method is in line with being responsive to a learner's profile, and is appropriate for differentiated learning and addressing underachievement as well. Using a SEL lens, educators assess a student's needs to determine a "prescription," or intervention, to address the needs of the student with the goal of maximizing potential. The major benefit of the diagnostic-prescriptive approach, which also uses precision teaching

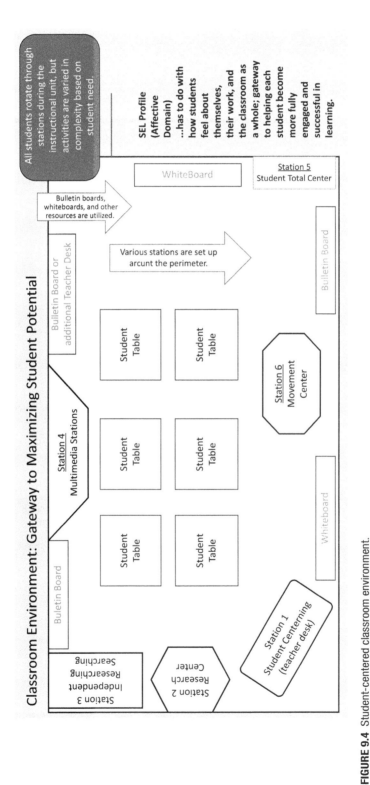

FIGURE 9.4 Student-centered classroom environment.

Source: Kubina (2019). *The Precision Teaching Implementation Manual.* Reprinted with permission. Availb https://centralreach.com/pt-myths/.

(see Figure 9.5: pinpoint, record, change, and try again) is that a facilitator can formatively re-examine the needs and findings of a student, and prescribe another course of treatment if a previous "prescription" is ineffective. From their observations, teachers then implement prescriptions that remediate underachievement (Figure 9.6). Because diagnostic-prescriptive teaching focuses on identifying students' strengths and weaknesses within several areas to include comprehension, it offers an alternative approach to determine academic readiness as well.

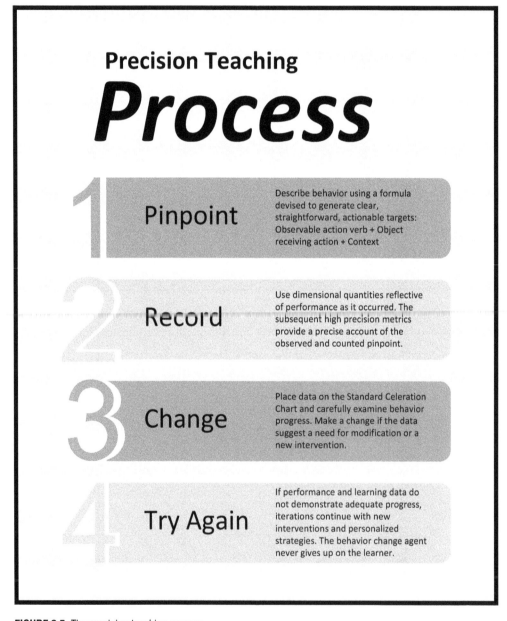

Precision Teaching
Process

1 Pinpoint
Describe behavior using a formula devised to generate clear, straightforward, actionable targets: Observable action verb + Object receiving action + Context

2 Record
Use dimensional quantities reflective of performance as it occurred. The subsequent high precision metrics provide a precise account of the observed and counted pinpoint.

3 Change
Place data on the Standard Celeration Chart and carefully examine behavior progress. Make a change if the data suggest a need for modification or a new intervention.

4 Try Again
If performance and learning data do not demonstrate adequate progress, iterations continue with new interventions and personalized strategies. The behavior change agent never gives up on the learner.

FIGURE 9.5 The precision teaching process.
Source: Reprinted with permission of Dr. Richard Kubina, Jr.

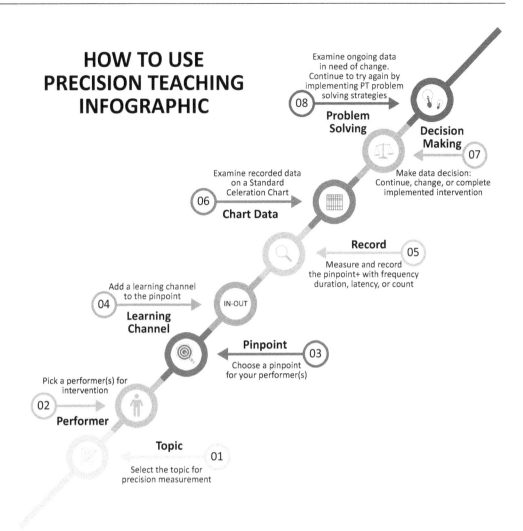

FIGURE 9.6 How to use precision teaching.

Source: Reprinted with permission of Dr. Richard Kubina, Jr.

Compacting for Student Mastery

Because diagnostic-prescriptive teaching focuses on identifying students' strengths and weaknesses within several areas to include comprehension, it offers an alternative approach to determine academic readiness as well (Figure 9.7).

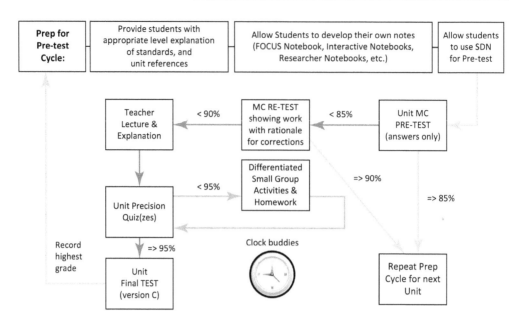

FIGURE 9.7 Classroom-level readiness: assessing student mastery and subject compacting using pre-test-treatment-post-test instructional strategy.

Source: Collins (2009). Reprinted with permission.

Conclusion

In a classroom, both the teacher and the student are engaged in the learning process. To maximize the student's potential, the practices of the educator to promote inquiry and active engagement are factors that are as critical as the motivation of the student to learn. As such, instruction design should be very cognizant of the learners' profile – academic readiness, cultural values and personal interests – to productively alter curriculum and instruction strategies in real time so that underachievement, which can only be diagnosed after an extended period of time, can be addressed through prevention rather than intervention after the fact.

REFLECTION QUESTIONS

Modeling a concept-based curriculum or lesson planning and its critical components, the following reflection questions and tasks are offered to demonstrate a balance of factual/content (F) and concept-based (C) engagement. They are based on the following generalizations (comparison of two or more concepts), which are meant to build knowledge and transfer into other topics, disciplines, and or areas of study.

Generalizations (=G) Enduring Understandings About PLS/M

1. G1. Preferred learning styles and sensory memory can be detected through observation.
2. G2. Teacher observations are an effective strategy to identify preferred learning styles.
3. G3. Language, culture and gender play an important role in students' preferred learning styles.

4.   G4. Preferred learning styles can be detected through effective communication, which also plays an important role in a student's preferred learning style and memory.
5.   G5. PLS/M is impacted by the unique qualities of the students.
6.   G6. PLS/M can be used to gauge readiness and development for student learning and understanding.
7.   G7. PLS/M can help detect how development in one area may affect performance in other areas.
8.   G8. PLS/M can be detected through evaluation of students' presented knowledge and can be used to identity learning gaps.

Essential (= E) Guiding Questions

1.   E1. What evidence is present when visual PLS/M is detected? (F)
2.   E2. What evidence is present when auditory PLS/M is detected? (F)
3.   E3. What evidence is present when reading/writing PLS/M is detected? (F)
4.   E4. What evidence is present in kinesthetic PLS/M? (F)
5.   E5. What strategies are used to identify a student's PLS/M? (C)
6.   E6. What evidence is present when communicating and identifying PLS/M?
7.   E7. What evidence is present when identifying readiness development and techniques to students?
8.   E8. What evidence is present when detecting learning gaps? (F)

Know (= K) Facts/Topics

1.   K1. Describe the four commonly noted preferred learning strategies and sensory memory (PLS/M).
2.   K2. Practitioners should possess a working knowledge of the different ways to observe students. Explain how at least two of the different PLS/M behaviors might manifest in each of the highlighted engagement types: passive, non-engagement; active engagement; and formal testing.
3.   K3. Explain how socialized concepts such as language, culture, and/or gender play a role in students' preferred learning or sensory memory.

Skill (= S) Do

1.   S1. What are examples of acceptable evidence of students' PLS/M identified through observations?
2.   S2. What are the most effective observation strategies to identify students' PLS/M when testing? Collaborating within a group project?
3.   S3. Can identification of students' PLS/M help an educator detect student's learning gaps? If so, give an example. If not, explain why not.
4.   S4. What is a "promising practice" when developing and organizing curriculum, including scope and sequence, to combat underachievement?
5.   S5. Use the Velasquez PLS/M Observation Checklist to help an underachieving gifted student understand their own PLS/M (see Figure 9.8).
6.   S6. Review Figure 9.4 on the student-centered classroom environment. How does this setting promote differentiated instruction? How does this setting foster SEL integrated in differentiated instruction? Explain how you would use each station in your classroom.

Velasquez Observation Checklist
Student Preferred Learning Styles and Sensory Memory

Name of Person Observed/ Participant ______________________________
Observation Date: ______________________________
Setting/Lesson/ Activity: ______________________________

Observation Techniques: Check all that apply:

- ☐ Passive learning,
- ☐ Non-engagement (whole or small group activity)
- ☐ Active engagement (whole or small group activity)
- ☐ Formal testing

Before Observing the Participant

1. Get to know your participant and/or write down what you already know about them. (Background information)
2. Optional: Conduct a brief PLS interview – use questions similar to the PLS Quiz to gauge preferred learning style from participant.
   (Do not ask the participant about their PLS directly; this may skew the results).

PLS Observation

During the lesson or activity, the observer should **tally** (using tally marks) how many times s/he observes traits that indicates and/or falls within the PLS category. Use the third column to provide context and/or reflection notes about the demonstrated traits.

PLS	Tally	Data Analysis/Comments
Visual		
Auditorily		
Kinesthetic		
Reading/writing		

Additional Notes

Encouragement	
Questions	

FIGURE 9.8 The PLS/M Observation Checklist.

References

Akkoyunlu, B., & Soylu, M. Y. (2008). A study of student's perceptions in a blended learning environment based on different learning styles. *Educational Technology & Society*, *11*(1), 183–193,

Anderson, I. (2016). Identifying different learning styles to enhance the learning experience. *Nursing Standard*, *31*(7).

Brady, C. L. (2013). Understanding learning styles. *International Journal of Childbirth Education, 28*(2), 16–19.

Collins, K.H. (2009). *ALANHS "3R" curriculum framework and program planning guide* [Unpublished Document], Adapted by Newton High School, Newton County Schools, Georgia.

Collins, K. H., Coleman, M. R., & Grantham, T. C. (2022). A bioecological perspective of emotional/behavioral challenges for gifted students of color: Support needed vs. Support received. *Journal of Emotional and Behavioral Disorders, 30*(2), 86–95. https://doi.org/10.1177/10634266221076466

Davis, S. (2007). Learning styles and memory. *Institute for Learning Styles Journal, 1,* 46–51.

Eissa, M. A., & Mostafa, A. A. (2013). Integrating multiple intelligences and learning styles on solving problems, achievement in, and attitudes towards math in six graders with learning disabilities in cooperative groups. *International Journal of Psycho-Educational Sciences, 2*(2), 33–45.

Furey, W. (2020). The stubborn myth of "learning styles": State teacher-license prep materials peddle a debunked theory. *Education Next, 20*(3), 8–12.

Kubina, R. (2019). *The precision teaching implementation manual.* Available at: https://centralreach.com/pt-myths

Metivier, A. (2022, September). Embrace sensory learning (so none of your students get left behind). Available at: https://www.magneticmemorymethod.com/sensory-learning/

Rolfe, A., & Cheek, B. (2012). Learning styles. *InnovAiT, 5*(3).

Sener, S., & Cokcaliskan, A. (2018). An investigation between multiple intelligences and learning styles. *Journal of Education and Training Studies, 6*(2), 125–132.

Sprenger, M. (2003). *Differentiation through learning styles and memory.* Corwin Press.

Sprick, M. (2019, March 13). The diagnostic-prescriptive reading teacher and foundational reading skills. EDVIEW360 Blog Series. Available at: https://www.voyagersopris.com/blog/edview360/the-diagnostic-prescriptive-reading-teacher-and-foundational-reading-skills

Tomlinson, C. A. (1999). *The differentiated classroom: Responding to the needs of all learners,* ASCD.

Vygotsky, L. S. (1987). The development of scientific concepts in childhood. In R. W. Reiber & A. S. Carton (Eds.). *Collected works of L. S. Vygotsky* (vol. 1, pp. 167–242). Plenum.

PART 3

Possibilities

Breaking the Glass Ceiling*
Equitable Leadership Practices to Help Alleviate Gifted Underachievement

Javetta Jones Roberson

Introduction

Many factors have been explored that affect gifted students' underachievement. Examining student self-perceptions, motivation concerns, and teacher relationships are a few topics that have been mentioned in previous research. Also included in the literature are varying factors contributing to underachievement in gifted students who are racially, culturally, ethnically, and linguistically different (RCELD). Educators are continuously trying to find ways to address underachievement among traditionally marginalized student groups. While acknowledging and recognizing the aforementioned factors, little discussion has been undertaken on the leadership practices needed to help mitigate gifted underachievement. Leaders of gifted programs need to be equipped with foundational strategies that support them in curbing underachievement for all gifted students. As US schools and gifted programs continue to evolve, educators' approaches to student achievement must also evolve to match the populations being served. That evolution not only affects teaching practices but also leadership behaviors. The intentionality of gifted leaders must adhere to program needs regarding underachievement to help reverse this trend among gifted students. Although previous chapters in this volume have focused on the implications of gifted educators and underachievement, this chapter focuses on the leadership of the gifted coordinator to support program practices to reinforce an equitable leadership stance essential for the twenty-first-century gifted student. With the reality that the populations being served in schools and gifted programs are increasing in diversity, the need for a leadership style that reflects this diversity must be a point of discourse to reflect the change in the student population.

How Underachievement Can Be Perpetual in RCELD Gifted Students

The plight of underachievement in the education of diverse student populations has been a topic of discussion for decades (Ladson-Billings, 2006; Milner, 2012). Many oppressive structures within our society have trickled down to our educational system, creating systemic inequities that continue to plague classrooms today. Many of

DOI: 10.4324/9781003369578-14

the ways traditionally marginalized student groups are treated in schools today are directly aligned with the treatment those individuals and their ancestors received in history. The remnants of segregation, racism, classism, and generational poverty, to name a few, still have a lasting effect on schools and special programs where RCELD students are enrolled. In return, these factors have played a major role in influencing student educational outcomes, including equitable representation for RCELD gifted and advanced placement programs.

Educators and stakeholders across the nation are continuously looking for ways to change the status quo and provide a more-just learning experience for students who fall into the aforementioned categories. Along with looking at systemic factors that have transitioned from our society into our schools, educators take into account structures within the school system internally that have affected schooling experiences for RCELD students. Examining instructional and curricular practices, professional learning of educators, and even considerations supporting the social and emotional needs of students, all have been points of discourse on student underachievement. Yet with few exceptions, the conversations are ongoing with minimal recommendations in research for students from diverse backgrounds who experience underachievement. The conversations are even briefer when referring to educational leaders addressing underachievement from an equity standpoint.

When discourse or research into the "why" behind RCELD students' underachievement or on the leadership attributes needed to support them in schools and gifted programs, occurs at a low rate, the perpetuity of inequity continues. Oppressive systems, such as ability tracking, a Eurocentric curriculum, and building the school-to-prison pipeline, are exacerbated. The establishment of student and community trust deteriorates. We know that the causes of underachievement are multifaceted. But when there is simply no discussion or measures in place to address underachievement consistently from all levels (teacher, parent, leader, community), then the problem continues to be a historic issue. This is not ideal for the progression of students who experience underachievement. Leaders must make it their mission to address underachievement as it plagues our schools and special programs. Equitable leadership practices are needed, but where do leaders start?

What Are Equitable Leadership Practices in Gifted Education?

When looking at equitable leadership practices, I believe it's important to break down the importance of understanding what the term equity means. Although a variety of definitions of equity are found in the literature, Campbell Jones et al.'s (2020) description is one that most resembles what true educational equity encompasses in the simplest form. Equity is fairness based on the individual differences or needs of a student (Campbell Jones et al., 2020). Equity in education is needed because each student has individual needs that must be addressed to ensure they are successful and have optional outcomes based on that accommodation need. Equity counteracts oppressive structures and systems in schools that can be perpetuated over time. When equity is implemented in education, it moves to disrupt those disparities meant to harm our brightest and most brilliant students. We know that gifted education, from its origins, was initially designed for the most elite in our society. That definition excluded students of color and other diverse backgrounds. Now, more than ever, equity is essential for a path to access and opportunity for each gifted student. Equity serves as a catalyst for positive change and growth in our gifted programs. In today's political climate, where there is a "war on education," all this inclusive equity is a necessity.

Gifted coordinators and leaders have played critical roles in the supervision and program improvement for gifted students. This includes understanding laws and policy updates to program services. Although gifted education is not mandated by federal law, each state dictates its policy and mandates for gifted services. The *2018–2019 State of the States in Gifted Education Report* (Rinn et al., 2020), noted that 38 states have legal mandates that require identification of students with gifts and talents, but only 24 states have legal mandates for gifted services for identified students. Gifted leaders are expected not only to be knowledgeable about this information but also serve as advocates in any proposed legislation that will benefit gifted students. The focus of the gifted leader has been policy, programming, and identification, to name but a few. Much of this is due to state funding being tied directly to these efforts. However, inclusive targeted measures in leadership styles have grown lax, as the precedent of state accountability, standardized testing, and other political agenda items, in recent years, has gained more attention.

For gifted education, incorporating equitable leadership practices gives leaders an opportunity to redefine the status quo with a more inclusive viewpoint and approach. An equitable leadership practice in gifted education that is strongly believed to help address underachievement is culturally responsive leadership (Khalifa, 2018; Roberson, 2020; Roberson & Floyd, 2020). Culturally responsive leadership is a leadership framework steeped in the research of Culturally Relevant Pedagogy (Ladson-Billings, 1995) and Culturally Responsive Teaching (Gay, 2010). Culturally responsive leadership practices are a unique set of behaviors that include: (1) being critically self-reflective; (2) promoting inclusive, anti-oppressive school contexts; (3) developing and sustaining culturally responsive educators and curricula; and (4) engaging students' Indigenous (or local neighborhood) community contexts (Khalifa, 2018). For gifted leaders, these behaviors are adapted to fit the needs to sustain an equitable gifted program. Table 10.1 describes how gifted leaders display culturally responsive behaviors and the possible impacts this could have on gifted programs.

For gifted programs, leaders who are culturally responsive are able to promote positive change while mitigating deficit thinking and oppressive structures that are meant to serve as a gatekeeper for RCELD students' entry into the programs. This includes those who suffer from underachievement. The philosophy, mission, and vision of the gifted program reflect the values, beliefs, and promise of supporting cultural responsiveness throughout the program for the greater good of each gifted student. Culturally responsive gifted leaders are intentional about each decision they make. They are strategic, holistic in nature, and are critically self-reflective of their actions and day-to-day operations. When gifted leaders are culturally responsive, they recognize the value of educators' professional learning being seeped in equity. They know those training experiences will help current and future gifted students thrive and create a positive narrative for informing the public that each gifted student is seen, served, and supported. Culturally responsive gifted leaders know the difference between the terms "each" and "all" when referring to the vision and mission of gifted programs. Sometimes, both terms are needed when describing student support. However, when used from the perspective of equity efforts, the phrase "each student will grow" versus "all students will grow" denotes a more inclusive tone that shows

TABLE 10.1 Examples of culturally responsive gifted leader behaviors and impacts for gifted/advanced level programs

Culturally responsive gifted leader behaviors/focus	Possible impact on gifted/advanced level program
Critical self-reflection of current practices (policy, procedures, program holistically and leadership style)	Increase school-based culturally responsive leadership protocols Require gifted program data on culturally responsive and competent practices (professional learning of staff, curriculum and instruction used, policy, etc.)
Developing and sustaining culturally responsive teachers and curriculum embedded within gifted programs	Increase diversity of gifted program and school curricula and activities Provide gifted educators with authentic examples of culturally responsive teaching in both theory and practice
Promoting inclusive and anti-oppressive educational contexts in gifted education	Students/community are mirrored in all facets of the gifted program Diversity is welcomed and incorporated
Engaging in students' Indigenous (or local) school community contexts through Improved participation and representation of diverse parents and community stakeholders in school/program culture	Establish a partnership between the school and community by inviting stakeholders into schools to visit gifted and advanced level programs and integrating the culture of students and community members into school/program activities
Incorporate equitable evaluation methods for gifted programs	Equity audits Equity teams Use data to drive evaluation (quantitative and qualitative) Inclusive evaluation of each portion of the gifted program

Source: Adapted from Roberson and Floyd's (2020) recommendations and suggested actions to promote culturally responsive leadership and advocacy for gifted English learners and Khalila's (2018) summary of effective culturally responsive school leadership behaviors and outcomes.

that gifted leaders are focusing more on the individual students being served within the program. Culturally responsive gifted leaders understand that their impact will continue beyond the classroom instruction and pedagogy. These leaders emphasize the importance of social–emotional learning and how educators must consider these factors as they too have an academic impact on RCELD gifted students. Ensuring that the social–emotional connections that gifted educators make with students and their families will build partnerships, and they can discuss societal inequities that may impact learning and that are meaningful for each student.

Students are able to thrive and grow in a gifted program as they have leaders who are dedicated to the cause of dismantling inequities through every facet of the program in general. These leaders understand the difference between "equality" and "equity." Equality is fairness for all, while equity focuses on fairness based on individual differences or needs. Gifted leaders who are culturally responsive know the two terms must be integrated together in order to strengthen programs. Being a culturally responsive gifted leader is a journey that requires a paradigm shift and for one to lead change. These leaders promote inclusivity in instructional and curricular practices, are aware of the various student populations they serve, and find multiple ways to connect students to instruction using real-world concepts (Roberson & Floyd, 2020).

Implications for Practice

Curricular and instructional practices for gifted underachievers must focus on incorporating activities that build on student strengths. We know that underachieving RCELD students can struggle with academic disengagement, motivation, peer pressure, and a plethora of other issues. Leaders can equitably support students by supporting teachers to alter the classroom environment and instructional practices based on student needs. Student-centered instructional and curricular alignment can provide a space directly designed with students being served in mind. Allowing talent development opportunities for students helps hone their gifts and channels untapped potential. Students must also feel like the curriculum reflects who they are as individuals. If students do not feel they are seen in the classroom, they'll most likely not respond to instruction. If students feel the curriculum or instructional practices are not adaptive or adjusted to their specific needs, they'll most likely not respond in a positive way. For example, students who are twice exceptional (2e) and thrice exceptional (3e) need leaders to ensure educators utilize equitable frameworks going beyond the typical gifted curriculum that involves enrichment and intervention. Collins et al. (2022) offered a culturally responsive multi-tiered system of supports (Collins' CR-MTSS) model that focuses on the whole child while systemically focusing on student learning objectives and the differentiation of curriculum and instruction from a culturally responsive lens (Figure 10.1).

The model reinforces the notion of "each" student versus "all" students, meaning its purpose is to view product, content, and process through a student's individual interest and cognitive ability. It is a way to still provide universal, intensive, and targeted support in the classroom to mitigate overrepresentation, underrepresentation, underserved and unidentified students in special and gifted education (Collins et al., 2022). As a culturally responsive gifted leader, you are continuously aware of the populations you serve and use models to adapt your program so students have a successful academic outcome.

Language, culture, and the school community of students should also be included in the learning environment as these aspects bring value to students' lives. Working with RCELD gifted learners requires leaders who will challenge educators to provide various opportunities for the students' lived experiences to come forth and flourish in the classroom. Real-world and life connections can tap into students' interests and could result in reversing the underachievement in RCELD gifted students. It is the hope that each gifted student will experience academic success. By using equitable teaching and curriculum support, educators and leaders can develop strategies and interventions to support underachieving RCELD gifted students.

Why Does Professional Learning Matter?

Gifted students benefit greatly from leaders and educators who are trained to support their unique learning experiences. Many leaders and educators, in general, have not been fully prepared to address inclusive, diverse student needs in gifted education. This could be due to several factors including a lack of training opportunities, the district/campus stance on equity-based professional learning, and possibly a vast focus on state accountability. Much of professional learning in education has been dependent on what educators believed the desired outcomes should be for students versus what is needed for their holistic growth. Despite the growing need for gifted teacher and leader training that is equity-based, it sometimes falls by the wayside and is not

	Remember (Know)	Understand (Comprehend)	Apply (Do)	Analyze (& Synthesis)	Evaluate (Critique)	Create (Products)
Contribution Approach (*Unpacking information as part of core instruction*)	Students **know and recall facts that** include cultural* reference, artifacts, events, groups, and/or other cultural elements.	Students **understand facts and concepts** that include cultural* reference, artifacts, events, groups, and/or other cultural elements.	Students **understand** and **apply facts and concepts** that include cultural* reference, artifacts, events, groups, etc.	Students **analyze relationship between concepts** learned, including cultural* references, artifacts, events, groups, etc.	Students **evaluate provocative questions, concepts, and theories** including cultural* context of references, artifacts, events, groups, etc.	Students **translate facts, concepts and theories** into new disciplines and/or **create products** from facts, concepts and theories, including cultural* references, artifacts, events, groups, etc.
Additive Approach (*Unpacking cultural themes as part of core instruction*)	Students **know and recall facts within a** cultural* context and framework.	Students **understand facts and concepts** within a cultural* context and framework.	Students **understand** and **apply facts and concepts** within a cultural* context and framework.	Students **responsively* analyze the relationship between concepts** learned within a cultural* context and framework.	Students **responsively* evaluate and critique** the cultural* context of **concepts and theories.**	Students **translate concepts and theories** into new cultural settings and disciplines and/or create culturally responsive products.
Transformation Approach (*Integrating multiple perspective and sources as a resource and part of the curriculum for additional support and targeted needs*)	Students **know and recall facts** from multiple and/or opposing cultural perspectives.	Students **demonstrate understanding of facts and concepts** from multiple and/or opposing cultural perspectives.	Students **apply their understanding** of **facts** and **concepts** from multiple and/or opposing cultural perspectives.	Students **responsively* analyze** and offer multiple and/or opposing cultural perspectives for **relationships between concepts.**	Students **responsively* evaluate, critique, and/or judge,** and/or offer multiple and/or opposing cultural perspectives for **relationships between concepts and theories.**	Students **translate the relationship between concepts and theories** into multiple and/or opposing cultural perspectives and disciplines, and/or **create** culturally responsive products.
Social Action Approach (*Integrating service learning as a resource and part of the curriculum for intensive and individualized support*)	Based multicultural contexts of **facts,** students **make connections** to appropriate and potential social action steps.	Based on their **understanding** of important multicultural **facts and concepts,** students **make recommendations** for appropriate and potential social action steps.	Based on their **understanding** of important multicultural facts **and concepts,** students **take actions** to disseminate, improve, and/or enhance a task or situation.	Students **responsively* analyze** the social and multicultural contexts **of the relationship between concepts** from multiple and/or opposing cultural perspectives, and **take actions** to disseminate, improve, and/or enhance a task or situation.	Students **responsively* critique provocative questions and** multicultural contexts of the **relationship between concepts** from multiple and/or opposing cultural perspectives, and **seek to impact** positive and collaborative **change.**	Students **create** a plan of social action and/or novel product that translate and integrate **concepts and theories** from multicultural and/or multidiscipline settings for the purpose **impacting** positive and collaborative **change.**

Overlay labels: Tier 1: Universal Support — Tier II — Tier III — Developmental Enrichments — Extended Enrichments

FIGURE 10.1 Collins' Culturally Responsive Multi-tiered System of Supports (CR-MTSS).

Source: Collins et al.'s (2022) Culturally Responsive Multi-Tiered System of Support (CR-MTSS) Framework. Reprinted with permission.

FIGURE 10.2 Roberson's Professional Learning Foundations Model for culturally responsive gifted leaders.

made a priority. Therefore, we need culturally responsive gifted leaders to advocate for such professional learning opportunities regarding their own development as well as other stakeholders within their building. Gifted leaders must ensure they foster a high standard of professional learning for the educators in their programs in order to reverse the underachievement of RCELD gifted students. Culturally responsive gifted leaders serve as the catalyst for enhancing the professional learning experience for educators related to content, pedagogy, appropriate learning environments, and accessible curriculum and courses throughout the year. I posit five foundational elements that serve as evidence and a guide for the development and implementation of culturally responsive gifted leadership within gifted programs (Figure 10.2).

Built on a Philosophy of Equity

The goal and overarching philosophy of the professional learning offered should be based on collaboration and equity-based efforts for all gifted educators. Equitable practices lead to equalized opportunities, which are a necessary component in combatting underachievement. Professional learning opportunities must be grounded in a principle of equity with the student in mind. This is vital for all stakeholders dedicated to serving RCELD gifted students and includes understanding the necessary coping and social/emotional skills to support students who struggle with underachievement. The learning received can dispel any preconceived misconceptions, biases, and myths about RCELD gifted students and underachievement in general.

Equitable Feedback and Evaluation

Formative feedback and evaluation should be implemented for growth and development. It is important that evaluations aren't always high-stake and/or attached to merit-based promotions. At minimum, evaluation of the program should occur at least once per year with feedback accepted from all stakeholders, including the gifted students themselves. This is in addition to traditional faculty evaluations. This is especially important for gifted students who have been identified as underachieving. Their feedback will give insight into their underachievement and appropriate solutions that match their needs. In Chapter 11, Martinez-Ortis et al. discuss best practices and sustainable ways to partner with universities for program evaluations that are also designed to build the capacity of the leaders and educators who serve gifted students.

Continuous Professional Learning

In educational settings, professional learning is the major approach for educators' skill development. Skill development is best learned and maintained when implemented on a continuous basis. This is especially important when addressing underachievement of RCLED students. Culturally sustainable professional development must be updated and current, constantly shifting as a response to student and program needs.

Synchronous and Asynchronous Learning Environments

As a result of the pandemic in 2020, educators and families were forced to embrace and take full advantage of the learning environments and technologies that were available to them. To accommodate what was a limitation for some school systems, asynchronous learning pedagogies and andragogy played a critical role in preventing gaps in learning for all students. As a benefit, students were allowed more opportunities than before to work at their own pace. This has long been proven as a benefit, especially to gifted students, whose curriculum can be compacted based on their learner profiles (see Chapter 9 to learn more about learner profiles). At the same time, a synchronous learning environment remains to offer its benefit cognitively and socially. As such, providing professional learning that allows educators and leaders to experience both of these learning environments offers an opportunity for them also to continually develop their skill in facilitating synchronous and asynchronous learning.

Culturally Responsive Content and Materials

Facilitators of professional learning should always be certified and/or have extensive experience in culturally responsive teaching and learning strategies. A culturally responsive leader should be skilled in multiple ways of knowing, teaching, learning, presenting, and engaging students. The tools – content and materials – used to complement the facilitation should also be inclusive and evidence-based, fostering equitable practices and cultural sustainability.

Conclusion

As gifted leaders embark on a new school year, it's imperative that they put equity at the forefront of their decision making for the growth of their programs. Although history has taught us that the inception of gifted programs was meant to serve and identify one type of gifted student, gifted leaders must use this information to shift the narrative and their thinking into a more equitable practice for the future. Leaders must realize the value in understanding diversity and aligning program needs to that diverse population. Considering students who are underachieving, we must first recognize the patterns of underachievement in gifted students, what those characteristics look like for RCELD students, and how our leadership practices affect the attitudes, beliefs, and motivation to support students as they matriculate through the program.

Equity work is work of the heart. Equity work is invigorating because it can leave leaders with a sense of hope and purpose, as you journey through it. It is tiring at times as others may not see the value in being a culturally responsive equity-driven leader in gifted. Sometimes, conflict can arise when integrating cultural responsiveness. But, as a gifted leader, it is a necessity and vital to an effective, holistic gifted program.

REFLECTION QUESTIONS

1. Describe some evidence-based strategies and/or promising practices that administrators and other gifted leaders can use to support RCELD students who struggle with underachievement.
2. What leadership practices are you currently using to mitigate gifted underachievement in your program?
3. Do you believe critical self-reflection as a gifted leader can impact student underachievement? Explain.
4. What curriculum and instructional supports or systems can gifted coordinators and other leaders put in place to support teachers and gifted students who struggle with underachievement?
5. What paradigm shift will gifted leaders and other stakeholders need to make as they move toward solutions for underachievement for all gifted learners?

References

Campbell Jones, B., Keeny, S., Campbell Jones, F. (2020). Culture, Class, and Race: Constructive Conversations That Unite and Energize Your School and Community. ASCD.

Collins, K. H., Coleman, M. R., & Grantham, T. C. (2022). A bioecological perspective of emotional/behavioral challenges for gifted students of color: Support needed versus support received. *Journal of Emotional and Behavioral Disorders, 30*(2), 86–95. https://doi.org/10.1177/10634266221076466

Gay, G. (2010). *Culturally responsive teaching: Theory, research, and practice* (2nd ed.). Teachers College Press.

Khalifa, M. (2018). *Culturally responsive school leadership*. Harvard Education Press.

Khalifa, M. (2019).

Ladson-Billings, G. (2006). But that's just good teaching! The case for culturally relevant pedagogy. *Theory into Practice, 34*(3), 159–165. https://doi.org/10.1080/00405849509543675

Milner, R. (2012). Beyond a Test Score: Explaining Opportunity Gaps in Educational Practice. *Journal of Black Studies,* 43 (6), 693–718.

Rinn, A., Mun, R. U., & Hodges, J. (2020). *2018–2019 State of the states in gifted education*. National Association for Gifted Children and the Council of State Directors of Programs for the Gifted. Available at: https://www.nacg.org/2018-2019-state-states-gifted-education

Roberson, J. J. (2020). The voice of leaders: Examining the underrepresentation of diverse students in advanced academics from a culturally responsive leadership lens. Doctoral dissertation. Texas A&M University-Commerce. ProQuest.

Roberson, J. J., & Floyd, E. (2020) Advocating for gifted English learners through culturally responsive leadership. *Teaching for High Potential.*

* **Note:** The use of terms RCELD (racially, culturally, ethnically, and linguistically different) in Chapter 10 and the use of the term CLED (culturally, linguistically, and economically diverse) in Chapter 12, more specifically, refer to individuals who have been historically discriminated against, marginalized and disadvantaged based on race/ethnicity, language, or socio-economic statuses as well as represent diversity that poses a standard, value, and/or belief, that is considered to be divergent or vastly "different" from and, oftentimes challenged by, the White middle class culture that dominates and influences the typical perspectives, policies, and practices in education. The contributors for this book acknowledge that the basic definitions of the words "different" and "diverse" separate from these acronyms simply make inference to a range of representation determined by distinctive characteristics within the named group or subgroup.

Program Evaluation as a Capacity-Building Tool in Gifted Education
A Call to Action to Maximize University-School Partnerships

Araceli Martinez Ortiz, Andrea Dennison, and Kristina Henry Collins

Introduction

The gaps in STEM and advanced learning courses are well documented. Overall low concentrations of women and minorities in STEM exist, relative to the number of women and minorities in the overall workforce, and low numbers o these groups hold STEM degrees (National Science Board & National Science Foundation, 2020). Science and engineering indicators from the National Science Board (NSB) showed that while in the last 25 years women's presence in the broad area of science and engineering has significantly increased by degrees and within the workforce, the enormous disparity between men and women remains largely unchanged. Hodge, Matthews, and Squires (2017) posited that gaps in STEM career paths become apparent by at least eighth grade. Whether categorized by workforce or STEM degrees, non-Hispanic White males make up the majority of individuals identified as scientists or engineers (National Science Board & National Science Foundation, 2020). The absence of diversity in STEM and other advanced programming such as gifted and talented education is not only an issue of recruitment and retention that negatively impacts career choices for underrepresented students (i.e., Black, Hispanics, and females), but also yields critical gaps in perspective necessary for an organization to maintain its competitive edge. As such, the authors assert that the persistence in long-standing underrepresentation among a plethora of nationwide initiatives and programming efforts suggests that we turn our focus from perceived deficits of students to critical evaluations of the programs that are designed to foster talent development.

To insert an equity focus into talent development calls for the use of social justice orientation (Lardier et al., 2021), Arthur et al. (2009) offered five principles to illustrate how social justice is foundational in career guidance:

DOI: 10.4324/9781003369578-15

1. Fair and equitable distribution of resources and opportunities.
2. Direct action to address oppression and marginalization within society.
3. Inclusion and participation of all members of society.
4. Fostering human development and potential.
5. Engaging people as co-participants in decision making.

All of these can impact students' achievement. Just as important as formative and summative assessment is the process of student learning, and program evaluation is important for program effectiveness. The same best practice for implementing holds true – start with the end goal and then follow a backwards design (Wiggins & McTighe, 2005) with the assessment, or evaluation plan as a priority and initial step in the curriculum/program planning process. Moreover, programs designed with social justice orientation as their framework should take careful planning, with formative evaluations conducted throughout. Collaborative evaluation is a responsive approach to evaluation that is participant-oriented. Participation in partnership-based program evaluation models helps to move effective equity-based STEM and advanced learning programming efforts forward. An evaluation culture emerges as a consequence of routine evaluation practice. Its responsive nature yields a diversity focus and skill development that are transformative because it considers the history, structure, culture, and context of the programming organization. To the benefit of community partners, capacity for sustained improvement and effectiveness of overall STEM and advanced learning programming are increased. Graduate students, as external program evaluators, become more culturally competent, increasing the validity and utility of the evaluation within a real-world context (Fitzpatrick et al., 2011). This was the goal as we, along with other stakeholders, designed PEACE GEMS (Pre-Engineering and Career Exploration for Girls interested in Engineering, Math, and Science) program and pilot study.

Background Information

Traditional program evaluation includes an internal evaluation conducted by an organization's members or an external evaluation conducted by outside consultants. The biggest challenge with either method is the amount of time and money needed to conduct them – luxuries which most schools do not possess. As an alternative to traditional program evaluation, utilizing a university-school partnership with a service-learning immersion approach can address issues in the STEM and other academic pipelines related to capacity-building, program effectiveness, resources, and shortages. Schools can enlist university partners to provide rigorous, authentic evaluations, benefitting matriculating graduate students with another opportunity to strengthen both cognitive and non-cognitive skills that will be useful later in life.

Priority in STEM Evaluation Training Programs

The issue of evaluation has also been a concern for the field of evaluation. The National Science Foundation (NSF) has funded many evaluations training fellowships, including those designed to close the gaps for underrepresented groups and to educate program evaluators. As far back as 1997, the NSF provided a grant to the

American Education Research Association (AERA) to fund universities for fellowships to graduate students in this area of study. They also funded AERA's Evaluation Training Program (ETP) that targeted underrepresented groups in STEM (AERA, 2002). They used this opportunity to evaluate their own program, and use the experience gained to assist NSF in developing new programs to train qualified evaluators. They particularly placed a priority on collaboration efforts to develop STEM evaluators who possess an understanding of STEM background as well as an understanding of educational practices.

Program Evaluation Development and Critical Theory

In 2011, the American Evaluation Association changed its standards to reflect an enhanced focus on equity and social justice. Since then, the field of program evaluation has been faced with new challenges, including the need to recognize the impact of injustice and historically perpetuated racism implicit in the systems and structures of American institutions (Caldwell & Bledsoe, 2019). This challenge is timely, as those who have been most impacted by racism and other structural inequalities continue to have unmet needs, and continue in many ways to suffer the insults of these inequalities. Caldwell and Bledsoe recommended remedies to program evaluators and researchers, so that we can be actively engaged in undoing these structural inequalities. The authors emphasize that theory, methods, and practice all present opportunities for change in the field, and that normalizing social justice as a desired result of evaluations will improve standards and practices across the field.

We must realize that the deep and persisting inequalities that exist in our world are also reflected in our profession, and investigate the history of this phenomenon. Then we can engage in transformative processes to uproot racism and other forms of oppression, beginning with transforming the pedagogical approach to teaching about social justice in program evaluation. Traditionally, social justice has been considered one of the frameworks that are available to program evaluators. We advocate for a change, placing social justice at the forefront of consideration of any program's inner workings. An anti-racist pedagogical orientation is necessary for the evolution of this perspective. This is especially important for programs designed to address underrepresentation in STEM, gifted, and other advanced learning programs.

Collaborative Evaluation as a Service-Learning Approach to Instruction

Service-learning can provide efficacious bridges for theory to practice through authentic real-world learning experiences (Brand, Brascia, & Sass, 2019; Collins, et al., 2020) and additionally provide opportunities for community and non-profit institutions to benefit from university-based students' learning experiences. Partnership-based evaluation complements the value and practical application of authentic and real-life problem-solving as it simultaneously develops the evaluation skills and capacity of K-12 educators as program facilitators and graduate students. More specific to the PEACE GEMS program, the evaluation model is linked to the university, community organizations, STEM educational faculty, and graduate students in ways that combine expertise and resources to address deficiencies in the STEM pipeline related to sustainability of programs designed to bridge the gaps in STEM for underrepresented students.

Formative and Summative Meta-Evaluations

The service-learning approach situates program facilitators and graduate students in a position to evaluate the evaluation team's effectiveness as external evaluators – using formative and summative meta-evaluation – while learning about program evaluation. In addition to the evaluation of the program itself, the students of a graduate-level program evaluation course self-assess their own processes (formative/internal meta-evaluation) and the program facilitators offer a summative meta-evaluation at the end of the program. The summative meta-evaluation serves to further scrutinize the effectiveness of the program evaluation and the formative/internal meta-evaluation.

Oftentimes, as part of the course, the graduate students will learn about different types of evaluations and their appropriate use. It is advised that program coordinators work with the professor and the graduate students who will make up their collaborating evaluation team to determine the type of evaluation that best fits the program. For the purpose of evaluating the PEACE GEMS pilot study, which included program facilitators, researchers, and evaluators as part of the evaluation team, we chose the participant-oriented evaluation approach for the program itself, and adapted a summative meta-evaluation checklist (Stufflebeam, 1999, 2012), based on program evaluation standards organized according to the original (1994) and updated (2010) Joint Committee on Standards for Educational Evaluation (Fournier, 1994; JCSEE, 1994; Yarbrough et al., 2010).

This original checklist is provided as a free service to users, who are encouraged to modify or adapt the checklist to fit their specific needs and to execute their own discretion and judgment when using the checklist. As written, it is designed to assess the program evaluation process to meet the requirement and determine the strength of the five core attributes of evaluation quality:

1. *Utility (U)* based on checkpoints for standards U1–U8: evaluator credibility, attention to stakeholders (stakeholder identification), negotiated purposes (information scope and selection), explicit values, relevant information (report clarity), meaningful process and products, timely and appropriate communicating and reporting (timeliness and dissemination), concern for consequences and influence (evaluation impact).

2. *Feasibility (F)* based on checkpoints for standards F1–F4: project management, practical procedures, contextual/political viability, and resource use (cost effectiveness).

3. *Propriety (P)* based on checkpoints for standards P1–P7: responsive and inclusive orientations/service orientation, formal agreements, human rights and respect (rights of human subjects and human interactions), clarity and fairness (complete and fair assessment), transparency and disclosure (disclosure of findings), conflict of interests, and fiscal responsibility.

4. *Accuracy (A)* based on checkpoints for standards A1–A8: justified conclusions (and decisions), valid information, reliable information, explicit program and context descriptions (program documentation and context analysis), information management (described purposes and procedures), sound designs and analyses (defensible information sources, analysis of quantitative data, and analysis of qualitative information), and communication and reporting (impartial reporting),

5. *Evaluation accountability (E)* (meta-evaluation standards) based on checkpoints for standards E1–E3: evaluation documentation, internal meta-evaluation, and external meta-evaluation.

For each of the 30 standards (or the number of pre-selected standards determined to be critical for your program's design), the checklist includes six checkpoints drawn from the substance of the standard. It is suggested that each standard be scored on each checkpoint. Then judgments about the adequacy of the subject evaluation in meeting the standard can be made as follows:

0–1 Poor
2–3 Fair
4 Good
5 Very good
6 Excellent

It is recommended that an evaluation be deemed invalid if it scores Poor on standards P1 Service Orientation, A1 Justified Conclusions, A2 Valid Information, or A8 Impartial Reporting.

The PEACE GEMS Program Design and Evaluation

The PEACE GEMS pilot program was a one-week residential program hosted by a regional university in the central part of Texas. Selected participants (16) were paired in teams of four and assigned to dormitory rooms where they resided for the entire week.

Organizational Framework: Backwards Design

Using a backwards design (Wiggins & McTighe, 1997, 2005) as the organizational framework for the program, we also referred to it for the design of the actual study and the design of their learning activities because of its usefulness for instructional intervention. Also known as understanding by design, backwards design emphasizes three main stages: (1) identifying the desired learning outcomes; (2) determining the acceptable evidence of learning; and (3) planning the experiences and instructional approach.

The Desired Outcomes

The overall goal for the PEACE GEMS program was to increase STEM awareness in terms of discipline areas, preparation, opportunities, and reflective identity/potential of participants throughout the STEM pipeline. Referencing the Content Learning and Identity Construction (CLIC; Varelas, Martin, & Kane, 2013) theoretical framework and race- and gender-based identity development models (Collins, 2018), desired outcomes included:

1. enhanced confidence in sense of STEM belonging and capacity to succeed in the STEM field for rising 9th grade participants; and
2. positive impact on STEM motivation and persistence for undergraduate students who served as program mentors.

Acceptable Evidence of Learning

PEACE GEMS also served as a pilot study to offer data and evidence needed for a grant application to conduct a bigger project. As such, program evaluation was a critical and necessary part of the program. A graduate course in program evaluation was scheduled to be taught at the same time as the study with its aim to encompass a culmination of authentic learning, collaboration, service to the field, and blended delivery. Together, the program evaluation course and the STEM pilot study evolved into a collaborative partnership with critical components of stakeholder engagement to evaluate a STEM program's capacity to redress STEM academic achievement, access to career exploration, and identity development. The purpose of the evaluation of the PEACE GEMS camp was to help evaluate the effectiveness of a week-long, overnight camp and whether the PEACE GEMS camp achieved the intended goals of offering more awareness of the STEM field to girls and young women.

Experiences and Instructional Approach

The students participated in hands-on classroom instruction within the context of engineering design, innovation and creativity, advanced academic preparation, and career exploration. Activities included, but were not limited to, team-building sessions, identity and talent development, academic and career coaching, mentoring, personal reflection, and industry tours. Throughout the week, they also planned for a student-centered showcase of their experiences and this was presented at the conclusion of the camp to the families and friends of the participants. Each showcase team highlighted a different field of engineering in their presentation.

Implementation Framework: Theories of Change and Action

Theory of change is defined as "a particular approach for making underlying assumptions in a change project explicit, and using the desired outcomes of the project as a mechanism to guide project planning, implementation, and evaluation" within the scope of a "single change initiative" that is "created and refined by the project team" (Reinholz & Andrews, 2020, p. 2). It is project-specific and responsive to evaluation. It provides the theoretical foundation upon which a diverse set of interventions can be built. It is important especially when these interventions are implemented simultaneously – as was the case with the PEACE GEMS program. Davenport and colleagues (2020) asserted specifically that this theory is one of planned behavior, or performance, as a result of changing attitudes as a predictor of intentions toward that performance, and "therefore can be used as a theoretical basis to explore the connection between a young person's intention to exhibit a particular career behavior" (p. 3), such as STEM persistence. This makes this framework ideal for addressing issues of underachievement within gifted education. As an example, Figure 11.1 outlines the scope and sequence for PEACE GEMS activities and evaluation that led to its desired outcomes.

Theory of change is operationalized for implementation by a theory of action. For PEACE GEMS, with an overarching goal of reducing the gap of underrepresentation in STEM, this process of creating the theory of change allowed facilitators and external evaluators to identify and codify a theory of action to understand the conditions and for whom components or interventions of an initiative work. The theory of action, or logic model, is a logical sequence of events or activities that results in the expected outcome (Martinek, 2017; Reinholz & Andrews, 2020). It outlines how the

Inputs	Activities	Outputs	Outcomes
• Ethnically diverse team of female professors focused on PE use w/ a Social Justice lens, volunteering time and resources • Small internal funding for summer camp from Dean of College • Girls from low-income areas recruited • On-campus resources • PE summer class taught by a SP professor w SJ focus • Community partnerships	• Summer Camp for Girls interested in STEM, planned over an academic year, conducted in summer • P.E. Team made of a diverse all-female group of graduate students • So many more activities... how in-depth should we be?	• PE conducted efficiently, turned report in to camp faculty within weeks of camp completion • This meta-evaluation was conducted • Next camp was planned (delayed due to COVID-19)	• Girls rated the experience highly, all want to return • SP Students got experience w PE (NASP competency) • Parent feedback positive • Community partnerships solidified, extended • Further funding sought • Capacity built across stakeholders

FIGURE 11.1 The PEACE GEMS theory of action.

program actually works; it offers a visual representation of the innermost workings of the program. The theory of change, and its operationalized theory of action, are most useful in evaluating existing programs or as a tool to develop new programs. By carefully conducting formative meta-evaluations as routine evaluations throughout the program, external evaluators can provide objective feedback about alignment of the activities to the behavioral outcomes, and offer advice on how the program might be improved and best evaluated. Figure 11.2 highlights the PEACE GEMS logic model, which provides a visual for the evaluative action plan.

A theory of action can also serve as the evidence-based "story" that explains the specific changes facilitators intend to make to improve the program.

- *Inputs.* Notice that the inputs outlined in the PEACE GEMS camp were the faculty members who organized the program; undergraduate and graduate-level student mentors; time; funding sources; an extensive research base; transportation to and from field trip locations; materials, equipment, and technology used in various workshops; and the classroom, dining, and dormitory facilities of hosting university.

- *Outputs.* The outputs included activities and participation in the program. The activities conducted throughout the week of camp were workshops designed to foster an interest in STEM activities, development of a curriculum for continued learning in STEM fields, field trips to locations where STEM career opportunities exist, and providing mentorship opportunities from undergraduate and graduate students. The intended audience for the PEACE GEMS program included the students, parents or guardians of the students, surrounding school districts, undergraduate and graduate mentors, and agencies and businesses in STEM career fields.

- *Outcomes.* The outcomes included the short-term, medium-term, and long-term results and impacts of the PEACE GEMS program. More specific to the goals, the intended short-term results were an increase in awareness of underrepresentation in STEM, as well as its consequences, among participants; an increase in knowledge

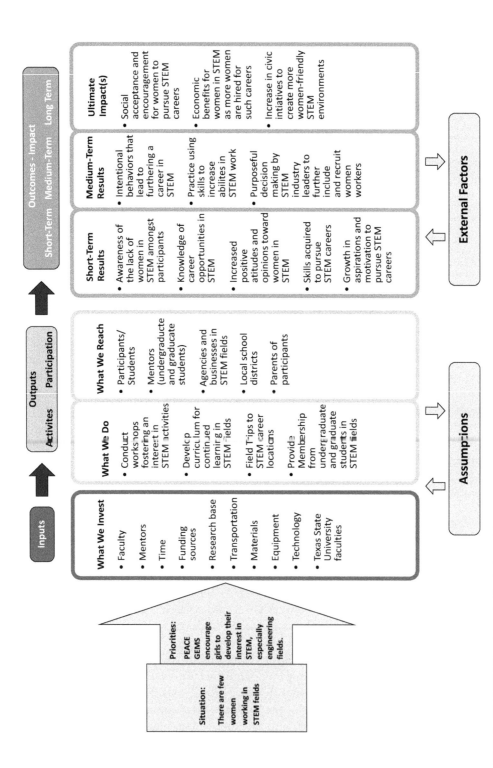

FIGURE 11.2 The PEACE GEMS meta-evaluation logic model.

of career opportunities in STEM; increased positive attitudes and opinions toward women in STEM; acquiring skills needed to pursue STEM careers; and growth in aspirations and motivation to pursue STEM careers. The intended medium-term results were the creation of intentional behaviors in female students that lead to furthering a career in STEM, the practice of using skills to increase abilities in STEM work, and purposeful decision-making by STEM industry leaders to further include and recruit women workers. The ultimate, long-term impacts of the program are social acceptance and encouragement for women to pursue STEM careers, economic benefits for women in STEM as more women are hired for such careers, an increase in civic initiatives to create more women-friendly STEM environments, and benefit to companies for global competitiveness that include important contributions that are accompanied by the socialized perspective and experience of women. Potential assumptions about the PEACE GEMS program by both the stakeholders in the program as well as the outside community are considered. External factors may affect the program as well as be impacted by the program itself. Both of these factors work in a codirectional relationship with the PEACE GEMS program, and serve as a source of limitations that may affect goals and outcomes.

Methods

The PEACE GEMS leadership team chose a social action approach to program evaluation that maximized the benefits of traditional evaluation and capacity-building for all stakeholders. The program facilitators for PEACE GEM program, which represented the "client" to the graduate course, participated in the evaluation process as summative meta-evaluators to build their own capacity for evaluation.

Program Participants

All facilitators and participants directly involved in PEACE GEMS self-identified as female. The program was coordinated by five professors with diverse backgrounds in science and engineering as well as curriculum and identity development. Sixteen rising 9th graders from three different neighboring school systems were selected to participate in a week-long university-sponsored, residential STEM program aimed at providing female students, as underrepresented students in STEM, with academic skill development, career exploration, and reflective-identity mentoring. Using a hybrid mentoring approach (Collins et al., 2020), the rising 9th grade students were directly mentored by three undergraduate STEM students and one graduate pre-service education student, focusing on evening and social engagement. The mentors along with two of the professors resided in the dorms with the participants. Formed as the formative meta-evaluation team, five school psychology graduate students, enrolled in a program evaluation course, served as evaluators throughout the planning and implementation of the program.

In addition to the team-based efforts, each member of the program evaluation team had a specific title and role as part of the team:

- Captain/External Reviewer (Contact Person)
- Evaluator I (Dominant and Paradigm Shifts)

- Evaluator II (Action Sequence and Logic Model)
- Data Analyzer
- Meta-evaluation Manager
- Summative Meta-evaluators.

Coupled with the guided program evaluation, formative meta-evaluations were conducted by the graduate students in the university classroom within the context of program evaluation as a service-learning project, and the program facilitators completed the summative meta-analysis after receiving the reports of the program evaluation. With this approach, we offered lessons and opportunity for building capacity for all stakeholders.

Evaluation Design: A Translational Platform for Theory to Practice

The program evaluation team used a cyclical inquiry model approach throughout the evaluation process. This included:

1. Explore pertinent school data, student background information, and program history (websites and program applications).
2. Implement familiarization of program goals as implications for the end-users, or female student participants.
3. Focus the evaluation, develop the instrumentation, and identify the analysis process.
4. Develop and implement a plan of action/activities to reach the goal.
5. Collect and analyze data.
6. Monitor and report the results.
7. Repeat.

These steps in the cyclical inquiry model are now described:

- *Explore pertinent information*: The PEACE GEMS program coordinators met together as a first step to be sure they understood and could communicate the goals and plans. They took this time to brainstorm potential partners, participation requirements, and potential activities informed by the data.
- *Familiarization of goals*: After one week (8 hours) and the program coordinators' initial meeting, the graduate students met with the program coordinators – as part of the next inquiry cycle – to examine the program's goals, its plan of action, and the implications as a preface to the evaluation.
- *Focus the evaluation*: A reflection of broad issues within the STEM pipeline compelled the development of the evaluation questions that led the investigation and the evaluation focus. Instrumentation and analysis procedures were created, as a plan of evaluation action, in order to further inform program coordinators' instructional plan of action to address problems that were identified. These were then used as a frame to also examine the activities planned for alignment to the goals set for the program.
- *Develop and implement the plan*: After the initial evaluation team meeting, the program coordinators solidified its program and session activities as well as its evaluation plan.

■ *Data collection and analysis.* The evaluation team conducted observations and interviews with various stakeholders throughout the program to gather quantitative and qualitative data that informed an analysis of effectiveness of the PEACE GEMS camp. They used qualitative-dominant mixed methods and a participatory action design.

   – *Data collection*: The faculty relied on the expertise of the graduate students to develop data collection instruments, including student surveys. Faculty *members* developed their own surveys to capture the voice of the faculty/ STEM mentors. Throughout the program, evaluators collected and analyzed data, including observations of select activities. At the end of the semester, a metrics report was prepared as a final deliverable by the program evaluation team that was shared with the program coordinators and summative meta-evaluation team. The evaluation data was collected through various methods, such as surveys, interviews, and observations throughout the week-long camp. The campers completed pre-program and post-program surveys provided by the PEACE GEMS faculty, as well as two additional surveys provided by the evaluation team – one mid-week and one on the last full day of camp. Parents were given a short survey on the first night of camp as well as a follow-up questionnaire sent via email. Faculty members and mentors also received post-camp questionnaires. The evaluation data was collected from 15 of the 16 campers.

   – *Data analysis.* An integrated mixed method design that included both quantitative and qualitative data was used to evaluate the data collected throughout the week. The quantitative data includes Likert-scale items evaluated on a scale from 1–5 (see Tables 11.1–11.5). Descriptive statistics were also calculated from the Likert-scale questions. The qualitative data includes information provided through faculty, student, parent, and mentor questionnaire responses.

■ *Report data findings.* The results of the evaluation were summarized by a formative and the summative meta-evaluation. Tables 11.1 and 11.2 show the pre- and post-program (treatment) Likert-scale raw scores and averages calculated on the surveys administered by program faculty and given to the students on their first and final day of the camp. The items were crafted to measure the girls' attitudes toward STEM for the purpose of uncovering and developing their STEM potential within formal and informal settings. They were based on Collins' (2018) identity development model for understanding the critical characteristics that positively influence motivation to learn and persist in STEM for underrepresented students who already show a high interest in STEM. These traits included a sense of belonging (reflective STEM identity) and STEM interest (value) along with self-perceptions regarding their own potential (STEM competence/ability), and necessary investment (risk/benefit of STEM cultural assimilation).

The evaluated results of participants' responses to statements that speak to their STEM identity (belongingness, knowledge, self-efficacy, motivation, etc.), reveal there was statistical and practical improvement in the participants' self-perception after participating in the PEACE GEMS program. A major shift (2- to 4-point positive scale rating difference) in perception from both categories of "disagree" to either category of "agree" (somewhat or strongly) reveals a significant positive impact of the PEACE GEMS program on all participants.

TABLE 11.1 PEACE GEMS participants' pre-program and post-program attitudes toward STEM

STEM identity development traits/ attitude toward STEM	Strongly disagree	Somewhat disagree	Neither agree nor disagree	Somewhat agree	Strongly agree
Pre-program attitude toward STEM					
I Belong in STEM (Self-concept)	1	2	2	5	5
I Can Succeed in STEM (Ability)	0	1	0	7	7
I Want to Succeed in STEM (Value/Interest)	0	1	0	5	9
I Know What It Takes to Succeed in STEM (Assimilation)	0	3	6	5	1
Post-program attitude toward STEM					
I Belong in STEM (Self-concept)	0	0	2	5	7
I Can Succeed in STEM (Ability)	0	0	1	3	11
I Want to Succeed in STEM (Value/Interest)	0	0	1	3	11
I Know What It Takes to Succeed in STEM (Assimilation)	0	0	2	9	3

TABLE 11.2 PEACE GEMS participants' average pre- and post-program attitudes toward STEM

STEM identity development traits/Attitude toward STEM	Pre-program participation	Post-program participation
I Belong in STEM (Self-concept)	3.96	4.26
I Can Succeed in STEM (Ability)	4.33	4.66
I Want to Succeed in STEM (Value/Interest)	4.46	4.66
I Know What It Takes to Succeed in STEM (Assimilation)	3.26	3.93

Tables 11.3–11.5 show the raw scores reported on the surveys designed by the graduate students from the evaluation course and distributed as part of the formative meta-evaluation. Surveys were distributed at mid-week to evaluate participants' perceptions and to adapt, as needed, implementation of select components of the program, and at the end of the camp to evaluate the overall program impact. Both surveys

TABLE 11.3 PEACE GEMS mid-week evaluation questionnaire results

Program components	Very negative	Somewhat negative	Neutral/ neither	Somewhat positive	Very positive
Comfortability	0	0	2	11	2
Academic coaching ratings	0	1	4	4	5
Career coaching ratings	0	1	2	5	7
Identity-development ratings	0	1	3	6	4

TABLE 11.4 PEACE GEMS end-of-week evaluation questionnaire results

Overall program impact	Very negative	Somewhat negative	Neutral/neither	Somewhat positive	Very positive
Camp influence on desired persistence in STEM	0	0	0	5	10
New information about STEM field	0	0	0	3	12
Acquired knowledge about STEM	0	0	0	2	13
Camp influence on confidence to persist in STEM	0	0	0	4	11

TABLE 11.5 Increased awareness of different engineering disciplines

Types of engineering	Number of responses
Industrial	7
Biomedical	6
Aerospace	3
Materials	3
Mechanical	3
Audio/Visual	2
Architectural	2
Software	2
Chemical	1
Civil	1
Electrical	1

included Likert-scale items rated on a negative to positive impact scale ranging from 1–5. These would be comparable to the same scale ratings from 1 disagree to 5 agree on items. Table 11.5 includes quantitative data extracted from the qualitative open-ended responses for the end-of-week questionnaire. This data included the girls' responses to the question, "What new engineering disciplines, if any, did you learn about this week?"

In addition to the quantitative data, qualitative data was gathered to provide a more in-depth evaluation of the program. Other qualitative data was gathered from questionnaires, interviews, and observations conducted by the evaluators and given to the girls, college mentors, and faculty members, and participants' families. Overall, all stakeholders responded to the post-camp questionnaire with positive feedback. All program participants (girls, college mentors, and faculty members) offered suggestions for improvement (see Tables 11.6–11.8). Faculty members provided additional information related to their perceived success of the program (see Table 11.8). Parents or guardians were asked questions related to their satisfaction with the program and their student's report of satisfaction to them. Example responses are detailed in Table 11.9.

In order to gather more data on the sustainability of PEACE GEMS, a post-camp interview was conducted with one of the faculty members. The data gathered during the interview included information about funding sources that contributed to this pilot study and reflecting on potential funding and grant applications.

TABLE 11.6 Sample of participants' responses

Positive feedback/benefits of the program	Negative feedback/suggestions for change
■ This experience has meant a lot to me because it has helped me learn things about engineering, I would otherwise never get the chance to learn about ■ This has been a great experience. It taught me that I can be anything I want to be, I just have to work hard and never give up. ■ I've learned from my mentors that it's possible to be a successful young woman in STEM, while also still being able to truly belong, and be yourself in a male-dominated field	■ The lecture style sessions were "boring" or "hard to stay focused during" ■ They would prefer more interactive activities ■ Mornings were "tough to be engaged in due to being tired"

TABLE 11.7 Examples of college mentors' responses

Positive feedback/benefits of the program	Negative feedback/suggestions for change
■ The lectures were filled with great information ■ The girls took very well to the identity pieces ■ Great communication between girls and mentors ■ Mentors and girls felt comfortable approaching faculty ■ Everything was well organized, any problems were quickly solved and were not seen by the girls ■ Everyone was welcoming to the girls and respected that they were all different and needed to be treated as such	■ The girls had a hard time staying attentive ■ Students would have enjoyed more time doing hands-on activities and fewer lectures ■ Not enough time for sleep and personal time ■ One idea is that the girls could have more time with the professors, maybe have an "interview" time for each professor where each girl asks a question ■ The girls expressed that they wanted to see more of the campus (maybe the girls find details about buildings and they present to parents on last day) ■ Start some kind of group message to keep in touch

TABLE 11.8 Examples of faculty's responses

Positive feedback/perceived success	Negative feedback/suggestions for change
Just about every single candidate mentioned attending the camp next summer. The girls were engaged throughout the camp.

They were clearly inspired and asked about what next year will be like. :) I think it was worth our time and resources, but the outcomes are a few years down the line, and will be seen by how many return to camp next year, and how many choose science as a career. | In the future there should be more of a cohesive curriculum that builds throughout the week. Each faculty member took their own area of expertise and shared within that area, but there was little connection and shared information regarding content leading up to the camp. Some of the sessions built on one another (Identity workshops), while others were more stand-alone. I would have liked to see all of the sessions build up to the end, collaborating across themes in each section. In the future, we also need to have a training session preparing faculty and camp mentors on logistics and responding to behavioral issues and other incidents. Other changes would include: fewer catered meals (cost), including additional items for participants on the packing list, and involving faculty more in preparation of the materials needed for camp.

More time for different activities

Reconsider the student schedule as the students were getting at max, 8 hours of sleep. This caused a few students to get drowsy throughout the day.

We need a funding mechanism to make this sustainable. I would also put more effort into social media; to use that as a marketing tool for funders we need more images and content. The communication in person and via email was good, but I would create a faculty text chain in advance next time, or perhaps Slack channel in the future. |

TABLE 11.9 Examples of parents' responses

Would you send your student back to PEACE GEMS camp? Why or why not?	How do you feel this camp has influenced your student?	First or most notable thing that your child reported when they came back from camp
Yes. Exposure to different fields and college major options, meeting friends with like interests and experience of being away from home.	Shown her there are options for her and other young women with like interests	The activities were fun and challenging, sometimes things come easy and it was nice to have challenges
Most definitely. My daughter enjoyed spending time on a college campus, getting to know girls from other schools with similar interests, and learned a ton in just a week	She has been a serious student for a while, but this camp made her passionate about engineering. She was really excited about the idea of coming again next year.	The first thing she told me when I picked her up was that she had the opportunity to return next year... obviously that was a clear sign that she loved the camp. The first thing she texted me from camp was that she wanted to be an engineer. The next night she told me she wanted to be a programmer. Her excitement for a STEM career path has to be the biggest take-away from camp.

Discussion and Limitations

The graduate students from the evaluation course conducted detailed discussions regarding the process and the evaluation results. They crafted metrics reports and presented their findings as part of their capstone project for the course. Copies of all relevant reports were also distributed to the PEACE GEMS program facilitators. Evaluators reported that use of mixed methods for this meta-evaluation was important to understand the complexity of the data and influence of several treatments being implemented simultaneously; the data worked in conjunction to explain the program's effectiveness so neither the qualitative or quantitative data should be analyzed independently. Purported benefits and strengths of a participant-oriented evaluation approach that uses a university-school partnership were confirmed. Additional benefits noted by the graduate students and evaluation team included:

■ Cooperation and camaraderie among all team members allowed for maximum investment of time and efforts for facilitators and external reviewers.

■ Proactive, mindful, and dynamic efforts toward theories of change and actions for improvement were continuously implemented.

■ Use of external evaluators in partnership with the program facilitators allowed for the objectivity of evaluation and full appreciation of the context of the goals, desired outcomes, and larger problem at hand – underrepresentation of women in STEM and positive self-concept as educated women in science and engineering fields of study.

■ Accessibility and engagement by all stakeholders in the program meetings and activities were helpful which permitted gaining important information needed for evaluation.

■ Efficiency and productivity were maximized within the time constraints.

■ Information was able to be gathered from all stakeholders, increasing feedback responses and perspective.

Limitations

Graduate students in program evaluation courses typically take them for one semester earning 3–4 credit hours. However, unlike this week-long residential program, some programs warrant commitment longer than a semester. Bringing in new students the following semester and/or consistent course offerings may be an issue. It is recommended for such programs that university professors seek funding from diverse sources to financially support their service-learning efforts. As such, the university may be able to offer an extended or special topics course, as a follow-up course, for select students to continue their work beyond the semester for additional credit hours. This would afford more time for graduate students to work with clients as an independent cohort. This could be an attractive model to attract graduate students who are particularly interested in program evaluation as a concentration or area of focus, offering more advanced learning possibilities in the form of a fellowship within the setting of the stakeholders. This would be beneficial to the client as well, especially those with limited funding, no budget, or no capacity for evaluation.

Implications for Practice

Benefits to the overall program included meaningful communications of results that go beyond the written report. Graduate students were able to reflect, in real time, on their ability to translate theory into practice in an authentic learning environment. Program evaluation added value to the program, credibility, and positionality for funding. Focus on accountability and results framed by intended outcomes, made the program and process more satisfying for the program coordinators and the evaluators.

Implications for Educational and Community Leaders

Considering our current data-driven K-12 educational environment that is dominated by high-stakes testing and rapidly advancing technology, it is critical that schools and graduate programs alike build evaluation capacity that is grounded in STEM and advanced academic programming. It engages all participants equally. A shift in thinking for educators is fostered, to focus on the things that they can control, such as instructional delivery and technique, giving more ownership in the process as well. Implications for educational and community leaders include engaging educators as researchers (action research) and empowering organizations to build capacity to internally evaluate programs with the benefit of familiarity of program, processes, and stakeholders.

The authors strongly recommend a call to action to transform STEM pedagogy and programming practices. Community- and school-based program coordinators of STEM projects and initiatives should research program evaluation courses and programs within their neighboring university. Reach out to the department and/or professor responsible for teaching the course to see if they include a service-learning approach in their class. Some universities may have a centralized service-learning office that could provide you with that information as well. If no such program exists, propose a partnership with the professor. Use this chapter as a reference to support your proposal. Next, prepare yourself for the partnership.

Recommendations

Ill-developed programs do not consider evaluation of the program until after the program has been developed or problems have occurred to warrant improvement that then lead to actions for change. However, in this strategy, it is probable that administrators will seek immediate actions for a focused problem and not fully examine or appreciate what is actually occurring to create the problem, leading to ineffective long-term solutions for change. It is imperative that program developers and facilitators have a well-developed and conceptual understanding of the complete situation or issues at hand to include what the value, interest, and background considerations are for the targeted participants. This creates a dynamic environment that compels formative evaluation and summative evaluations processes that must be designed at the forefront of the program. The authors offer the following general recommendations as a framework for participant-oriented evaluation between university and community/school partners that also builds capacity among all stakeholders.

Recommendation #1: Backwards design/planning. Begin with the desired outcomes and use reverse engineering, or backward planning (see also Loberti & Dewsbury, 2018; Vidal, Dos Santos, & Carvalho, 2016; Ziegenfuss & LeMire, 2019), to organize proposed components and activities of the program that are intended to foster the desired outcomes. Think, first, about the evaluation process and instruments for measuring to what extent those goals have been met. Program developers who are in the process of designing a STEM program should incorporate backwards planning with an evaluation process conceptualized at the beginning of that program to guide the alignment and focus of the program. If a program is already underway and does not include this critical component, it is not too late to begin this process, and it should be incorporated into the program as soon as possible.

Recommendation #2: Develop a theory of action. Informed by backwards design and planning, develop a theory of action. Use a visual representation, or logic model, for your theory of action. Educators and/or faculty members, as "clients" of the program evaluation service, should generate concept maps that reflect issues or problems that negatively impact STEM recruitment, retention, and achievement of underrepresented students within your district that are also tied to student assessment data. These are essential to determine the focus of the program evaluation. Be prepared to share them with your potential partners.

Recommendation #3: Collaboration. Coordinate a meeting to develop a compact and/or services agreement. The program coordinators should be prepared to meet with the professor and the student team to share the vision as well as negotiate shared roles and responsibilities during the evaluation process. Share the theory of action with a university partner. Meet with the university faculty and graduate team of evaluators. Revise the theory of action as needed, and solidify the evaluation process. With the theory of action as your blueprint, determine the measurement strategies (surveys, interviews, observations, etc.).

Recommendation #4. Foster data-driven decision making. Even though the graduate students are responsible for developing data collection instruments, the faculty, as primary users of the evaluation, should create their own teaching and learning surveys as well. These can be used to assist educators in their own decision making.

Conclusion

Program evaluation fosters systematic intentional changes to improve teaching and learning outcomes. The PEACE GEMS evaluation process fostered a process that included constant self-examination, observation, and reflection. It also developed relationships of different cultures in partnership. Program evaluators must consider the impact and not simply the program in which they are evaluated, adding additional value and meaning to their own learning.

The concept of participant-oriented program evaluation as an immersion approach to teaching program evaluation at the graduate level could very well serve as a template for standardizing and fostering authentic practice among all stakeholders in the evaluation process. Coupled with AERA's and NSF's commitment to foster evaluation capacity building (ECB) as well, STEM learning and programming could be enhanced.

REFLECTION QUESTIONS

1. The authors strongly recommend a call to action to transform STEM pedagogy and programming practices. How does program evaluation address this call to action as well as underachievement in gifted and STEM education programs?

2. Describe the individual differences, including purpose and processes, for program evaluation, formative meta-evaluation, and summative meta-evaluation. How do these, collectively, strengthen overall program evaluation?

3. Conduct a research of graduate-level program evaluation courses within your neighboring university. List the course and contact information for the department and professor responsible for teaching the course. Is there a centralized service learning office that could provide you with that information as well?

4. Use this chapter as a reference and support to craft a proposal for partnership to conduct a program evaluation of your STEM or gifted education program (it can be formal or informal).

5. The authors recommend that K-12 schools or specific programs prepare themselves for a partnership in program evaluation. What tasks are included to do this and what might it "look like" in your district and/or program?

References

American Education Research Association (AERA). (2002). Evaluation Training Program (ETP). Available at: https://www.nsf.gov/awardsearch/showAward?AWD_ID=0092641

Arthur, N., Collins, S., McMahon, M., & Marshall, C. (2009). Career practitioners' views of social justice and barriers for practice. *Canadian Journal of Career Development, 8*(1), 22–31.

Brand, B. D., Brascia, K., & Sass, M. (2019). The community outreach model of service learning: A case study of active learning and service learning in natural hazards, vulnerability, and risk class. *Higher Learning Research Communications, 9*(2). Available at: https://eric-ed-gov.libproxy .txstate.edu/contentdelivery/servlet/ERICServlet?accno=EJ1233498

Caldwell, L. D., & Bledsoe, K. L. (2019) Can social justice live in a house of structural racism? A question for the field of evaluation. *American Journal of Evaluation, 40,* 6–18.

Collins, K. H. (2018). Confronting colorblind STEM talent development: Toward a contextual model for Black student STEM identity. *Journal of Advanced Academics, 29*(2), 143–168. https:// doi.org/10.1177/1932202X18757958

Collins, M. A., Totino, J., Hartry, A., Romero, V. F., Nava, R., & Pedroso, R. (2020). Service-learning as a lever to support STEM engagement for underrepresented youth. *Journal of Experiential Education, 43*(1), 55–70.

Davenport, C., Dele-Ajayi, O., Emembolu, I., Morton, R., Padwick, A., Portas, A., Sanderson, J., Shimwell, J., Stonehouse, J., Strachan, R., Wake, L., Wells, G., & Woodward, J. (2020). A theory of change for improving children's perceptions, aspirations and uptake of STEM careers. *Research in Science Education,* 2020 (online, April 20). doi:10.1007/s11165-019-09909-6.

Fitzpatrick, J. L., Sanders, J. R., & Worthen, B. R. (2011). *Program evaluation: Alternative approaches and practical guidelines* (4th ed.). Pearson, Inc.

Fournier, D. M. (1994). Review of the program evaluation standards: How to assess evaluations of educational programs. *Journal of Educational Measurement, 31*(4), 363–367.

Hodge, A., Matthews, M., & Squires, A. (2017). Eureka! STEM: Hands-on, minds-on STEM for at-risk middle school girls. In L. R. Wiest, J. E. Sanchez, & H. G. Crawford-Ferre (Eds.),

Out-of-school-time STEM programs for females: Implications for research and practice, vol. I: *Longer-term programs* (pp. 127–154). Information Age Publishing.

JCS EEE (Joint Committee on Standards for Educational Evaluation) (1994). *The program evaluation standards: How to assess evaluations of educational programs* (2nd ed.). Sage.

Lardier, J. D. T., Opara, I., Garcia-Reid, P., & Reid, R. J. (2021). The mediating role of ethnic identity and social justice orientation between community civic participation, psychological sense of community, and dimensions of psychological empowerment among adolescents of color. *The Urban Review: Issues and Ideas in Education*, *53*(3), 403–423. https://doi-org.libproxy.txstate.edu/10.1007/s11256-020-00573-z

Loberti, A., & Dewsbury, B. (2018). Using a logic model to direct backward design of curriculum. *Journal of Microbiology and Biology Education*, *19*(3), 1–4. doi:10.1128/jmbe.v19i3.1638.

Martinek, T. (2017). Enhancing youth development programs through logic model assessment. *Revista Internacional de Ciencias del Deporte*, *13*(49), 302–316.

National Science Board & National Science Foundation. (2020). Science and engineering indicators 2020: The state of U.S. science and engineering. NSB-2020-1. NSF. Available at: https://ncses.nsf.gov/pubs/nsb20201/

Reinholz, D. L., & Andrews, T. C. (2020). Change theory and theory of change: What's the difference anyway? *International Journal of STEM Education*, *7*(2), 1–12. https://doi.org/10.1186/s40594-020-0202-3

Stufflebeam, D. L. (1999). Program evaluations metaevaluation checklist. Available at: https://wmich.edu/sites/default/files/attachments/u350/2014/eval_model_metaeval.pdf

Stufflebeam, D. L. (2012). Program evaluations metaevaluation checklist. Available at: https://usaidlearninglab.org/sites/default/files/resource/files/mod3_summary_meta_evaluation_checklist_1.pdf

Varelas, M., Martin, D. B., & Kane, J. M. (2013). Content learning and identity construction: A framework to strengthen African American students' mathematics and science learning in urban elementary schools. *Human Development*, 55(5–6), 319–339. https://doi-org.libproxy.txstate.edu/10.1159/000345324

Vidal, T. C., Dos Santos, S. C., & Carvalho, R. S. (2016). PBL-tutor canvas: A tool based on backward design to plan PBL in computing education. *2016* IEEE Frontiers in Education Conference (FIE), Frontiers in Education Conference (FIE), 2016 IEEE, 1–8. https://doi-org.libproxy.txstate.edu/10.1109/FIE.2016.7757386

Wiggins, G., & McTighe, J. (1997). *Understanding by design*. Association for Supervision and Curriculum Development.

Wiggins, G., & McTighe, J. (2005). *Understanding by design*. (2nd ed.). Association for Supervision and Curriculum Development.

Yarbrough, D. B., Shula, L. M., Hopson, R. K., & Caruthers, F. A. (2010). *The program evaluation standards: A guide for evaluators and evaluation users* (3rd ed.). Corwin Press.

Ziegenfuss, D. H., & LeMire, S. (2019). Backward design: A must-have library instructional design strategy for your pedagogical and teaching toolbox. *Reference & User Services Quarterly*, *59*(2), 307–112.

Identifying and Serving Culturally, Linguistically, Economically, and Geographically Diverse Gifted Underachievers*

Rachel U. Mun, Grizelle Larriviel, Robin Johnson,

and Andrea Stewart

Introduction

Underachievement in gifted students, particularly for the *culturally, linguistically ,economically, diverse* (CLED), and geographically diverse is a conundrum that has perplexed parents, educators, and researchers alike. Too often, students who show some of the greatest promise to succeed academically, perform at levels that do not reflect their inner potential (Reis & McCoach, 2000; Snyder & Wormington, 2020). Gifted underachievement can be conceived as an unanticipated discrepancy between the fulfillment of potential and performance based on ability (National Association for Gifted Children, n.d.). The reasons for underachievement can be complicated and look different for different students (Siegle, 2018; White et al., 2018). Some cases of underachievement result from lack of opportunity, while others are more voluntary. Gifted learners may be said to be underachieving when the opportunities are present, yet the students fail to manifest potential, and the presence of learning differences has been ruled out (Siegle, 2018; White et al., 2018).

Gifted underachievers may see school experiences as lacking meaning (McCoach & Siegle, 2003). These learners need to see value in assignments and believe that they can apply effort and succeed (Siegle, 2018). CLED gifted learners often face the additional struggle of marginalization resulting from deficit thinking and microaggressions. For these students, underachievement can involve a combination of involuntary and voluntary factors – involuntary in that many in this group have difficulty accessing programming and resources, and voluntary in the sense of a set of learned behaviors to an academic environment that does not match their needs or abilities. When student needs are not adequately met, students become unmotivated and disengaged.

Furthermore, when considering underachievement in CLED populations, the phenomenon denotes unique attributes that include cultural identity, language,

DOI: 10.4324/9781003369578-16

topography, and socioeconomic status. Diverse populations underachieve for various reasons and identifying the specific factors within a population determines the relevant resolutions. Thus, recognizing barriers within the gifted program for these underrepresented communities will narrow the appropriate interventions and methods to reduce the increasing excellence gap between their White and/or dominant language-speaking peers (Mun et al., 2020; Siegle et al., 2016; Subotnik et al., 2012).

In this chapter, we review literature for CLED and geographically diverse populations in gifted education who are also underachieving. In particular, we consider barriers and best practices in gifted identification and services. We also examine ways to foster a successful learning environment and discuss the importance of essential gifted pedagogy to address student needs for these special populations.

Literature Review

Underachievement in Gifted Racially and Culturally Diverse Students

According to the 2020 U.S. Census, the population characteristics have not only expanded but also shifted in population rates. Racial and cultural groups include Hispanic or Latino (18.5%), African-American (13.4%), Asian (5.9%), American Indian and Alaska Native (1.3%), and Native Hawaiian and other Pacific Islanders (0.2%) (U.S. Census Bureau, 2020). Students are classified under these broad labels in American schools, which may mask heterogeneity related to heritage, national origin, culture, language, and social capital. This has led some scholars to advocate for the need for disaggregation of racial/ethnic data within the field of gifted education to better address student needs (Yeung & Mun, 2022). Furthermore, many racially and culturally diverse students are underrepresented in gifted programming, experience difficulty performing well on major tests, earn below-average grades, and resign before completing their academic journey (Hodges et al., 2018; Moore III et al., 2005). Although there is limited research, the theme of underrepresentation and underachievement appears to be connected due to unintentional bias in schools and identification practices (Reis & McCoach, 2000).

Gifted psychometrics use unidimensional instruments that forgo flexibility and heterogeneity during the screening process, disregarding behavioral elements of underachievement. Cut-off scores and heavy reliance on standardized cognitive assessments are some of the most significant barriers for special populations in gifted education (Mun, 2016; Mun, Ezzani, Lee, et al., 2021; Siegle et al., 2016). When schools or districts use standardized tests as the major criterion to participate in gifted programs, biases are formed against traditionally underrepresented students who may exhibit the attitude-achievement paradox, a positive mindset toward learning but lower performance commonly found in African-American students (Reis & McCoach, 2000). These students are also less likely to be referred by teachers for gifted assessment as they may not exhibit behaviors considered gifted by the dominant culture (Mun et al., 2016).

African-American Students

The attitude-achievement paradox is specific to the achievement gap between African-Americans and White students, presenting three main influences; literature and research attribute *school*, *family*, and *social* influences as part of the discussion (Ford et al., 2008). School influences include subtractive factors, such as lack of curricular rigor, few technology-supported learning opportunities, and using less qualified and experienced gifted educators serving African-Americans. When away from school, family, and community, factors include limited parental availability or participation. There is minimal opportunity for how often parents read to their children in their early years in this setting, and inversely, more time is allocated to watching television or other activities. Lastly, the social variable impacts two significant learning strands: engagement, and motivation. African-American students may have an oppositional attitude about academic performance. They believe that speaking Standard American English (SAE), valuing high grades, and studying can be interpreted as "acting White" rather than "acting Black." Such views contribute to peer pressure and increase the achievement gap. The dominant White culture and linguistics present in assessment development, curriculum objectives, and its delivery by K-12 educators may create a school culture that rejects African-American Vernacular English and perceives an incapacity or illegibility when identifying students for gifted services (Smith, 2019).

Additionally, the lack of representation of African-American educators in the gifted classroom and awareness of the African-American culture by White educators can lead to feelings of inadequacy, and lack of motivation. The social and emotional variables affect identity and norm assimilation through the development stages, becoming a juggling act as well as a power struggle within the African-American student and manifesting in poor performance, recruitment, and retention rates (Ford et al., 2011).

Hispanic-American Students

The Hispanic community is a diverse group of 20 Spanish-speaking countries and one U.S. Commonwealth (i.e., Puerto Rico) (U.S. Census Bureau, 2020); not to be confused with Latino, or Latinx that involve all Latin American countries, including non-Spanish-speaking territories (Salinas & Lozano, 2019). Hispanics come from five different continents, many historical and political backgrounds, and have immigrated for involuntary and voluntary reasons. The fundamental commonality is language. However, values within family settings range from high educational aspirations to basic levels due to socioeconomic status. Additionally, many different motivational achievement gap issues exist from generation to generation based on the Hispanic narratives (Crosnoe, 2005). Research within gifted education is either homogeneous or identifies the most significant Hispanic demographic subgroups in the United States: Mexicans, Puerto Ricans, and Cubans (U.S. Census Bureau, 2020). Like African-Americans, they are underrepresented in gifted education in 43 out of the 50 states (Yoon & Gentry, 2009). Analysis of any kind related to gifted education and student underachievement variables for Hispanic subgroups is also woefully lacking (Henfield et al., 2016).

Those who have recently immigrated and are in the process of learning a new language also grapple with how to navigate the American educational system. Hispanics will find themselves unfamiliar with the process more often than those who are second- or third-generation Hispanic-Americans. Starting with the recruitment process, criteria like standardized test scores may disqualify Hispanics from participating in gifted services based on poor educational circumstances (Hurt, 2018; Vega & Moore III, 2018). Teacher awareness of cultural backgrounds can also be a limiting factor for referrals due to biases if students struggle with language acquisition (Lohman, 2005; Mun et al., 2020). Moreover, the familiarization of a district's demographic subgroups is necessary to provide appropriate interventions, community support, and a meaningful curriculum to meet their needs.

Underachievement varies from generation to generation, with the family experience being a contributing factor. For example, research does explain that Mexican-Americans who struggle with English generally underachieve and are different from those who become proficient or are second- and third-generation immigrants (Rumberger & Larson, 1998). However, many Mexican-Americans struggle with home-school obligations. Often, families working to provide for their children can lead students to become caretakers for siblings at home and miss school for a variety of reasons; and depending on migration within the United States for work opportunities, there are significant gaps that occur in education from K-12 (Landale et al., 1998; Matute-Bianchi, 1986; Valenzuela, 1999). Mexican-Americans have strong academic beliefs, but immediate economic circumstances take precedence. Non-Hispanic teachers in and outside the gifted programs may consider the difference in the value system as a reason for underachievement and, without the proper support or training, omit interventions, enrichment opportunities, identification, and intentionally or unintentionally circumvent adjusting their views (Reis & McCoach, 2000).

Native American Students

Native Americans over the last 40 years have been considered a homogeneous ethnicity despite great variation (Gentry et al., 2014). Native Americans (i.e., American Indians, Alaska Natives, Native Hawaiians, Chamorros, American Samoans, Canadian First Nations, and Indigenous societies from Mexico and Central and South America) have many Tribes and live on 56 million acres across the continental US and 44 million acres in Alaska (NCAI, 2020). The United States recognizes 574 Indigenous Nations, meaning 574 subcultures under the Native American umbrella (NCAI, 2020). When looking for underachievement in gifted research across these diverse ranges, the limitations are great, and the number of studies are few. Hence, American Indian/Alaska Natives are among the most underrepresented in gifted education.

Undoubtedly, the shortage of data and overgeneralization of the Tribes make it challenging to assess the underlying issues for gifted Native American underachievers. Obstacles include ill-preparedness for elementary education rigor, competitive performance school culture with an increased focus on grades, and less one-on-one attention from teachers toward student progress. These factors are related to the oversight of sociocultural influences, including family relationships, student-teacher, peer relationships, and anxiety with school transition. Gifted education currently undermines the focus needed on these determinants, especially for those living on reservations (Willeto, 1999) who potentially become unidentified and less likely to graduate from high school (Aud et al., 2011; Yoon & Gentry, 2009).

The data that does exist directs gifted underachievement primarily toward motivation, specifically within the Navajo Indians. The Navajo People refer to themselves as the Diné, the largest Nation (NCAI, 2020). Many of the Diné are from rural, mountainous areas living in poverty. The poverty/rural barrier is considered a "triple threat" to students' academic potential. A decrease in their lack of readiness in elementary (Bauch, 2001; Bryant Jr., 2019) is the first peril leading to unidentified academic gifted or talent potential during the screening process. The estrangement of their culture by the educational system is the second attributed threat. Those identified to enter the program may not be motivated to stay and drop out due to feelings of alienation and lack of peer representation in the classroom. According to the National Center of Educational Statistics (NCES), the 2017 dropout rate was 9.5% for Native Americans and Alaska Natives, the highest of all race/ethnic groups; 8.1% for Pacific Islander, 8.0% for Hispanics, 6.4% for African-Americans, 4.2% for Anglo-Americans, and 1.9% for Asian (National Center of Educational Statistics, 2018). Remote areas are the third threat. The infrastructure in these Indigenous communities is below formal education, where gifted programs would be considerably underfunded, without primary resources and technology (Gentry & Fugate, 2012).

Asian-American Students

In 2018, Asian-Americans made up over 5% of the total US population (U.S. Census Bureau, 2018) and were the most rapidly growing racial or ethnic group between 2000 and 2010 with a growth rate of 72% between 2000 and 2015 (Hoeffel et al., 2012; Lopez et al., 2017). Asian-Americans have diverse cultures, languages, histories, and sociopolitical conditions with heritages in over 20 countries in East Asia (China, Japan, and Korea), South Asia (Bangladesh, Bhutan, India, Nepal, Pakistan, and Sri Lanka), and Southeast Asia (Cambodia, Indonesia, Laos, Malaysia, Myanmar, the Philippines, Singapore, Thailand, and Vietnam) (U.S. Census Bureau, 2018; Wu et al., 2019). Despite this heterogeneity, they are often perceived as a homogeneous group and stereotyped as "model minorities" or successful in academic programs, overrepresented in gifted and talented programs, self-sufficient, and mentally healthy (Mun & Yeung, 2022; Museus & Kiang, 2009).

Asian-Americans are a unique category as they are the only racial/ethnic group considered to be overrepresented along with their White peers in gifted programs (Yoon & Gentry, 2009). This overrepresentation can be partly attributed to mainstream cultural behaviors perceived by teachers as favorable (i.e., mastery of English, classroom participation) and the acculturation process by families into mainstream American education. However, the needs of Asian subgroups such as Southeast Asian students who do not perform as well academically are often overlooked (Yoon & Gentry, 2009). The oversight due to the model minority stereotype prevents many in gifted education from addressing the individual struggles of Asian-American students who experience many of the same difficulties as other marginalized populations (Mun & Yeung, 2022; Yu, 2006). Additionally, Asian-American students, especially in high school, will experience added anxiety, feelings of incompetence, and denial of intervention services (Gym, 2011; Oyserman & Sakamoto, 1997).

In one case study, Andy, a Korean high school student, felt that he fell through the cracks because no one saw the at-risk indicators (attendance, tardiness, grades, transfer of school history, and disengagement) until he was in the process of withdrawing (Wexler & Pyle, 2012). He believed the model minority stereotype contributed to the lack of intervention and sabotaged his potential. As academic achievement is one of many identifiers in the gifted program, teachers did not provide opportunities to improve educational outcomes (enrichment, extra study opportunities, credit recovery, acceleration programs). Andy felt nobody cared and that he was on his own. He adds that the competitive nature of his first high school and the lack of family and school climate contributed to him dropping out, creating personal and family shame.

Underachievement in Gifted Linguistically Diverse/English Learners

English Learners (ELs) are the most rapidly growing student population in the United States. This group represents speakers of over 350 different languages. They are diverse in socioeconomic status, acculturation, levels of English proficiency, and learning needs (Siegle et al., 2016). Included in this group are immigrants, children of immigrants, and Native Americans. The majority have been born in the United States to parents who do not speak English. Many recent immigrant families are coming from Asia and Latin America (Mun et al., 2020). The largest group of ELs consists of Hispanic students (Castellano & Frazier, 2011).

If underachievement is defined as a discrepancy between actual performance and potential performance, potential performance is revealed through test results (McCoach & Siegle, 2003; Siegle, 2018). On a personal level, students caught in a cycle of underachievement lose their sense of self-efficacy and fail to develop a sturdy academic self-concept. This is important because students' life accomplishments are more closely related to school performance than raw IQ (Siegle, 2018). ELs are often discussed as an "at-risk" population and viewed as requiring remediation to build language proficiency (Brulles et al., 2011). And yet, for many ELs, potential goes undetected due to issues with language proficiency and testing. Gifted ELs too often find themselves cut off from opportunities to develop their talents and find school unmotivating. They become stuck in a path of underachievement. It is not always fully evident to teachers that the student is underachieving due to issues with language proficiency and testing.

One source of underachievement in this student population is the failure of the school system to identify and nurture talent correctly. Gifted ELs face the unique challenge of having to adjust to a new culture at the same time as learning a new language. Language learning status can mask their giftedness, resulting in many in this student population going unidentified. Unfortunately, some teachers still operate under deficit thinking models, impacting referrals for this student population (Ford et al., 2008; Mun et al., 2020). Teachers may also assume that students need to develop proficiency in English before participating in gifted programming. However, the "proficiency-first" attitude only hinders student progress and marginalizes students (Hurt, 2018). In addition, teachers may have a stereotyped view of what giftedness should look like that is based on their cultural expectations. This causes teachers to overlook students whose class participation styles may be more reserved, without considering that the students' cultures emphasize different values (Aguirre & Hernandez, 2011). Further, ELs may not feel comfortable expressing themselves in English due to their level of proficiency and remain quiet for that reason (Mun et al., 2020).

Testing as a method for placement and identification presents more issues. Students' English learning status often results in the students not receiving the level of instruction that matches their abilities; thus, their standardized cognitive ability scores often fail to accurately reflect their true understanding (Brulles et al., 2011; Mun et al., 2016). Students may also lack familiarity with cultural references on the test items themselves and incorrectly interpret questions or answer choices (Brulles et al., 2011). The validity of the tests is then questionable. It has been shown that test scores correlate with socioeconomic status and parental education, which calls into question their reliability (Mun et al., 2020). While non-verbal tests offer alternatives and can reduce bias, there are also questions about their efficacy and efficiency (Mun et al., 2020).

All of these factors contribute to the exclusion of ELs from gifted programming. The most rapidly growing student population is also the least represented group in gifted education (Mun et al., 2020). While English Learners constitute 10% of public school enrollment, they account for only 3% of gifted program enrollment (Hamilton et al., 2020). When gifted students are not supported by their need for rapid learning, do not have adequate resources, or teachers are unresponsive to the gifted student's potential, student development is hindered (Cross & Coleman, 2014; Vega & Moore III, 2018). The result is diminished self-esteem and self-efficacy, disengagement with school, and underachievement.

Underachievement in Gifted Rural Students

Sixty million people (about 19% of the US population) live in rural America (U.S. Census Bureau, 2017). Rural areas are isolated areas of population that lie outside urban clusters (U.S. Census Bureau, n.d.). The U.S. Census Bureau (n.d.) defined rural school districts as those not in a metropolitan area. Schools in rural areas are geographically isolated from towns and cities. In the United States, approximately 9.6 million students are enrolled in rural school districts. That equates to 20% of the student population (Puryear & Kettler, 2017).

The underachievement of gifted and talented students in rural schools can often be attributed to the school system's structure. The educational experience of gifted and talented students is often different from the educational experience of gifted and talented students in urban and suburban schools. Challenges, which can vary from school district to school district, can be divided into three categories: educational factors, socioeconomic factors, and cultural factors (Burton, 2011).

Educational factors can lead to underachievement. Many rural gifted and talented students lack appropriate educational opportunities (Burton, 2011; Van Tassel-Baska & Hubbard, 2016). A low student population and lack of funding per student requires school districts to appropriate funds for mandated curriculum rather than specialized classes. Educators are often required to assume multiple roles, leaving little time for training or differentiation for gifted and talented students (Van Tassel-Baska et al., 2020). The continuous lack of challenging opportunities within the education system can lead to less school enjoyment and underachievement for gifted learners (Burton, 2011).

Socioeconomic factors play a role in underachievement. Gifted students struggle to choose between loyalty to their community or leaving the community to have access to abundant opportunities in urban areas. Remaining in the community can limit gifted students to opportunities traditionally found within the community (Lewis & Boswell, 2020). Choosing to leave in order to move to urban areas is a difficult decision (Burton, 2011). The majority of young people who leave rural communities never permanently return (Howley et al., 2009).

Cultural factors play an important role in the educational decisions of gifted and talented students. Traditionalism is important to rural communities. Careers outside of the community may be discouraged (Lewis & Hafer, 2007, as cited in Burton, 2011). In addition, stereotypes of people who live in rural communities can inhibit young people from pursuing careers outside of the community, as rural people are often stereotyped as backwards, ignorant, and unintelligent (Howley et al., 2009; Lawrence, 2009).

Gagné's Model of Giftedness and Talents describes the relationship between high potential and high performance where gifts are transformed into talent (Gagné, 2008, as cited by Merrotsy, 2013). Disadvantaged children can fall short in developing talents due to low socioeconomic status, racial/ethnic status, or living in isolated communities. Gifted students from disadvantaged backgrounds can become invisible (Merrotsy, 2013). Invisible gifted and talented students can appear to be average students yet are underachievers because their potential goes unnoticed. Their parents and teachers may be unaware of their potential; therefore, their individual academic needs are unmet (Merrotsy, 2013). Underachievement may not be an appropriate term for invisible gifted students because the cause for not meeting one's potential can often be placed on the school system rather than the student (Funk-Werblo, 2003).

Invisibility can result from several causes. First, a rigid and inflexible curriculum does not allow students to explore their potential (Ashman & Merrotsy, 2011). Second, the students may live in a culture that does not support intellectual pursuits. Third, the student may lack cultural capital and social capital that encourage pursuing passions and different career choices from those available in rural communities. Finally, the students may fear failure while searching for self-identity or have low self-efficacy due to being forced to choose between community and career (Ashman & Merrotsy, 2011).

Implications for Practice

Supporting Underachieving Gifted CLED and Geographically Diverse Students

Supporting underachieving gifted CLED and geographically diverse students requires developing a gifted program with essential components to address learning needs, equitable identification methods, strong academic support, and building relationships between schools, family, and the community. It is also about educators in the United States moving beyond seeing schools as "English-only" spaces (Early & Kendrick, 2020). Professional development needs to cultivate culturally responsive teaching and linguistically responsive teaching, demonstrating respect and positive attitudes toward diversity (Charity Hudley & Mallinson, 2017; Muniz, 2020; Pereira & de Oliveira, 2015). Ladson-Billings' (1995) theory of culturally relevant pedagogy is defined as a "theoretical model that not only addresses student achievement but also helps students to accept and affirm their cultural identity while developing critical perspectives that challenge inequities that schools (and other institutions) perpetuate" (p. 469). The model is a promising approach with CLED students and has been found to support academics and cultural identity. Attention to cultural awareness and effort toward building relationships from the pedagogical community and their specific diverse demographics are also indispensable to avert underachievement and underrepresentation.

The actions taken to move beyond the current climate will require the cooperation of all stakeholders, especially those in leadership (Ezzani et al., 2021). The first step is through gifted programming supporting district demographics. A culture-inviting environment in schools that leads to building communities between schools, families, and their community is the second step. The final step is a professional development community that goes beyond cultural awareness toward cultural implementation. A list of recommendations to support CLED and geographically diverse students in elementary and in secondary education includes:

1. Build gifted programming around equity and student support, including talent development.
2. Develop a culturally relevant and responsive curriculum to affirm student identity.
3. Provide multiple pathways for identification and advanced learning in and out of school.

4. Build relationships with families and support parents/caretakers through services that allow family learning opportunities, collaboration, and cultural contributions.

5. Provide family education and resources on gifted children's needs, characteristics, and services.

6. Build a professional development community that goes beyond cultural awareness toward cultural implementation.

Addressing barriers using these recommendations can help reduce and eliminate the achievement gap and retain students in the gifted program. The relationship between students, parents, and schools continues to be a key component. According to the focus groups in Mackety and Linder-VanBerschot's (2008) qualitative study, establishing home and school-oriented involvement can begin to remove barriers. A responsibility to attend school events, open lines of communication on both sides, and participate and support their child by showing an interest can motivate students to succeed. Sociocultural intelligence in gifted education must serve potentially gifted students and provide services for them through the educational trail. In conjunction with student services, gifted education must collaborate with CLED and geographically diverse families through awareness of values and historical knowledge so that the school culture is respectful and inviting.

For ELs, teachers should be encouraged to view their students as bilingual and bicultural instead of being deficient in English (Szymanski & Lunch, 2020). Educators need to be aware of the strengths that ELs possess. Students who demonstrate the ability to integrate two cultural systems through code-switching have greater levels of cognitive and social flexibility (Bialystok, 2011; Blom et al., 2017; Hughes et al., 2006). Further, bilingual students often also have greater mental flexibility (Garcia & Michie, 2005). One area of focus is the development of academic language. Students can be allowed the use of translation applications and dual-language texts (Early & Kendrick, 2020). Research suggests that teaching academic language should not be the target goal. Instead, the focus should be on use, making meaning, allowing students to use the language of the discipline to effectively communicate (Schall- Leckrone, 2016; Swanson, 2016). Students need ample practice; therefore, class activities where teachers do less talking are preferable (Garcia & Michie, 2005). Inquiry-based pedagogies provide opportunities for students to learn content and practice language skills at the same time through discussion (Early & Kendrick, 2020). Socratic-style discussions also help foster self-efficacy and help students self-identify as successful students (Verplaetse, 2014). Teachers can also pair ELs with fluent peers for various activities (Pereira & de Oliveira, 2015) and provide scaffolding such as sentence starters, context-specific words, or guided textual analysis (Schall -Leckrone, 2016). There are various ways that ELs can be supported in learning advanced content and language alongside each other so that the gifted learner gets the benefit of a curriculum with complexity and depth.

In addition, teachers should aim to incorporate the student's home language. Teachers who are practicing linguistically responsive teaching should also strive to create an inclusive learning environment. For example, ELs may be asked to share essential vocabulary from their first language so that the whole class can share in the learning experience. Students also should be given a choice and opportunity to explore interests in their home language (Aguirre & Hernandez, 2011). Offering choice increases student engagement. Allowing students opportunities to use their home language shows the value of their native language and diversity in the classroom (Bianco & Harris,

2014; Early & Kendrick, 2020). Interestingly, teachers may actually hinder students' cognitive development in approaching their first language only as a tool for learning English instead of building on prior knowledge and experiences (Garcia & Michie, 2005). Affirming student identity is an integral part of providing the social and emotional support that students need to succeed academically (Muniz, 2020).

We should also keep in mind that effective gifted and talented programs implement essential components. Essential components include acceleration and flexibility, differentiation of curriculum, quality teaching, and out-of-school learning opportunities. Critical components should be implemented regardless of school district, grade level, or location (Van Tassel-Baska, 2005). Acceleration is a cost-effective way to meet the instructional needs of gifted students (Assouline et al., 2015; Olthouse, 2015). Children learn at different rates in different subjects (Van Tassel-Baska, 2005). Flexibility with curriculum in lieu of the mandated "magic age" for grade level and curriculum levels traditionally adopted by most schools is more effective in meeting learning needs. Early entrance programs into kindergarten and high school accommodate different rates at which children learn (Van Tassel-Baska & Hubbard, 2016). Subject content acceleration at all levels should be available for all gifted learners. Research shows positive outcomes of acceleration opportunities on enhanced learning, motivation, and extracurricular engagement (Assouline et al., 2015; Van Tassel-Baska, 2005.

A differentiated curriculum is essential for all gifted students. Curriculum should link the general curriculum to more advanced, complex, in-depth, and creative instruction differentiated to meet individual student's needs. Problem-based learning is a way to connect the general curriculum with real-world problems. Problem-based learning allows students to inquire about and study a problem while locating data sources relevant to the problem (Van Tassel-Baska, 2005). In rural schools, students can use problem-based learning to solve world problems and problems within their school or community. Advanced study, if differentiated to meet individual students' needs, is an effective way to specialize curriculum for CLED and geographically diverse gifted students (Gagnon & Mattingly, 2016; Van Tassel-Baska, 2005). Distance learning is an alternative to traditional gifted and talented services. Distance learning aims to expand services and give gifted and talented students an opportunity to extend learning beyond the classes offered at their schools (Washington, 1997). Distance learning is flexible and can be tailored to the needs and schedules of individual students (Adams & Cross, 2000). Finally, out-of-school learning opportunities are essential components of an effective gifted and talented program (Van Tassel-Baska, 2005). Most colleges and universities offer summer and weekend programs where students can select programs of interest. Many local libraries have summer programs. Internships help older students pursue areas of interest. If the community and school work together, a powerful experience can be created for gifted learners.

Conclusion

The United States of America has become the refuge and the home of many people. For some, it has become a place of personal and environmental identity battles due to involuntary assimilation. Regardless of the causes, their ipseity is in question when looking at gifted research in underachievement that is minimal and perceived as a homogeneous society. As Benjamin Franklin echoed, misperceptions, stereotypes, and biases have created many doubts about ability and created barriers to success.

Retention and consideration for underachieving and underrepresented populations require removing obstacles in gifted education and addressing preventative measures. A gifted and talented program that fosters positive student self-concepts of our CLED and geographically diverse learners will help them thrive within the school and community. If teachers respect students' abilities, value their interests, and work to meet their unique needs, the bond created will help students succeed and fulfill their potential. Ensuring students' academic as well as social and emotional needs are met is not affected by geography (Gear, 1984) but by the teachers, parents, and community members who guide them (Mun, Ezzani, & Yeung, 2021). We must acknowledge the special assessment and learning needs within these various subgroups and ensure our colleagues in the field understand the idiosyncrasies and cultural nuances within this population.

Furthermore, key components include a need for cultural awareness and cultural intelligence of the population being served (Lockhart & Mun, 2020). Understanding political, economic, and geographical aspects of the family and societal backgrounds will provide insight into building relationships inside the school structure and the community (Castellano & Frazier, 2011). Educator self-awareness of biases and the educational transition from a singular or static curriculum view to multiple perspectives of historical accounts (Jimenez, 2019) and instructional methods can influence motivation, engagement, and language acquisition. Hence Franklin's, "doubt about ability" could include "myths about ability" (e.g., model minority stereotype).

Finally, the personal acknowledgment of a student's social, emotional, and academic needs is crucial. Students from diverse cultures face enormous pressures from family, peers, and school. The root cause of students struggling with achievement will have underlying factors that come from one or all of these environments. Immediate attention by gifted educators and appropriate interventions like mentorship, fellowship activities, collaborative events between all three partnerships will provide opportunities for communication, family educational processes, and a culture of inclusivity (Murray et al., 2020). Through a support system of all three communities, we can recognize CLED and geographically diverse students' gifts and talents and help them realize their full academic potential.

REFLECTION QUESTIONS

1. How does the culture of your school support diverse learners and recognize their strengths? In what ways does the culture of your school contribute to some students not being seen?

2. How familiar are you with the cultural context of your classroom or school demographics? How has your personal experience contributed to possible implicit or explicit biases? In what ways can the school or district increase equity in gifted student identification and services, especially for diverse students who may underachieve?

3. Are there programs or plans in place to help build parent knowledge of the educational system and gifted services for parents to advocate for their children and seek resources for identification? What are some organizations (e.g., family center, liaison) within the school or district to provide support and resources for marginalized groups?

4. How might giftedness look for different students (ELs, ethnic/racial groups, rural/urban students)? How can you scaffold lessons to support these students? How can their language and culture be included in your lessons?

5. What are your assumptions about underachievement and giftedness? How do your cultural expectations shape your view of giftedness? How can you construct your curriculum to include more student choice and voice? What are some ways you can help students experience meaningful learning to increase engagement with learning? How does the culture of your school support diverse learners and recognize their strengths?

6. How can acceleration in the gifted curriculum be implemented for bilingual and bicultural students in your school and district? How often are cross-cultural enrichment opportunities included in a culturally responsive curriculum?

References

Adams, C. & Cross, T. (2000). Distance learning opportunities for academically gifted students. *The Journal of Secondary Gifted Education, 9*(2), 88–96. doi:10.4219%2Fjsge-1999–61

Aguirre, N. M., & Hernandez, N. E. (2011). Differentiating the curriculum for gifted second language learners: Teaching them to think. In J. Castellano & A. D. Frazier (Eds.), *Special populations in gifted education: Understanding our most able students from diverse backgrounds* (pp. 273–286). Prufrock Press.

Ashman, A., & Merrotsy, P. (2011). Learners and environments. In A. Ashman & J. Elkins (Eds.), *Education for inclusion and diversity* (4th ed.; pp. 63–95). Pearson Education Australia.

Assouline, S. G., Colangelo, N., Van Tassel-Baska, J., & Lupkowski-Shoplik, A. (Eds.). (2015). *A nation empowered,* vol. 2: *Evidence trumps the excuses holding back America's brightest students.* University of Iowa Press.

Aud, S., Hussar, W., Kena, G., Bianco, K., Frohlich, L., Kemp, J., & Tahan, K. (2011). *The condition of education* 2011. National Center for Education Statistics. Available at: https://nces.ed.gov /pubs2011/2011033.pdf

Bauch, P. A. (2001). School-community partnerships in rural schools: Leadership, renewal, and a sense of place. *Peabody Journal of Education, 76*(2), 204–221. https://doi.org/10.1207/ s15327930pje7602_9

Bialystok, E. (2011). Reshaping the mind: The benefits of bilingualism. *Canadian Journal of Experimental Psychology, 65*(4), 229–235. https://doi.org/10.1037/a0025406

Bianco, M., & Harris, B. (2014). Strength-based RTI: Developing gifted potential in Spanish-speaking English language learners. *Gifted Child Today, 37*(3), 169–176. https://doi.org/10 .1177/1076217514530115

Blom, E., Boerma, T., Bosma, E., Cornips, L. M. E. A., & Everaert, E. (2017). Cognitive advantages of bilingual children in different sociolinguistic contexts. *Frontiers in Psychology, 8,* 1–12. https:// doi.org/10.3389/fpsyg.2017.00552

Brulles, D., Castellano, J. A., & Laing, P. C. (2011). Identifying and enfranchising gifted English language learners. In J. Castellano & A. D. Frazier (Eds.), *Special populations in gifted education: Understanding our most able students from diverse backgrounds* (pp. 305–316). Prufrock Press.

Bryant Jr., J. A. (2019). Killing Mayberry: The crisis in rural American education. *The Rural Educator, 29*(1). https://doi.org/10.35608/ruraled.v29i1.947

Burton, J. (2011). Small ponds: The challenges facing gifted students in rural communities. *Northwest Journal of Teacher Education, 9*(1), 113–118. https://doi.org/10.15760/nwje.2011.9.1.11

Castellano, J. A., & Frazier, A. D. (2011). *Special populations in gifted education: Understanding our most able students from diverse backgrounds.* Prufrock Press.

Charity Hudley, A. H., & Mallinson, C. (2017). "It's worth our time": A model of culturally and linguistically supportive professional development for K-12 STEM educators. *Cultural Studies of Science Education, 12*(3), 637–660. https://doi.org/10.1007/s11422-016-9743-7

Crosnoe, R. (2005). The diverse experiences of Hispanic students in the American educational system. *Sociological Forum, 20*(4), 561–588. https://doi.org/10.1007/s11206-005-9058-z

Cross, T. L., & Coleman, L. J. (2014). School-based conception of giftedness. *Journal for the Education of the Gifted*, *37*(1), 94–103. https://doi.org/10.1177/0162353214521522

Early, M., & Kendrick, M. (2020). Inquiry-based pedagogies, multimodalities, and multilingualism: Opportunities and challenges in supporting English learner success. *The Canadian Modern Language Review/La revue canadienne des langues vivantes*, *76*(2), 139–154. https://www.muse.jhu.edu/article/754998.

Ezzani, M. D., Mun, R. U., & Lee, L. E. (2021). District leaders focused on systemic equity in identification and services for gifted education: From policy to practice. *Roeper Review*, *43*(2), 112–127. https://doi.org/10.1080/02783193.2021.1881853

Ford, D. Y., Grantham, T. C., & Whiting, G. W. (2008). Culturally and linguistically diverse students in gifted education: Recruitment and retention issues. *Exceptional Children*, *74*(3), 289–306. https://doi.org/10.1177/001440290807400302

Ford, D. Y., Moore, J., & Scott, M. (2011). Key theories and frameworks for improving the recruitment and retention of African American students in gifted education. *The Journal of Negro Education*, *80*(3), 239–253. http://www.jstor.org/stable/41341131

Funk-Werblo, D. (2003). The invisible gifted child. In F. J. Smutny (Ed.), *Underserved gifted population*. Hampton Press.

Gagnon, D. J., & Mattingly, M. J. (2016). Advanced placement and rural schools: Access, success, and exploring alternatives. *Journal of Advanced Academics*, *27*(4), 266–284. https://doi.org/10.1177/1932202X16656390

Garcia, E. E., & Michie, G. (2005). *Teaching and learning in two languages: Bilingualism and schooling in the United States*. ProQuest Ebook Central. Available at: https://ebookcentral.proquest.com

Gear, G. H. (1984). Providing services for rural gifted children. *Exceptional Children*, *50*(4): 326–331. https://doi.org/10.1177/001440298405000405

Gentry, M., & Fugate, C. M. (2012). Gifted Native American students: Underperforming, under-identified, and overlooked. *Psychology in the Schools*, *49*(7), 631–646. https://doi.org/10.1002/pits.21624

Gentry, M., Fugate, C. M., Wu, J., & Castellano, J. A. (2014). Gifted Native American students. *Gifted Child Quarterly*, *58*(2), 98–110. https://doi.org/10.1177/0016986214521660

Gym, H. (2011). Tiger moms and the model minority myth. *Rethinking Schools*, *25*(4), 34–35.

Hamilton, R., Long, D., McCoach, D. B., Hemmler, V., Siegle, D., Newton, S. D., Gubbins, E. J., & Callahan, C. M. (2020). Proficiency and giftedness: The role of language comprehension in gifted identification and achievement. *Journal for the Education of the Gifted*, *43*(4), 370–404. https://doi.org/10.1177/0162353220955225

Henfield, M. S., Woo, H., & Bang, N. M. (2016). Gifted ethnic minority students and academic achievement. *Gifted Child Quarterly*, *61*(1), 3–19. https://doi.org/10.1177/0016986216674556

Hodges, J., Tay, J., Maeda, Y., & Gentry, M. (2018). A meta-analysis of gifted and talented identification practices. *Gifted Child Quarterly*, *62*(2), 147–174. https://doi-org.libproxy.library.unt.edu/10.1177/0016986217752107

Hoeffel, E. M., Rastogi, S., Kim, M. O., & Shahid, H. (2012). *The Asian population: 2010*. United States Census Bureau. Available at: http://www.census.gov/prod/cen2010/briefs/c2010br-11.pdf

Howley, A., Rhodes, M., & Beall, J. (2009). Challenges facing rural schools: Implications for gifted students. *Journal for the Education of the Gifted*, *32*, 515–536. https://doi.org/10.1177/016235320903200404

Hughes, C. E., Shaunessy, E. S., Brice, A. R., Ratliff, M. A., & McHatton, P. A. (2006). Code switching among bilingual and limited English proficient students: Possible indicators of giftedness. *Journal for the Education of the Gifted*, *30*(1), 7–28. https://doi.org/10.1177/016235320603000102

Hurt, J. W. (2018). "Why are the gifted classes so white?" Making space for gifted Latino students. *Journal of Cases in Educational Leadership*, *21*(4), 112–130. https://doi.org/10.1177/1555458918769115

Jimenez, R. M. (2019). Community cultural wealth pedagogies: Cultivating autoethnographic counternarratives and migration capital. *American Educational Research Journal*, *57*(2), 775–807. https://doi.org/10.3102/0002831219866148

Ladson-Billings, G. (1995). Toward a theory of culturally relevant pedagogy. *American Educational Research Journal*, *32*(3), 465–491. https://doi.org/10.3102/00028312032003465

Landale, N. S., Oropesa, R. S., & Llanes, D. (1998). Schooling, work, and idleness among Mexican and non-Latino White adolescents. *Social Science Research*, *27*(4), 457–480. https://doi.org/10.1006/ssre.1998.0631

Lawrence, B. K. (2009). Rural gifted education: A comprehensive literature review. *Journal for the Education of the Gifted*, *32*(4), 461–494. https://doi.org/10.1177/016235320903200402

Lewis, K. D., & Boswell, C. (2020). Perceived challenges for rural gifted education. *Gifted Child Today*, *43*(3), 184–198. https://doi-org.libproxy.library.unt.edu/10.1177/1076217520915742

Lockhart, K., & Mun, R. U. (2020). Developing a strong home-school connection to better identify and serve culturally, linguistically, and economically diverse gifted students. *Gifted Child Today*, *43*(4), 231–238. https://doi.org/10.1177/1076217520940743.

Lohman, D. F. (2005). The role of nonverbal ability tests in identifying academically gifted students: An aptitude perspective. *Gifted Child Quarterly*, *49*(2), 111–138. https://doi.org/10.1177/001698620504900203

Lopez, G., Ruiz, N. G., & Patten, E. (2017, September 8). Key facts about Asian Americans, a diverse and growing population. Pew Research. Available at: https://www.pewresearch.org/fact-tank/2017/09/08/key-facts-about-asian-americans/

Mackety, D. M., & Linder-VanBerschot, J. A. (2008). *Examining American Indian perspectives in the Central Region on parent involvement in children's education*. Institute of Education Sciences (IES) Home Page, a part of the U.S. Department of Education. Available at: http://ies.ed.gov/ncee/edlabs/projects/project.asp?projectID=159

Matute-Bianchi, M. E. (1986). Ethnic identities and patterns of school success and failure among Mexican-descent and Japanese-American students in a California high school: An ethnographic analysis. *American Journal of Education*, *95*(1), 233–255. https://doi.org/10.1086/444298

McCoach, D. B., & Siegle, D. (2003). Factors that differentiate underachieving gifted students from high-achieving gifted students. *Gifted Child Quarterly*, *47*(2), 144–154. https://doi.org/10.1177/001698620304700205

Merrotsy, P. (2013). Invisible gifted students. *Journal of Talent Development and Excellence*, *5*(2), 31–42. http://iratde.com/index.php/jtde/article/view/33

Moore III, J. L., Milner, H. R., & Ford, D. (2005). Underachievement among gifted students of color: Implications for educators. *Theory into Practice*, *44*(2), 167–177. https://doi.org/10.1207/s15430421tip4402_11

Mun, R. U., Ezzani, M. D., Lee, L. E., & Ottwein, J. K. (2021). Building systemic capacity to improve identification and services in gifted education: A case study of one district. *Gifted Child Quarterly*, *65*(2), 132–152. https://doi.org/10.1177%2F0016986220967376

Mun, R. U., Ezzani, M. D., & Yeung, G. (2021). Parent engagement in identifying and serving diverse gifted students: What is the role of leadership? *Journal of Advanced Academics*, *32*(4), 533–566. https://doi-org.libproxy.library.unt.edu/10.1177/1932202X211021836

Mun, R. U., Hemmler, V., Langley, S. D., Ware, S., Gubbins, E. J., Callahan, C. M., McCoach, D. B., & Siegle, D. (2020). Identifying and serving English learners in gifted education: Looking back and moving forward. *Journal for the Education of the Gifted*, *43*(4), 297–335. https://doi.org/10.1177/0162353220955230

Mun, R. U., Langley, S. D., Ware, S., Gubbins, E. J., Siegle, D., Callahan, C. M., McCoach, D. B., & Hamilton, R. (2016, December). *Effective practices for identifying and serving English learners in gifted education: A systematic review of the literature*. National Center for Research on Gifted Education (NCRGE).

Mun, R. U., & Yeung, G. (2022). Gifted identification and services for Asian Americans. In J. A. Castellano & K. L. Chandler (Eds.), *Identifying and serving diverse gifted learners: Meeting the needs of special populations in gifted education* (pp. 164–187). Prufrock Press and the National Association for Gifted Children.

Muniz, J. (2020, September 23). Culturally responsive teaching: A reflection guide. *New America*. Available at: https://www.newamerica.org/education-policy/policy-papers/culturally-responsive-teaching-competencies/

Murray, B., Domina, T., Petts, A., Renzulli, L., & Boylan, R. (2020). "We're in this together": Bridging and bonding social capital in elementary school PTOs. *American Educational Research Journal, 57*(5), 2210–2244. https://doi.org/10.3102/0002831220908848

Museus, S. D., & Kiang, P. N. (2009). Deconstructing the model minority myth and how it contributes to the invisible minority reality in higher education research. *New Directions for Institutional Research, 142,* 5–15. https://doi.org/10.1002/ir.292

National Association for Gifted Children. (n.d.). Underachievement. Available at: https://www.nagc.org/resources-publications/resources/achievement-keeping-your-child-challenged/underachievement

National Center for Education Statistics. (2018). Dropout rates. A part of the U.S. Department of Education. Available at: https://nces.ed.gov/fastfacts/display.asp?id=16.

National Congress of American Indians (NCAI). (2020). Tribal nations & the United States: An introduction. Available at: https://www.ncai.org/about-tribes.

Olthouse, J. M. (2015). Improving rural teachers' attitudes towards acceleration. *Gifted Education International, 31*(2), 154–161. https://doi.org/10.1177/0261429413507177

Oyserman, D., & Sakamoto, I. (1997). Being Asian American. *The Journal of Applied Behavioral Science, 33*(4), 435–453. https://doi.org/10.1177/0021886397334002

Pereira, N., & de Oliveira, L. C. (2015). Meeting the linguistic needs of high-potential English language learners: What teachers need to know. *Teaching Exceptional Children, 47*(4), 208–215. https://doi.org/10.1177/0040059915569362

Puryear, J. S., & Kettler T. (2017). Rural gifted education and the effect of proximity. *Gifted Child Quarterly, 61*(2), 143–152. doi:10.1177/0016986217690229

Reis, S. M., & McCoach, D. B. (2000). The underachievement of gifted students: What do we know and where do we go? *Gifted Child Quarterly, 44*(3), 152–170. https://doi.org/10.1177/001698620004400302

Rumberger, R. W., & Larson, K. A. (1998). Student mobility and the increased risk of high school dropout. *American Journal of Education, 107*(1), 1–35. https://doi.org/10.1086/444201

Salinas, C., & Lozano, A. (2019). Mapping and recontextualizing the evolution of the term *Latinx*. *Critical Readings on Latinos and Education,* 216–235. https://doi.org/10.4324/9780429021206-14

Schall-Leckrone, L. (2016). Genre pedagogy: A framework to prepare history teachers to teach language. *TESOL Quarterly, 51*(2), 358–382. https://doi-org.libproxy.library.unt.edu/10.1002/tesq.322

Siegle, D. (2018). Understanding underachievement. In J. L. Roberts, T. F. Inman, & J. H. Robins (Eds.), *Introduction to gifted education* (pp. 323–336). Prufrock Press.

Siegle, D., Gubbins, E. J., O'Rourke, P., Langley, S. D., Mun, R. U., Luria, S. R., Little, C. A., McCoach, D. B., Knupp, T., Callahan, C. M., & Plucker, J. A. (2016). Barriers to underserved students' participation in gifted programs and possible solutions. *Journal for the Education of the Gifted, 39*(2), 103–131. https://doi.org/10.1177/0162353216640930

Smith, P. (2019). "How does a Black person speak English?" Beyond American language norms. *American Educational Research Journal, 57*(1), 106–147. https://doi.org/10.3102/0002831219850760

Snyder, K. E., & Wormington, S. V. (2020). Gifted underachievement and achievement motivation: The promise of breaking silos. *Gifted Child Quarterly, 64*(2), 63–66. https://doi.org/10.1177/0016986220909179

Subotnik, R. F., Olszewski-Kubilius, P., & Worrell, F. C. (2012). A proposed direction forward for gifted education based on psychological science. *Gifted Child Quarterly, 56*(4), 176–188. https://doi.org/10.1177/0016986212456079

Swanson, J. D. (2016). Drawing upon lessons learned: Effective curriculum and instruction for culturally and linguistically diverse gifted learners. *Gifted Child Quarterly, 60*(3), 172–191. https://doi.org/10.1177/0016986216642016

Szymanski, A. T., & Lynch, M. (2020). Educator perceptions of English language learners. *Journal of Advanced Academics, 31*(4), 436–450. https://doi.org/10.1177/1932202X20917141

U.S. Census Bureau. (2017). What is rural America? Available at: https://www.census.gov/library/stories/2017/08/rural-america.html

U.S. Census Bureau. (2018). About race. Available at: https://www.census.gov/topics/population/race/about.html

U.S. Census Bureau. (2020, October 16). Population. Available at:. https://www.census.gov/topics/population.html.

U.S. Census Bureau. (n.d.), Rural America. Available at: https://mtgis-portal.geo.census.gov/arcgis/apps/MapSeries/index.html?appid=49cd4bc9c8eb444ab51218c1d5001ef6#:~:text=At%20the%20time%20of%20the,areas%20of%20the%20United%20States

Valenzuela, A. (1999). Subtractive schooling: U.S.-Mexican youth and the politics of caring. *Contemporary Sociology*, *30*(2). https://doi.org/10.2307/2655442

Van Tassel-Baska, J. (2005). Gifted programs and services: What are the nonnegotiables? *Theory into Practice*, *44*(2), 90–97. https://doi.org/10.1207/s15430421tip4402_3

Van Tassel-Baska, J., & Hubbard, G. F. (2016). Classroom-based strategies for advanced learners in rural settings. *Journal of Advanced Academics*, *27*(4), 285–310.

Van Tassel-Baska, J., Hubbard, G. F., & Robbins, J. I. (2020). Differentiation of instruction for gifted learners: Collated evaluative studies of teacher classroom practices. *Roeper Review*, *42*(3), 153–164. https://doi.org/10.1080/02783193.2020.1765919

Vega, D., & Moore III, James L., (2018). Access to gifted education among African-American and Latino males. *Journal for Multicultural Education*, *12*(3), 237–248. http://dx.doi.org.libproxy.library.unt.edu/10.1108/JME-01-2017-0006

Verplaetse, L. S. (2014). Using big questions to apprentice students into language-rich classroom practices. *TESOL Quarterly*, *48*(3), 632–641. https://doi-org.libproxy.library.unt.edu/10.1002/tesq.179

Washington, M. F. (1997). Real hope for the gifted. *Gifted Child Today Magazine*, *20*(6), 20–22. https://doi.org/10.1177/107621759702000607

Wexler, J., & Pyle, N. (2012). Dropout prevention and the Model-Minority stereotype: Reflections from an Asian American high school dropout. *The Urban Review*, *44*(5), 551–570. https://doi.org/10.1007/s11256-012-0207-4

White, S., Graham, L., & Blaas, S. (2018). Why do we know so little about the factors associated with gifted underachievement? A systematic literature review. *Educational Research Review*, *24*, 55–66.

Willeto, A. A. A. (1999). Navajo culture and family influences on academic success: Traditionalism is not a significant predictor of achievement among Navajo youth. *Journal of American Indian Education*, *38*(2), 1–24.

Wu, Y., Outley, C., & Matarrita-Cascante, D. (2019). Cultural immersion camps and development of ethnic identity in Asian American youth. *Journal of Youth Development*, *14*(2), 166–182. https://doi:10.5195/jyd.2019.708

Yeung, G., & Mun, R. U. (2022). A renewed call for disaggregation of racial and ethnic data: Advancing scientific rigor and equity in gifted and talented education research. *Journal for the Education of the Gifted*, *45*(4), 319–351. https://doi.org/10.1177/01623532221123795

Yoon, Y., & Gentry, M. (2009). Racial and ethnic representation in gifted programs. *Gifted Child Quarterly*, *53*(2), 121–136. https://doi.org/10.1177/0016986208330564

Yu, T. (2006). Challenging the politics of the "Model Minority" stereotype: A case for educational equality. *Equity & Excellence in Education*, *39*(4), 325–333. https://doi.org/10.1080/10665680600932333

★ **Note:** The use of terms RCELD (racially, culturally, ethnically, and linguistically different) in Chapter 10 and the use of the term CLED (culturally, linguistically, and economically diverse) in Chapter 12, more specifically, refer to individuals who have been historically discriminated against, marginalized and disadvantaged based on race/ethnicity, language, or socio-economic statuses as well as represent diversity that poses a standard, value, and/or belief, that is considered to be divergent or vastly "different" from and, oftentimes challenged by, the White middle class culture that dominates and influences the typical perspectives, policies, and practices in education. The contributors for this book acknowledge that the basic definitions of the words "different" and "diverse" separate from these acronyms simply make inference to a range of representation determined by distinctive characteristics within the named group or subgroup.

Translating Athletic Talent for Gifted Identification and Academic Talent Development
Expanding Frasier's New Window for Looking at Gifted Children

Tony D. D. Collins II and Kristina Henry Collins

Collins' Unhyphenated Scholar-Athlete Story

Soon after I started my public education career in elementary school, I was identified as a gifted student with high academic achievement and also identified as a talented athlete who lettered in football and track. I also went on to play Division 1 football and track at a highly-selective, private research 1 institution with a full academic scholarship that also paid for my master's program. As such, I chose to refer to myself as a scholar athlete (without the hyphen). I found that the hyphen, which is meant to link two words together, did not appropriately describe how the K-12 educational system approached my identity. I found that many of my classroom teachers, including those who had been trained and taught courses in gifted education programs, lacked awareness about the fundamentals of sports and how to recognize and/or assess the cognitive skills that I used in sports, and they used that against me as they maintained stereotypical views about athletes. In addition, my coaches often would criticize my "overthinking" on the field even though my position as a linebacker is often referred to as "the quarterback of the defense," insinuating that it too is a position that requires a high level of cognitive ability. In both settings, the teachers and coaches wanted me, for the most part, to drop the other identifier attached to the hyphen when I was in their spaces. My coaches would often proclaim that I was not "maximizing my potential" and teachers would blame my multiple interests as a reason for my academic "underachievement," both of which I found to be very subjective observations as judgments that did not include my voice for how I saw my life unfolding.

— Tony Collins II

DOI: 10.4324/9781003369578-17

Introduction

As a Black male who stood at 6'1" at 230 lbs., Tony Collins' scholar athlete identity and expectations for his future positioned him in very singular ways (aka Split Identity Development; Beamon & Bell, 2006) through the narrative that has been told and retold in American society (Collins, 2017; Collins II, 2021). We assert that the teachers' and coaches' claims of untapped potential and underachievement could have been addressed, had the educators responsible for nurturing his gifts and talents also understood the compounded impact of intersectionality (Crenshaw, 2018), a construct which explains the interconnected nature of social categorizations as they apply to a given individual or group, and, when regarded with a deficit lens, creates overlapping and interdependent systems of discrimination or disadvantage. Furthermore, in Tony's case, we posit that peak performance, or maximum potential, occurs when he tapped into the intersection of his academic gifts, athletic talents, and artistic interests (see Figure 13.1).

This chapter is grounded in the supposition that competitive, varsity-level sports serve as a source that has not been utilized to identify academically gifted students who may have been overlooked and/or underserved, due to the discriminatory nature in which educational systems have historically regarded and identified giftedness in students. There are some scholar-athletes whose kinesthetically gifted traits may otherwise go undervalued and be misperceived as physical talent only. As such, this is a lost opportunity to translate these strengths for academic success, resulting in incomplete development of the gifts and talents, which is another form of underachievement that affects potential in and out of the classroom.

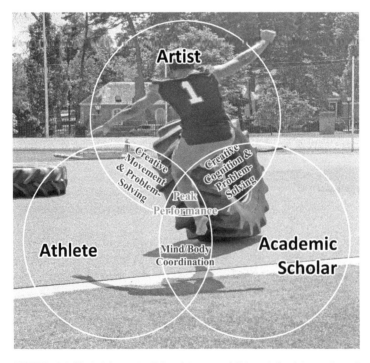

FIGURE 13.1 Maximizing potential: existence and living at the intersection of multicultural self-concepts and multipotentiality.

Source: Tony Collins II (2022). Author's personal photo. Printed with permission. Photo Credit: Danae Theocharaki.

Untapped Potential: Student-Athletes' Diverse Expression of Gifts and Talents

It is well documented that Black students are underrepresented in gifted and advanced programming (U.S. DOE & Office of Civil Rights, 2020). It is also common knowledge that African-Americans are well represented in American sports at all competition levels, including professional. Both of these facts, together, feed a stereotype about African-Americans, and particularly African-American males – since the emergence of eugenics as a study, "racist scientists have often equated physical prowess with intellectual deficiency" (Entine, 2001, p. iv). Thus arose the term "dumb jock" and the cultural practice of defining athletes solely by their physical abilities and strengths. For example, the focus on the running ability of a quarterback such as Michael Vic, Cameron Newton, and Lamar Jackson often overshadows the intellectual skillset often noted when speaking about White quarterbacks. Intellectual and cognitive strengths and traits like theirs become undervalued, and education professionals do not recognize and/or acknowledge these strengths during competition. If the educational professional cannot recognize diverse expressions of gifts and talents, then they will not be able to develop and nourish them. Moreover, as the next step after recognition of a scholar-athlete's intellectual and cognitive strengths, the educators must be competent enough to translate athletic skillset into academic and potential development. This is important to complement the personal development of the student-athlete since academic achievement is a requirement for eligibility to play in all school-based amateur sports, and all kinesthetic talent includes a cognitive component that enhances the physical abilities. In addition, an increased awareness will positively impact educators' value and priority for holistic identification of diverse talents in multiple settings, particularly in those environments that are readily accessible and already being performed within the scope of the educational setting.

Understanding Athletic Skills Using Frasier et al.'s (1995) TABs Assessment Tool

Recognizing and understanding the cognitive aspect of the gifts and talent of student-athletes can serve as a resource for gifted recruitment and identification of so many students, especially Black students, who are often overlooked for the gifted programs. This will help move past the stereotype (and stereotype threat) that sometimes come with being a student-athlete. With no widespread, and agreed-upon definition of giftedness, we focus on the concept of skill/skillset, and what it means to be a skilled player. Dictionary.com (2020) defines a skill as a person's ability to do something, and a skillset is the range of these abilities. Sports require players to possess certain skills. American football even classifies skilled positions, implying a requirement of cognitive abilities for them more than for other players. For example, there are three skilled positions on the offense and three on the defense. One of the most obvious and most recognized offensive skilled positions is the quarterback, as mentioned above. On the defensive side, the linebacker skilled position is comparable to the quarterback, and is referred to as "the quarterback of the defense." A linebacker is expected to manage the defensive strategies as the quarterback does to the offense. These and other skilled positions (i.e., wide receiver, running back, cornerback, and safety) require physical and cognitive skills. These skillsets are very similar to the traits, aptitudes, and behaviors (TABs) that are valued in an academic or classroom setting, and they are transferable.

Frasier et al.'s (1995) TABs assessment tool has been used to identify and develop gifted students with math-specific talents, ADHD, multilingual language learners, and more (Lovecky, 1999). Collins (2009) developed and adopted Frasier's TABs as an evaluation tool to assess student progress in academic places, leadership, and community service in a magnet school program for gifted and highly talented academic students. Students, mentors, and teachers were required to use TABs to measure students' skill levels (the scale used was: not addressed; formally introduced; systematically developing; applied by learner) for required and expected TABs. However, competency is required in educators to recognize and translate athletic skills, or TABs, to academic traits for the purpose of nurturing them in the classroom.

Collins (2020b) developed the Scholar Ballers Assessment Tool (SBAT; see Table 13.1). This evaluation instrument was designed to identify giftedness of student-athletes through the traits, aptitudes, and behaviors displayed through their on-field cognitive skills that can be translated for academic development. It shows alignment of Athletic TABs to Academic TABs within Frasier's Framework. A completed SBAT assessment, by trained evaluators, serves as a more inclusive and equitable screening method (1) to support student-athletes referred for gifted education, and/or (2) to confirm the validation of Frasier's TABs as an identification tool to recommend student-athletes, as an underrepresented subgroup, for gifted identification and programming services. This validated evaluation tool can also be replicated and put into practice for other sports, consistent with the sample for the desired population. The following are focused questions that we have posed and continue to explore as a guide to address underachievement in the context of underserved students and undervalued talent.

1. Can educators identify, understand, and serve diverse expressions of gifts and talents?
2. Are athletic TABs similar to academic TABs?
3. Can athletic TABs be validated for translation as academic strengths?
4. Can athletic TABs be nurtured for success in the classroom?

The Scholar Baller (SB) Construct

In sports, as students make forward progress through educational levels, a higher level of skill and talent must be exhibited. Highly competitive sports such as football are one of many extra-curricular activities that can serve as a great source for collecting evidence on the gifts and talent of students. At the highest level of football is the National Football League (NFL), for those who are deemed elite athletes. Students get to this level through the National Collegiate Athletics Association pipeline, starting at middle/high school. Harrison et al. (2010) defined a Scholar-Baller (SB; hyphenated) as a person who is educated and participates in extra-curricular sports; they later developed SB as model and a program. Dexter et al. (2021) reconceptualized and extended the Scholar-Baller model to present its dual strategy capacity to offer characterized support for academic success of student-athletes, particularly gifted Black males; these factors (pre-college experiences, goals and commitment, academic and social environment integration, and cultural inclusion) are used by gifted educators to forge a

TABLE 13.1 Collins' (2020) Scholar-Ballers Assessment Tool (SBAT)

TABs category	Definition and general description	Academic achievement (Collins, 2009)	Leadership	Athletic skillset
Motivation	Evidence of desire to learn Forces that initiate, direct and sustain individual or group behavior in order to satisfy a need or attain a goal	Manages time and activities for task completion	Engages and addresses situational gaps within groups	Extremely high level of self-expectations and standard of achievement. Understands and plays individual role toward overarching team goal.
Interests	Intense interests (sometimes unusual) Activities, avocations, objects, etc., that have special worth or significance and are given special attention	Explores topics beyond scope of learning (self-efficacy)	Serves as an "expert" in a particular area for peers	Intense attention toward several sports; unusual in-depth knowledge about several teams and players – stats, background, position, etc.
Communication skills	Highly expressive with words, numbers and symbols Transmission and reception of signals or meanings through a system of symbols, codes, gestures, language and numbers	Demonstrates appropriate use of resources and research material	Serves as a role model for others	Excellent non-verbal, physical communication and expression. Manages game and other players, player coach; exhibits high level of mental, physical and visual coordination.
Problem-solving ability	Effective (often inventive) strategies for recognizing and solving problems. Process of determining a correct sequence of alternatives leading to a desired goal or to successful completion or performance of a task.	Develops multiple and alternative methods of reaching solution	Foresees possible problems or issues of concern	Makes critical and immediate play adjustments in high-intensity and time-limiting situations
Memory	Large storehouse of information (on school or non-school topics) Exceptional ability to retain and retrieve information	Possesses a working and appropriate usage of vocabulary	Considered a source for information and guidance	Creates effective schemas for rapid learning; great retention and recall ability for extensive and comprehensive play books

(Continued)

Inquiry	Questions, experiments, explores Method of process of seeking knowledge, understanding or information	Constructs explanations and generates more questions as a result of research	Create learning opportunities for self and others	Constantly revisiting and replaying alternative action, reaction, and outcomes; understands individual role in context and in addition to all other positions and roles beyond their own
Insight	Quickly grasps new concepts and makes connections; senses deeper meanings Sudden discovery of the correct solution following incorrect attempts based primarily on trial and error	Understands the "bigger picture" of conceptual knowledge	Exhibits efficiency more often than sufficiency	Makes quick connections to grasp written, graphic, and audible directions and game strategies. Intuitive situational awareness – uses foresight and split-second "reading" skills for quick evaluation of opportunity, threat, within immediate and surrounding environment
Reasoning	Logical approaches to figuring out solutions. Highly conscious, directed, controlled, active, intentional, forward-looking and goal-oriented thought	Provides a clear methodology in problem-solving	Leads an activity from conception to completion	Demonstrates cognitive mindfulness of body control and expression. Implements appropriate transition between mindfulness and purposeful mindlessness of physical commitment and engagement
Imagination Creativity	Produces many ideas; highly original. Process of forming mental images of objects, qualities. Situations, or relationships which aren't immediately apparent to the sense; problem-solving through nontraditional patterns of thinking.	Interprets situations/ ideas in an unique manner	Achieves similar goals through various paths	Skillful at integrating impromptu ideas and strategy redesign; seeks novel and unique alternatives for compromised plays
Humor	Ability to synthesize key ideas or problems in complex situations in a humorous way; exceptional sense of timing in words and gestures	Connects abstract meaning and origin of ideas/content	Promotes and contributes to a healthy environment	Risk taker; willing to make mistakes for sake of learning; ability to quickly give perspective to, move beyond, and learn from mistakes; adapts and meshes quickly to diverse personalities, positions, and player backgrounds

Source: Collins (2020).

partnership with coaches and parents to support dual identity. While this strategy is useful, it still positions the student's academic identity as the primary or central identity, which does not help the teacher to appreciate the value of the students' athletic talent, which can equally support strengthening of academic skills. For the purpose of serving as a defined construct, a scholar-baller is a student-athlete, who demonstrates an ability to perform at a very high level of competition when compared to other players. Scholar-ballers are often overlooked for placement in gifted programs because their gifts and talents are unrecognized and/or undervalued by academic-focused educators and professionals. This is, in part, due to educational professionals' misperceived notion or not understanding the embedded cognitive attributes of kinesthetic ability.

Collins' Scholar-Baller Assessment Tool (SBAT)

Extending Frasier et al.'s (1995) traits, attitudes, and behaviors (TABs), which has been validated and proven to combat the disregard, in educational practice, for whole-child and holistic development, we introduce Collins' Scholar-Baller Assessment Tool (SBAT) as a new window through which educators can also address the disparaging lack of identification and underrepresentation of Black students in gifted education and advanced courses, especially for gifted Black males who are dominant figures in America's most popular sports (Entine, 2001).

The Validation of Collins' Scholar-Baller Assessment Tool (SBAT)

To translate theoretical knowledge into practical application in the field of education, the collected evidence must go through a validation process. Validation refers to the process of collecting validity evidence to evaluate the appropriateness of the interpretations, uses, and decisions based on assessment results. Following Cook and Hatala's (2016) eight-step practical approach for validation of educational assessments, Frasier's TABs were confirmed as key elements embedded in Collins' SBAT to generate useful interpretations for scoring, generalization, extrapolation, and implications/decisions (Kane, 2006). Extending Collins' (2009) evaluation tool for nurturing gifted and talented students' TABs in academic achievement, leadership, and community service, Collins' SBAT offers an added column with a description for athletic skillset (Athletic TABs) that aligns with academic achievement and leadership (Academic TABs). This alignment and the proposed interpretation confirm the cognitive nature of an athletic skillset, and suggest that the athletic factors in the scholar-baller model offer the same support that the academic factors offer. Table 13.1 shows the alignment of athletic TABs to academic TABs, which serves as the foundation for SBAT assessment criteria, and Table 13.2 highlights the select skillset that educators should possess to access and translate Athletic TABs into Academic TABs. [*Validation step 1: Define the construct and proposed interpretation.*]

For validation purposes, identified scholar-ballers were those who competed in a state or national championship game (MS, HS, collegiate), at the D1 general collegiate level and/or D2–D3 collegiate level at academically highly selective research institutions (HSRI). For consistency with existing evidence of gifted athleticism, championship 7 v 7 game play was used as the setting for this project. Championship-level game

TABLE 13.2 Select NAGC Standards used to guide educators in accessing and translating Athletic TABs

Professional Standard	Accessing and translating Athletic TABs
Standard 1: Learning and developing, through evidence based practices	
1.61: Educators design interventions for students to develop cognitive and affective growth that is based on research of effective practices, in order to reach outcome	■ Honor the unique experiences gained from Black students' academic and athletic involvement ■ Leverage the value and interest of sports to maximize academic development
1.6: Cognitive and Affective Growth. Students with gifts and talents benefit from meaningful and challenging learning activities addressing their unique characteristics and needs.	■ Integrate culturally responsive models of teaching into the curriculum ■ Infuse culture as a means to cultivate academic, athletic consumption into existing curriculum frameworks
Standard 2.1: Assessment through evidence based practice – Identification. All students in grades PK-12 have equal access to a comprehensive assessment system that allows them to demonstrate diverse characteristics and behaviors that are associated with giftedness.	
2 2.1.1: Educators develop environments and instructional activities that encourage students to express diverse characteristics and behaviors that are associated with giftedness	■ Empower and affirm Black student-athletes to personify their academic and athletic identities into one ■ Foster a more positive convergence of gifted Black students' academic and athletic identities ■ Translate athletic talents as a tool for academic development and achievement
2.1.2: Educators provide parents/guardians with information regarding diverse characteristics and behaviors that are associated with giftedness for the result of outcome	■ Cultivate more positive educational outcomes and career options for gifted Black athletes (i.e., academic and athletic scholarships) ■ Collaborate with parents and coaches in integrated talent development ■ Holistic talent development for increased opportunity to be a gifted scholar-athlete in college

play ensures observation of scholar–ballers who are considered highly cognitive, based on progression in rank and eliminating all other competitive players.

The current observation rubric (Table 13.3) developed for Collins' SBAT was used to assess this level of performance in a simulated game of "7 v 7," which is a series of tasks and performances designed to assess the skilled positions within football. "7 v 7" competitions are often used during the spring and summer training season for football at all levels, including national championship tournaments whereby recruiters at the next level can observe them. As evidence for interpretation of academic skill and ability, SBs are able to showcase traits, aptitudes, and behaviors (TABs) through their kinesthetic ability in a simulated game activity that sufficiently shows a level of cognitive processing that warrants further gifted identification testing.

Based on the construct and proposed interpretation (*Validation step 1*), a determination can be made about the recommendation and eligibility of an SB for further gifted identification testing based on the strengths shown during the SBAT assessment. The interpretation is based on the foundation grounded in the translation of Frasier et al.'s (1995) TABs within the context of athletic performance. The intended decision from this assessment is meant to (1) address inadequately recognized and under–identified talents of student-athletes by educators who lack the understanding of the significance in nurturing these talents in the classroom, and (2) build on the understanding that

TABLE 13.3 Offensive and Defensive Evaluation Rubric

Evaluator Competition Level							
Skilled Position							
Jersey #							
Motivation – verbal self-talk; non-management, <u>reactive</u> communication to encourage							
Communication - verbal and non-verbal proactive management of game/player							
Problem solving – play/body adjustment; fundamental and/or secondary read							
Interest – using in-depth of knowledge in ways that a coach would (non-play situations)							
Memory – memory recall from previous action; different variations of play; urgent <u>reactive</u> reposition of players							
Inquiry – reaction to oppositional cues							
Insight – non-fundamental situational awareness							
Reasoning – obvious mental decision for physical movement using foresight, consequences, and other cognitive analysis							
Imagination/Creativity – impromptu; unorthodox actions or training							
Humor – risk (e.g., deviations and high-stake risk; celebrations) ***Note*** - *Be careful not too many celebrations with exception of flagged - identified as humor (not imagination/creativity as perhaps seen in other settings – it's about the risk)*							
Total							

gifted athleticism is directly tied to cognitive ability. [*Validation Step 2: Explicit intended decisions.*]

A number of assumptions are made in the interpretation of the collected evidence and its use in the decision-making process. The assumptions for Collins SBAT are: (1) 7 v 7 allows SBs to showcase gifts and talents through standardized, replicated game play performance; and (2) scoring is similar across the board for trained evaluators; and that SBs who showcase an exceptional performance on the field have a cognitive ability that drives their athletic ability, comparable to those identified as gifted by traditional means. In response to these assumptions, the evidence features prioritized for validity were scoring, generalization, extrapolation, and implications. [*Validation Step 3: Define the interpretation-use argument, and prioritize needed validity evidence.*]

- *Scoring*: The rubric serves as a basis for the collection of data and is numerically represented to be interpreted for use in identification decision making. In order to ensure that the assessment is consistently translating skillset performance into numerical values that accurately represent the talent presented, calibration should always be conducted to ensure that the scoring rubric is understandable by evaluators. These trained evaluators submit similar results, and the SBAT identifies the relevant skills of scholar-ballers that are translatable in an academic or core curricular setting.

- *Generalization*: In order to show that the results of the assessment are able to be used in multiple facets, validation of the evidence is conducted through multiple observations of SBs in various skilled positions, over multiple 7 v 7 activities, and by multiple evaluators, trained in coaching and/or gifted programming. As priority for needed evidence, interpretation and reporting of the results should be aligned to other TABs-based assessment tools and their uses for gifted identification and service.

- *Extrapolation*: extrapolation is validity of Collins' SBAT because it is an extension of a pre-validated evaluation tool used to assess student progress in academic places, leadership and community service (Collins, 2009) using Frasier's TABs, which has also been validated, tested, and used with much success in identifying students overlooked by other means of identification.

- *Implications*: The SBAT has important and favorable effects on improving the quality of education of learners and creating more inclusive and equitable gifted and advanced learning programs. In addition, it serves as a practical professional development tool for educators in identifying and nurturing gifts and talents of underrepresented subgroups in culturally responsive ways that are likely to maximize the potential of each student. Evidence will ideally show that athletically gifted SBs exhibit TABs that can be nurtured for success in advanced and gifted programs.

Research Design

Video-recordings of 7 v 7 games, shared within the public domain, were used for observation to allow for easy access to evaluators who do not have access to those games behind a pay-wall used by recruiters and coaches. This also allowed for observation of SBs across multiple schools and regions of the country in an attempt to obtain a larger representation for exhibition and awareness of diverse talent to be considered for identification in gifted programs. Participants in the validation study serve as the base-level skillset for SBs. They range in age from 13–18 and were members of a national championship team for their age group and consisted of multiple races. Approximately 40 male scholar-ballers were evaluated during the assessment, observed in both offensive and defensive performance tasks. Skilled positions are already defined and identified by NCAA. However, as a translated definition to foster generalization and practical interpretation-use agreement, we offer the definition of skilled work to further explain these positions. Skilled work is defined as a job where the workers are required to use their judgment built from experience to make decisions based on measurements, estimations, reads, and/or calculations. Scholar-ballers, in these skilled positions, are asked to do skilled work in the athletic setting. The positions that we evaluated included defensive side (linebackers and defensive backs – safeties and cornerbacks) and offensive side (quarterbacks, wide-receivers, running backs, and tight-ends).

As a first step toward interpretation-use agreement (validation statements) and prioritizing validation evidence, the research design was determined. Collins' SBAT, as an adopted tool and assessment instrument, was designed through a thoughtful process identifying the best ways to assess the undervalued talents displayed by underrepresented students in gifted education as already validated and proven through Frasier's TABs. This tool is consistent with the design of Frasier's TABs, which is a more inclusive form of identification for unidentified gifted talents from minority populations and serves to significantly increase identification across all races. The traits, aptitudes, and behaviors designed to evaluate SBs' gifts and talents directly correlate to the Academy of Liberal Arts at Newton High School (ALANHS) students' leadership, community service, and academic gifts and talents that were identified and nurtured as required components for successful completion of that HS gifted program (Collins, 2009).

Three SBAT evaluators were trained using an informational PowerPoint, *Fostering dual identity*. They are also certified and trained in K-16 coaching (evaluators #1, #2) and/or in gifted education (evaluators #1, #3). Adapting the same process that Collins (2009) used to calibrate a clear understanding of TABs within the magnet school setting, a championship 7 v7 game was used as evidence to calibrate and triangulate the data collected by three trained evaluators in the validation process. For this video, the evaluation team was informed that one of the students had been referred for a gifted program and they were to use the SBAT as a screening tool to support this referral. As such, the evaluation focuses on the referred student-athlete, but used documented evidence of TABs in other players in conjunction with that of the referred student to also calibrate TABs in diverse students at the same level. Timestamps were used in this step to calibrate understanding of the tool and its definitions of each TAB within the context of 7 v 7. As a final appraisal, the ability of the evaluators to consistently and similarly identify TABs was substantiated and their appraisal of the referred student was triangulated as part of the validation process. As validated evidence, the tool should also serve as a qualifying assessment within a multiple criteria identification process. The validation study relied heavily on the extent to which the evaluators' identified TABs matched each other for this step in the validation process. Based on their evaluation, the student exhibited TABs consistent with gifted characteristics and should be considered for further testing.

Different from the first game, another video-recorded game was used as evidence for the post-calibrated assessment tool. For the other video, timestamps were used again to double-check understanding of TABs by each evaluator. However, since overlap and exhibition of different TABs may show up differently and in consideration of the fast pace of the game at this high level of competition, there was no requirement for evaluators' identification of TABs to match each other. Even though timestamps were used, they represent and should subsequently be denoted using tally marks to translate the identified TAB into a numerical representation. Since the tool is not meant to be used as a cutoff score, the value and qualification of the numerical representation should be determined by the local school in similar ways and following the same guidance found in the existing Frasier's FTAP guide (see Frasier et al., 1995). [*Validation Step 4: Identify candidate instruments and/or create/adapt a new instrument.*]

In light of existing validated assessment tools based on Frasier et al.'s (1995) TABs, there was no need to collect more evidence before the adoption of this instrument. However, we collected our own evidence during implementation of the validation study to solidify the process and directions for use of the SBAT, and to identify any important gaps between existing use and this new use for TABs. It is recommended that extensive training for evaluators is conducted to also ensure inter-rater reliability. These videos and their assessment (and others like them) can be used as exemplars for training prior to official assessments. [*Validation Step 5: Appraise existing evidence and collect new evidence as needed.*]

Findings

Practical issues with the use of SBAT include the prior training necessary to have evaluators who can assess TABs in an athletic setting. Prior knowledge or training in coaching and/or gifted programming increases the chances for inter-rater reliability that is acceptable to use the interpretation of the results for decision-making purposes. In addition, personal biases (e.g., adultification of students who show athletic talent) and system cultural views related to football (e.g., race-related biases about certain players in certain sports and positions) within our society and internally within the sport (e.g., the value that each side, defensive and offensive, as well as certain players bring to the game) should be addressed in the training.

For this validation study, the evaluators found it necessary to discuss the lens through which they chose or did not choose to highlight TABs. Evaluators #1 and #2 were stricter in their assessment when potential TABs (gifted characteristic) did not result in a desired outcome toward the team winning the game. However, when asked to think about it from a core curricular or classroom setting, the coach who was also trained in gifted programming could see the bias and translate that bias into ways that the coach without gifted education training could recognize as well. As such, we recommend that for calibration purposes, that evaluators are also refreshed in any area that they formally trained in as part of the SBAT training. Consequently, consider time and/or money to afford time off for such training when expertise in any one of these areas can be an issue. [*Validation Step 6: Keep track of practical issues including cost.*]

After completing the evaluation, we compared the evidence available with Frasier's FTAP and Collins' SBAT (the validity argument) against the evidence we identified up-front as necessary to support the desired interpretations and decisions (the interpretation-use argument). Through comparison, we found adequate scoring, generalization, extrapolation, and implication evidence:

1.   The rubric serves as a basis for collection of data and is numerically represented to be interpreted for use in identification decision making.

2. As priority for needed evidence, interpretation of the results can be aligned to other TABs-based assessment tools and their uses for gifted identification and service.

3. Extrapolation validity is present.

4. Evidence shows that athletically gifted SBs exhibit TABs that can be nurtured for success in advanced and gifted programs.

Although some gaps remain as they do in any validation process, an appropriate amount of evidence showed favorable to the assumptions, interpretation-use agreement, and priorities. [*Validation Step 7: Formulate/synthesize the validity argument in relation to the interpretation-use argument.*]

Resulting from an analysis of the evidence in this validation study, we have determined that the validation argument adequately meets the demands of the interpretation-use argument. After cost-benefit analysis, we also determined that the money, time, and effort involved in training evaluators and to include this assessment as a feasible tool in identification of gifted students are adequate for the expected results and broader impact. [*Validation Step 8: Make a judgment: Does the evidence support the intended use?*]

Implications for Practice

We submit goals and a call to action as implications to educators to address underachievement as a consequence of incomplete development of the gifts and talents. The goals are: (1) to address specific and intricate needs of Black male student-athletes who are both academically and athletically gifted; (2) intentionally to design and implement programs which accelerate academic and social integration in grades 7–12, specifically for Black scholar-athletes; and (3) to recruit and retain these underrepresented SBs in gifted and advanced programming.

Future plans and a call to action to finalize Collins' SBAT involve creating a complementary guide (similar to Frasier's FTAP, which can be used in the interim) to clearly explain and direct its intended use. As with many other educational assessments, the guide is needed to help standardize the tool for use across different states, within districts with various policies for identification, and for educators at different levels of expertise and background in gifted education, awareness of kinesthetic talents, and/ or sports knowledge.

The SBAT serves as an exemplar for coaches and educators to recognize and nurture complementary and corresponding TABs for scholar-ballers within core-curricular and extra-curricular settings. Progressing toward practical application, we have presented to multiple educators and integrated their feedback into revisions.

Conclusion

In a discourse of underachievement it is also important to discuss underserved students and undervalued talent – both of which lead to untapped potential. Untapped potential contributes to underachievement. Highly competitive sports, such as football, are one of many extra-curricular activities that can serve as a great source for collecting evidence of the gifts and talents of students. The example explored in this chapter offers an ethnographic and anecdotal vignette that is provided by the first author. It illuminates the positive impact of the intersectionality (compounded effects of overlapping conditions) of a student-athlete's diverse expression of gifts and talents. The authors have laid out evidence and processes that support observing and translating athletic talent as an identified gift to address unidentified and academically-undervalued talents of gifted scholar-athletes. They integrate kinesiology to understand the psychology and cognitive processes behind athletic talent as displayed by on-field cognitive skills.

Already validated as an appropriate assessment tool to identify diverse manifestation of talent, especially in minority students, Frasier's TABs (Frasier et al., 1995) is further extended to be an ideal framework using Collins' SBAT for identification of gifts, talents, and performance in an environment with which almost every American across every culture is familiar. Not only does this strategy (1) confirms the validation (Cook & Hatala, 2016) of Frasier's TABs as an identification tool to recommend student-athletes, as an underrepresented subgroup, for gifted identification and programming services, but also (2) it supports student-athletes referred for gifted education, and (3) offers a new way to address underachievement that may be influenced by the limitations of antiquated policies, inequitable practices, and ill-trained pre- and in-service educators in gifted identification.

REFLECTION QUESTIONS

1. Collins' SBAT and the strategy for identifying athletic talent as an indicator for academic gifts are introduced here for the first time. What are your initial thoughts regarding this strategy?
2. How comfortable would you be in using this tool in real time for evaluation of gifts and talents? What additional training or information, if any, would you need to be extremely comfortable and/or to show others how to use it?
3. Specific to a topic that you teach or enjoy most, offer a description for how Frasier's TABs might look in that setting when exhibited by students within that environment.
4. Using the descriptions offered in #3, explain how each of the athletic descriptions align with or can be indicators for your descriptions.
5. Prepare an "informational" sheet (single one-sided page) on what is outlined in this chapter that could be used to share the information with other teachers, coaches, athletic directors, etc. Briefly discuss this chapter with a coach and share your informational sheet. Report their reactions and feedback.

References

Beamon, K., & Bell, P. (2006). Academics versus athletics: An examination of the effects of background and socialization on African-American male student-athletes. *The Social Science Journal, 43*, 393–403.

Cook, D. A., & Hatala, R. (2016). Validation of educational assessments: A primer for simulation and beyond. *Advances in Simulation, 1*, 31. https://doi.org/10.1186/s41077-016-0033-y

Collins, K. H. (2009). *"3R" curriculum framework and program planning guide.* Academy of Liberal Arts at Newton High School (ALANHS), Newton County Schools, GA.

Collins, K. H. (2017). From identification to Ivy League: Nurturing multiple interests and multi-potentiality in gifted students. *Parenting for High Potential*, 6(4), 19–22.

Collins II, T. D. D. (2020a). Talking about racism in America: The retrospective voice of a gifted Black young adult. *Parenting for High Potential*, 9(3), 2, 3, 4.

Collins II, T. D. D. (2020b). Performance task: Student-athlete (SA) talent search. [Unpublished paper for EPSY 7060]. University of Georgia.

Collins II, T.D.D. (2021, August). Foster dual-identity & holistic talent development of gifted Black scholar athletes. Workshop presentation for Seattle Public Schools Talent Development Institute [online].

Crenshaw, K. (2018, August). What is intersectionality? Available at: https://youtu.be/ViDtnfQ9FHc

Dexter, M., Collins, K. H., & Grantham, T. (2021). Extending the scholar-baller model to support and cultivate the development of academically gifted Black male student-athletes. *Gifted Child Today*, 44(4), 203–215. https://doi.org/10.1177/10762175211030528

Dictionary.com (2020). Skillset. Available at: https://www.dictionary.com/browse/skill-set?s=t

Entine, J. (2001). *Taboo: Why Black athletes dominate sports and why we're afraid to talk about it*. Public Affairs.

Frasier, M. M., Martin, D., García, J. H., Finley, V. S., Frank, E., Krisel, S., King, L. L., & National Research Center on the Gifted and Talented (1995). *A new window for looking at gifted children*. National Research Center on the Gifted and Talented.

Harrison, C. K., Bukstein, S., Mottley, J., Comeaux, E., Boyd, J., Parks, C., & Heikkinen, D. (2010). Scholar-Baller®: Student athlete socialization, motivation and academic performance in American society. In P. Peterson, E. Baker, & B. McGaw (Eds.), *International encyclopedia of education* (vol. 1; pp. 860–865). Elsevier.

Kane, M. (2006). Validation. In R. L. Brennan (Ed.), *Educational measurement* (4th ed., pp. 17–64). Praeger.

Lovecky, D. V. (1999). Gifted children with AD/HD. Paper presented at the Annual CHADD International Conference, Washington, DC.

U.S. DOE & Office of Civil Rights (2020). Civil rights data collection. Available at: https://ocrdata.ed.gov

Transitioning from Highly Talented Student to Highly Capable Adult
The Intersection of Lifewide Learning

Joslyn Johnson

Introduction

As individuals reach early adulthood, navigating a career is often an expected next developmental phase (Erikson & Erikson, 1998). The developmental period of early adulthood brings about thoughts of the future and having the means to reach desired goals (Erikson & Erikson, 1998) as well as serving as a time of defining and redefining life roles (Merriam et al., 2007). Oftentimes, this is also a period when individuals are still exploring career options and/or their perceived "purpose in life." Gifted individuals with multipotentiality can find this time to be very stressful in trying to decide on a career or the "right" path to take. Over-analysis of options and indecision can lead them to jobs that do not maximize their potential or match their talents, leaving them feeling that they are underachieving. The study[1] highlighted in this chapter viewed the lifewide learning experiences that helped high-achieving individuals in early adulthood successfully transition into careers, as well as find a sense of purpose in their work. Furthermore, it sheds light on how types of lifewide learning – formal, self-directed, and non-formal – intersect. Findings from this study focused on how relational learning, connected learning, and identity capital were key factors in a successful transition to adulthood.

A constructivist approach to grounded theory was used to conduct this study. "Grounded theory research does not normally proceed in the usual iterative manner of literature search, hypotheses development, followed by field research. As a rule, grounded theory evolves from tentative literature base to begin with" (Goulding, 2002, p. 163). The goal of grounded theory is to construct an "integrated and comprehensive grounded theory that explains a process or scheme associated with a phenomenon" (Birks & Mills, 2011, p. 12). Whereas other qualitative research approaches are more focused on describing and exploring a phenomenon, grounded theory is concerned with explaining a phenomenon, with an emphasis on understanding processes (Birks & Miller, 2011; Charmaz, 2006). Process in this case is defined by Corbin and Strauss (2008) as "ongoing action/interaction/emotion taken in response to situations or problems" (p. 96). The aim of this study was to understand the process of lifewide

DOI: 10.4324/9781003369578-18

learning and how it has helped to create a sense of purpose and high achievement in the careers of high-potential individuals in early adulthood.

Early Adulthood and the Push Toward Meaningful Work

In this study, the process of transition was a primary focal point as I researched lifewide learning experiences that helped to spur success and a sense of purpose in early adulthood. Lifewide learning is the second dimension of lifelong learning, which consists of intentional (formal, self-directed, non-formal) and unintentional learning (informal, impromptu, teachable moments) that takes place in different settings across the lifespan (Reischmann, 2014). In Levinson's adult development model, he refers to the process of adulthood as a life structure shaped by the social and physical environment, and early adulthood as one of the most pivotal periods of the life structure. In Levinson's model, early adulthood consists of ages 17–45, with five distinctive periods: transitioning into early adulthood (17–22), grasping life structures for early adulthood (22–28), the transition into the thirties (28–33), settling into early adulthood (33–40), and transitioning into middle age (40–45) (Levinson, 1996). Levinson's theory is primarily focused on the process of constant change toward one's ideal life, referred to as "the dream"[2] (Aktu & Iihan, 2017).

Juxtaposing Levinson's theory, Gould's *transformations in adult development* theory highlights the social and emotional aspect of development and its impact on the decision-making process in early adulthood. In Gould's theory, individuals at ages 22–28 focus on developing independence and commitment to a career, with ages 29–34 typically being a period of questioning and vulnerability to career dissatisfaction. In this theory, individuals aged 35–43 have an urgency to attain life goals (Gould, 1978). Both theories posit early adulthood as a time of change that directly impacts the vision that individuals have for their lives. As I spoke with the participants in this study, I also recognized how it would be advantageous for me to be attentive to the information they shared pertaining to their aspirations and decision-making process. For example, Ben (pseudonym) knew that he wanted to help underserved populations, but initially he did not think he would work within the prison system. When Ben was presented with an opportunity to work for a state prison institution that would also allow him to enter a special loan repayment program, it fit in with his goal of being debt-free and providing the desired lifestyle for his family. Moreover, the position at the prison met his desire to help people who are often forgotten. Levinson would refer to Ben as adjusting his career as part of the process toward reaching "the dream." Another participant, Jessica (pseudonym), grew up in a family where she was taught that she should not pursue further education beyond her homeschooling due to her family's religious background. Nevertheless, Jessica had high aspirations and wanted to help women on a larger scale outside of the home. Initially she did not feel prepared to pursue further education, but when she learned about midwifery school she saw an opportunity to continue her education in a non-traditional way. Gould would recognize this as the process of developing independence and committing to a career field. Overall, there were numerous examples where participants in this study exemplified forward-thinking as they navigated their decision-making process in order to reach their life goals.

In addition to Levinson and Gould's theories, another prominent adult development theorist is Erikson (1968), who proposed an eight-stage psychosocial model of adult development. Erikson envisioned adolescence as the period prior to early adulthood, which consists of discovering one's identity and asserting one's independence as an adult by age 20. Consequently, in Erikson's theory, it is expected that during early adulthood (ages 20–39) an individual should be settled into their identity and seeking strong partnerships through love and friendships as he or she works out the conflict between intimacy and isolation (Erikson & Erikson, 1998). However, economic woes and societal changes have made settling into one's identity and transitioning into adult independence a difficult feat for many young adults, especially with regards to securing employment that will enable stable independence. As a result, many would argue that the adolescent phase has been prolonged (Côté, 2005). According to Arnett (2016), this shift has caused a new phase of adult development to evolve, called *emerging adulthood* (ages 18–25), defined as "an exceptionally unsettled time" (p. 1). Previously the age range of 18–28 was historically considered a time of settling into adulthood and family. However, in more recent years there has been great attention given to the concept of emerging adulthood. Arnett (2016) suggests that marriage, procreation, career goals and other dynamics associated with adulthood are being delayed as a result of economic factors, prolonged education, and societal changes. Essentially, emerging adulthood helps to address what could be considered a period situated between adolescence and early adulthood.

These different perspectives of early adulthood provide a contextual lens, as the participants' age range fell within all of the aforementioned models of early adulthood development (including a portion of emerging adulthood). Having participants between the mid-twenties to mid-thirties allowed me to learn about early adulthood transitions in a fresh way. The mean age of the 14 participants in this study was 30, which, according to many adult development theories, can often be a turbulent time as it marks another major transition. During this study, I listened to participants share their stories about their life transitions ranging from discovering themselves, coping with a hard break-up, connecting with new people, finding their purpose, rediscovering their purpose, testing the waters in a career field, and, for some, transitioning into marriage and parenthood. As expected, with multiple life transitions also came a multiplicity of challenges. Yet, all of the participants successfully navigated transitions associated with both emerging adulthood and early adulthood. As a result of the participants collectively identifying as being successful and having a sense of purpose in early adulthood, it was possible to focus on the lifewide learning experiences that helped make their transition successful.

The Role of Lifewide Learning

Lifewide learning, also known as the second dimension of lifelong learning, consists of intentional (formal, self-directed, non-formal) and unintentional learning (informal, impromptu, teachable moments). Lifewide learning occurs in different settings across the lifespan (Reischmann, 2014). As the participants reflected on their vast lifewide learning experiences, they saw them as investments toward their growth. The most prevalent way that their growth-mindset manifested was through the high value placed on learning. Participants expressed a humble, open disposition toward learning new things (as outlined in the findings section). One of the participants, Ian, provided the best example as he shared how he is "intentional and conscious about learning," recognizing that in every room that he enters he is both a "student of learning" from others as well as a "teacher for others" around him. Applying intentionality to lifewide learning experiences was a common thread among the participants. From a positive standpoint, the participants used exemplary role models as illustrations they could learn from, and experiential learning as ways to discover, strengthen, and build confidence in their own abilities. Moreover, no learning experience was considered wasted; as such, many of them considered their mistakes as an opportunity for greater growth, with one of the participants calling it "failing forward." Even in the participants' indirect experiences, the phrases "I learned by watching others' mistakes" or "I used it as an example of what not to do" were echoed by the majority of the participants. Though the participants' love for learning was evident, tackling the concept of lifewide learning itself was an immense undertaking. The concept of lifewide learning recognizes life itself as a place of learning: every space, also known as a learning ecology, is a space where learning takes place. When it came to assessing the breadth of lifewide learning experiences that took place in multiple settings, Bronfenbrenner's (1979) Ecological Model helped illustrate how different learning ecologies affect human development (Bronfenbrenner & Morris, 2006), as well as bringing the broad concept of lifewide learning into focus. Bronfenbrenner's theory consists of the following layers: the individual, the microsystem, the mesosystem, the exosystem, and the macrosystem. He believes that one's own biology is a factor and that the other layers interact with the individual, impacting his or her development. The microsystem consists of one's immediate surroundings (family, friends, teachers), the mesosystem pertains to connecting structures between the immediate surroundings and the individual (home, school, neighborhoods, church), and zooming out to a broader view, the exosystem accounts for the impact of social systems, while, finally, the macrosystem looks at broad ideas that help to shape such systems' impact on an individual (Berk, 2000). Figure 14.1 presents Bronfenbrenner's ecological model.

Based on the findings of the study, the participants spoke most frequently about their lifewide learning perspectives through the lens of the microsystem (family, friends, mentors, professors, school settings, the workplace, organizations, church groups, etc.). However, there were opportunities to gauge the impact of the mesosystem and beyond when the participants discussed their purpose, touching on topics relating to the impact their cultural upbringings had on their mindset, as well as how spirituality and overarching belief systems impacted their decisions. Bronfenbrenner's model provided an opportunity to look at the impact of the different layers and discover how the participants interacted with each system; however, the task of identifying the different types of lifewide learning experiences within the categories would prove to be a meticulous feat.

Initially, as I listened to the participants' stories, I thought it would be easy to separate their formal, non-formal, and informal learning experiences, but I quickly began to notice how much their lifewide learning experiences overlapped. One participant discussed a homework assignment given to him by his professor to do something "out of the norm" and keep a record of the experience. In this case, the participant decided to get his ears pierced. When he shared what he learned from the experience, he mostly spoke about how his family reacted negatively (unaware that it was part of an assignment). He recognized the learning experience as a pivotal moment that helped him realize how quickly people can judge someone based on the surface, even despite knowing a person on an intimate level. In this case, the assignment was given in the classroom, but the bulk of the learning took place outside of the classroom. This was a common trend observed as participants shared how formal education had impacted

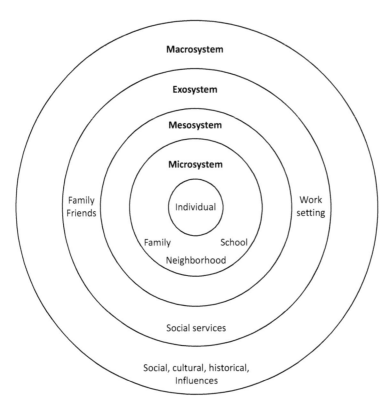

FIGURE 14.1 Bronfenbrenner's ecological model.
Source: Adapted from Bronfenbrenner (1979).

their learning. In some cases, the reverse would occur: a participant would learn as a result of their own self-education outside of the classroom. They would speak with a professor or mentor in their field regarding their newfound knowledge, which later led to a more formal or non-formal experience. In other words, I began to notice that, based on the participants' experiences, the concept of lifewide learning itself could not be segmented into categories, but rather, formal, non-formal, and informal settings were often simply starting points to learning experiences that eventually intertwined with one another. This discovery is closely related to discussions by LaBelle (1982), who in *Formal, Nonformal, and Informal Education: A Holistic Perspective on Lifelong Learning,* looked at the relationship between all three modes of learning and concluded that individuals are constantly engaged in learning experiences whether planned, voluntary or unintended, functioning all together; therefore formal, non-formal, and informal learning are always interacting with one another.

In the same way that our lives cannot simply be segmented into neat categories because of intersections, our lifewide learning follows suit. Nonetheless, despite the overlapping (of the types of learning), there were distinctions between what was gleaned by the participants from the different forms of learning based on their starting points. For instance, participants primarily recognized the starting point of formal education experiences as a *life trainer* that pushed them out of their comfort zones, and as an environment to further explore areas of interest. Conversely, when participants acknowledged informal learning as a starting point, it was chiefly identified as a catalyst for learning through connecting with others and developing a strong support system. However, in some cases it is hard to recognize the starting point when the types of learning are both so closely intertwined. For example, when I asked the participants about their formal learning experiences, they typically spoke about going away to college and echoed each other when sharing their experiences about the first time away from home. They noted that this experience led them to become more independent, find where they fit, and learn life lessons along the way. In fact, one of the main lessons the participants spoke about was how going to college introduced them to diversity and becoming culturally competent as a result of being in a space with people from different backgrounds. Although the experiences mentioned were within their school settings, they were more informal in nature, yet if you removed the institution, the likelihood of their experience would also be removed. It was the environmental change that the participants referred to the most as it related to their growth in formal settings, versus the teaching taking place in the classroom itself (which is what I initially expected to hear). The overlap of formal and non-formal learning also showed as the participants relayed their learning experiences. In some instances, the participants joined organizations chartered by their schools, or attended leadership development programs that they were made privy to through faculty members or co-workers.

As a result of the participants being introduced to new ideas in more formal or non-formal settings, it led to the desire to explore areas of interest through self-education and to share their knowledge with others. Bronfenbrenner's model acknowledges the overlapping and interplay of multiple domains by showing how each layer is continuously impacting the development of the individual, and vice versa, and refers to this as *bi-directional influences* (Paquette & Ryan, 2001). What I especially found interesting, as it relates to how learning experiences impacted the participants, was their ability to see their experiences in pixel form, but then zoom out and apply the lessons they learned from their experiences to progress toward their big picture goals. Such an ability lends itself to their learning intentionality. Maya Angelou once stated, "I come as one, but I stand as 10,000," referring to her presence and success being the result of her ancestors' experiences. A similar concept can be applied to the participants, but as it relates to the synthesis of their learning experiences. It is the multitude of lifewide learning experiences that the participants were able to connect together that positioned them to thrive when rewarding opportunities presented themselves.

Connected Learning

The ability that the participants showed in using their learning experiences to progress toward a goal is strongly centered on the principles of *connected learning*, which includes being socially embedded, interest-driven, and oriented toward opportunity. The participants were particularly skilled at connecting their informal learning experiences to their more non-formal and formal learning experiences in pursuit of their purpose. In *Connected Learning: An Agenda for Research and Design*, Ito et al. (2013) describe the realization of connected learning as "when a person is able to pursue a personal interest or passion with the support of friends and caring adults, as is in turn able to link learning and interest to academic achievement, career success or civic engagement" (p. 4). The lifewide learning experiences of the participants were undergirded by strong support systems (friendships, mentors, family), delving deeper into areas of interest through self-education, and exploring opportunities through organizations, internships, conferences, and formal learning experiences. While lifewide learning looks at the breadth of learning that takes place, connected learning helps to connect intentionality to the learning experiences so that the learner benefits at the highest levels from their lifewide learning experiences. Research suggests that a connected learning approach leads individuals to be more resilient and able to adapt when provided with the right social support (Ito et al., 2013). Even though it may not have been through an intentional curriculum, their experiences indeed mirror connected learning. This helps to explain why the participants were able to transition successfully, as strong connected learning experiences led them to be more resilient and adapt as needed. Whereas the literature on connected learning is typically tied to a curriculum and thought of as a process that an educator uses to link information together for their students, in this case, it was evident that connected learning is an ability that the participants exercised in their daily lives, through what I call *learning synthesis*. Perhaps the greatest link to the participants' ability to synthesize their learning is their self-directed learning abilities. Brookfield (1986) states, "The most complete form of self-directed learning occurs when process and reflection are married in the adult's pursuit of meaning" (p. 58). When Miranda (pseudonym) gave a simple example about personal development it confirmed how self-directed learning served as a link to connected learning:

> I would say a lot of my professional development connects to my personal development. [for example] Just like listening to interesting podcasts, I rarely just kind of sit and veg out. I do sometimes, but normally if I do, I do that in small doses, so I guess I'm always trying to do something that is somewhat enhancing to my life.

It is the mindset of connecting informal learning experiences to formal or non-formal experiences that allows the participants to receive the highest return on their learning investments. When the participants reflected on learning, they placed high esteem on its role, and when asked about the major contributing factors to developing their talents and abilities, they spoke of drawing from their everyday life experiences. Dan (pseudonym) shared how his life experiences helped his development:

> The major contributing factors that impact my talents and abilities [pause], I moved around a lot as a kid. So, with [my] dad getting a promotion every two and half years that would take us to a new city, sometimes a new state, so I was always the new kid in the class but I never had, like, a weird awkward [phase]. I guess when you're the brand new kid and have to figure it out, I would just always try to be nice with everyone and I made friends quick and I played a lot of sports in all those different communities. So, I made friends there, but I think that goes a lot into, kind of, always being a new person and sometimes feeling a little bit out of place but being okay with that. I think that's probably one of the greatest things that has contributed to my people skills and flexibility and just having to put myself out there.

Dan is an example of using his life experience to learn a skillset that has served him well in connecting with others in the field of government relations. It would have been easy to use being the new kid as an excuse to become more reclusive; however, he used his early life experiences as an opportunity to learn how to connect with people in new environments. This trend was not just observed in Dan's example, but similar sentiments were shared by others. Dave (pseudonym) shared:

I think maybe the biggest contributing factor to who I am and my approach to life is the fact that I needed to be more self-reliant from a very early age. I had a relatively unstable childhood in the sense that my folks, my mother in particular, were very loving but we were super poor, so I got a job. I think I have [a] Social Security record going back to when I was 10, but I got a job very early and was more or less an adult at a very early age and learned both in terms of day-to-day existence and personal relationships, how to be an adult really early, so that gave me a head start on working on and improving a lot of the things that people may take for granted.

Mentoring

For connected learning to take place, a prominent piece is the support of caring adults, communities, friends, and family, which correlates with the strong theme of mentorship that was prominent in informal learning settings. In this study as well as others, it has been shown that successful adults who were able to navigate and overcome challenges can also reflect back on key mentors who helped lead them in the right direction (DuBois & Silverthorn, 2005; Spencer, 2007). Spencer (2007) referred to this phenomenon as *natural mentoring relationships* that span family members, friends, coaches, teachers, neighbors, community leaders, and spiritual leaders, who are able to have a positive impact on youth and emerging adults during pivotal times in their lives. In *natural mentoring relationships*, rather than a more formalized partnering together of mentor to mentee, the relationship between mentor and mentee evolves out of everyday life situations. Furthermore, while mentoring has been shown to help navigate challenges, mentoring has also been shown to help early career professionals successfully transition.

Relational Learning

Along with mentorship, there was an emphasis on being surrounded by good people, having a positive impact on others and an immense appreciation of mentors and support groups. Subsequently the high value that is placed on people caused the participants to be relational learners. *Relational learning* subscribes to the idea that relationships are core to learning, whether inside or outside of the classroom (Otero, 2016). While the thread of formal, non-formal, and informal learning was encompassed in the participants' stories, the experiences that the participants mentioned the most were their relational learning experiences that often fell in the category of informal learning. One of the participants gave a great example of how relational learning has been at the core of his process, stating:

> Where I get most of my learning is through talks with my peers and challenging each other's view on different policy, political policy topics, and having my views challenged. I think that's where my growth and learning mostly come from.
>
> *(Dan)*

Likewise, Cindy (pseudonym) shared how she has been impacted in her learning by others: the impact of relational learning was evident:

> Some of the early experiences, I would say, of learning, would be learning what not to do by watching others, also social situations, and of course teachers, definitely.

I find myself very blessed to have most of [the] time teachers especially in college that I always felt comfortable enough to go to them if I didn't feel I was grasping the material or something like that. I had the kind of professors I could go to and find out what I wasn't catching or had opportunities for PAs or sessions or things like that I could take advantage of to be able to learn that way. Basically, people who were able to teach me things, are people who had a major impact. Also, my pastor and his wife, just the way that they interact with people and with each other, and also my parents, the way they interact and the way they help each other, have helped me try to be a better wife. So also learning from relationships from other people, some things I should do, some things I shouldn't do, to make my relationship work.

Pat (pseudonym) further highlighted how relational learning can take place through a spouse when naming one of the major contributions to her learning:

One of the most important [learning environments] is my husband because he can challenge me, he can tell me no, he knows what buttons to press and I mean this in a very good way of making me be better at what I'm doing. I couldn't even tell you how it works out but he and I have a great relationship to where he's one of the only people that really call me to the mat on figuring out how something could work better. I love that and appreciate that.

Their relational learning, combined with their ability to translate their lifewide learning experiences into connected learning, positioned the participants to be successful when faced with career opportunities.

Intersections of Adult Development, Lifewide Learning, and Career Development

When looking at the vast lifewide learning experiences of the participants and how they have navigated transitions in early adulthood, it is important to understand some of the basic principles of being an adult learner. While pedagogy is focused on the learning process of children, andragogy is concerned with the process of teaching adults and how they learn. The term andragogy was first coined by a German high school teacher in 1833 (Reischmann, 2005), but was introduced in America almost a century later by Eduard Lindeman (1926), who introduced andragogy as a key method for teaching adults. Lindeman's concept of adult education steered away from teachers as the gatekeeper of knowledge and the student as the receiver and embraced an engaged way of learning that is collaborative and focused on living a purposeful life (Lindeman, 1926). Ultimately Lindeman saw life itself as the classroom in which adults learn, causing a paradigm shift from a more traditional pedagogical perspective. Perhaps one of the most prominent voices and advocates for andragogy was Malcolm Knowles, who developed the Theory of Andragogy. As part of the theory, Knowles (1984, p. 12) introduced six adult learning assumptions of andragogy:

1. *Self-concept*: When we get older, our concept of who we are shifts from dependence toward independence and self-direction.
2. *Adult learner experience*: As we grow and experience more life, we accumulate knowledge based on this experience that then becomes a more valuable resource

for future learning. By the time we are adults, we have an abundance of experience to draw upon across a variety of contexts.

3. *Readiness to learn*: Our readiness to learn becomes more oriented to the developmental tasks of our social and work-related roles.

4. *Orientation to learning*: As adults, our perspectives change from one postponed application of knowledge to immediate application, and, as such, our orientation shifts from one of subject-centered to one of problem-centered.

5. *Motivation to learn*: As we mature, the motivation to learn is internal.

6. *Reason why*: Adults need to know why they need to learn something.

As high-potential adult learners, the push toward engaging in one's own learning process was heightened among participants. The core components that encompass being a high-potential individual include having high abilities, a push and motivation toward high achievement, and a commitment to growth and reaching goals. The combination of self-directed learning and traits associated with high ability amplified how the participants used their learning experiences in their push toward growth.

Identity Capital

The participants' view of learning experiences as investments toward growth closely aligns with ideas surrounding identity capital. While *emerging adulthood* aims to address the societal changes that have contributed to prolonged entry into what was previously considered adulthood (age-wise), James Côté and Charles Levine (2002) introduced a different perspective on transitions into adulthood that center around identity formation. The contextual aspects that underline Côté and Levine's theory of identity formation include:

1. *social structure*, which can include political and economic systems;

2. *interaction*, comprising patterns of behavior that characterize day-to-day contacts among people in socializing institutions like the family and schools;

3. *personality*, which encompasses terms like character, self and psyche, including subcomponents like ego identity (Côté, 1996, p. 1).

Rather than focus on age brackets to define adulthood, Côté builds on his concept of identity formation by introducing the *identity capital model*, focused on coping with challenges associated with transitioning from higher education into the workforce (Côté, 1997). Based on the findings of this study, participants' experiences strongly aligned with many of the aspects mentioned in the identity capital model, which asserts that certain resources (known as identity capital) are necessary in order to make a strong transition despite societal barriers. Broadly speaking, identity capital consists of both tangible (social class, parents, gender, organization memberships, etc.) and intangible (personality, advanced intellectual and social development) resources (Côté & Levine, 2002). Forms of identity capital include: advanced forms of personal development, making progress in one's life project, resolving adult-identity issues, securing community memberships that provide identity validation and social capital, and attaining an occupation that is personally and financially gratifying (Côté & Levine, 2002, p. 120).

In the list of things that constitute identity capital, most of them fall within the following three categories: (1) personal development; (2) progressive core traits; and (3) validating support systems. The prevailing themes in the findings of the study also closely align with the aforementioned categories. Traits associated with high potentiality align with advanced intellectual and social development, a push toward purpose that intersects with personal development, and meaningful lifewide learning experiences that align with having validating support systems. See Table 14.1 for a comparison of components of identity capital and the study findings.

Dave exemplified the intersections between his traits associated with high potentiality, personal development, and support systems as part of his learning experience, as he articulated:

> There are a few practices of personal development that I try to focus on. One is just looking for opportunities to find growth every day whether large or small, whether it's interactions with people that go particularly well or particularly not well, or situations where I think I could have done something different or better. I always try to stay very mindful and present in what's happening and then break those things down on a regular basis every day or week or couple of weeks, and then I find talking to people who I respect, like mentors or coaches, really helpful. I go to, like, a psychiatrist about things, just to check, like the mental tune-up.

In just a few sentences Dave's traits of being a forward-thinker, having an open disposition toward learning, and the push toward high achievement that are associated with high potentiality shine through in how he approaches life. To that end, Dave is focused on progressing forward based on what his lifewide learning experiences present and he understands the importance of leaning on the support systems around him (mentors, coaches, and psychiatrist). Each participant demonstrated a sense of identity,

TABLE 14.1 Comparison of components of identity capital and the study findings

Identity capital	Findings
Core traits	■ High aspirations and ability ■ Gifted ■ Forward-thinkers ■ Love and openness toward learning ■ Purpose-driven people ■ Centric ■ Courteous, self-aware
Personal development	■ Self-educators ■ Utilize books ■ Continued education courses ■ Leadership development ■ Spiritual development ■ Professional development ■ Mental health care
Support systems	■ Family ■ Expert to novice ■ Mentorship ■ Peer mentors ■ Friendships ■ Organization member ■ Assistantships/internships

clearly articulating their skillsets, personality traits, and the value that they bring as an individual. In Vaillant's (2002) model of adult development, one of the concepts that he expounds on is *career consolidation*, describing it as "expanding one's personal identity to assume a social identity within the world of work" (p. 36). Interestingly participants did not separate being successful in life from their career; in fact, when I attempted to ask questions that separated the two, the participants still did not make a distinction. As I noticed this trend of identity and career success aligning, I began directly asking the participants if they viewed being successful in life and successful in their career as two separate entities. Participants predominantly saw them as one and the same. This trend lends itself to the idea that the participants had merged their personal identity into the work that they were doing, which helped to give them a sense of purpose. Levinson's Life Structure theory speaks of an idea called "the dream," the idea that everyone has an ideal life that they are trying to achieve and as they go through transitions in life, they modify their goals as their perceptions of reality also adjust (Dean, 2007). The concepts of career consolidation and "the dream" in many aspects can be directly associated with purpose.

Career consolidation speaks to the process of synching one's identity with one's career and the process of reaching the dream is all about the lifewide learning experiences that contribute to the perception of reaching one's "dream."

Results of the Study

Based on the findings of the study that addressed the lifewide learning experiences of the participants, their formal, informal, and non-formal experiences overlapped heavily. However, there were distinctions to the roles that each type of experience played which are highlighted in Table 14.2.

It was through the breadth of lifewide learning experiences of the participants that they performed connected learning, relational learning, and experiences that provided them identity capital to step into their desired career roles in order to reach "the dream." The participants matched their breadth of learning with intentionality by practically applying their experience.

TABLE 14.2 Lifewide learning key findings

Lifewide learning	Main role	Key elements	Notable trend
Formal learning	Learning that serves as a place of exploration and life trainer	K-12 school settings, higher education institution, teachers, professors	Most notable for being an environment that helped participants view life from a different perspective
Non-formal learning	Supplemental and experiential learning	Organizations, church setting, conferences, seminars/workshops, internships/assistantships, continued education	Most notable for helping to further explore purpose
Informal learning	Catalyst for learning through support systems and self-education	Mentorships, family, friends, and books	Most notable for developing talents and abilities and providing "aha moments"

Implications for Practice

Lifelong learning has been a prominent term in education, but it is time for its counterpart of lifewide learning to be brought to the forefront to help build the body of knowledge and inform practices that incorporate all of life's learning ecologies. The findings from this study highlight lifelong and lifewide experiences that are beneficial to a student's successful transition into a career field in early adulthood. The following key concepts of *connected learning*, *relational learning*, and *identity capital* underpinned the participants' lifewide learning experiences. The strong support systems of the participants closely related to relational learning, empowering them to have connected learning experiences, which then led to strong identity capital. A further review of these concepts can be found in Table 14.3.

As such, it is recommended that skillsets are developed within the K-12 setting to foster the following.

1. *Connected learning*: A breadth of lifewide learning experiences are comprised of connected learning – most notably reinforced by strong support systems. Connecting academic learning to cultural values and interest-driven pursuits allows learners to match educational goals, and consequently career options, to that which gives them a sense of purpose to flourish and maximize their potential.

2. *Identity capital*: A strong identity capital exists – most notably underpinned by the push toward personal and professional development. Connecting students to inspiring peers and mentors who reflect their identities gives them opportunities to engage in a social exchange of shared contribution and feedback to strengthen students' own identity capital.

3. *Relational learning*: Relational learning experiences produce social capital – most notably reinforced by a love for learning and a high esteem of people. It creates learning opportunities for shared learning experiences in multiple settings that allow students to selectively engage with caring adults and peers who share their same interests, common goals, and purpose. As a benefit for skillsets for transitioning in a work environment, these experiences can model a "working alliance."

4. *Career consolidation*: Opportunities that allow an individual to merge their identity capital and social capital together result in career consolidation, which drives high levels of productivity by producing a sense of purpose in work. Experiential learning and independent studies promote merging of identity and social capital as students transform their passions into a career-style experience, demonstrating career consolidation.

TABLE 14.3 Concepts underpinning lifewide learning experiences

Concept	Definition
Connected learning	"Connected learning is realized when the learner is able to pursue personal interest or passion with the support of friends, caring adults, and/or expert communities and is in turn able to link this learning and interest to academic achievement, career success, or civic engagement." (Kumpulainen & Sefton-Green, 2014, p. 10)
Relational learning	"Learning through collaboration and relationships with others." (Wang, 2012, p. 25)
Identity capital	"Identity capital is the currency we use to metaphorically purchase jobs and relationships … [it] is our collection of personal assets. It is the repertoire of individual resources that we assemble over time." (Jay, 2013)

Conclusion

Tackling the concept of lifewide learning in this study was a substantial undertaking, because its width appeared boundless. The concept of lifelong learning from the cradle to the grave can be viewed linearly, however, the second dimension of lifelong learning, lifewide learning, encompasses every learning space across the lifespan and operates in a circular manner, regardless of time. Lifewide learning encompasses all three elements of formal, informal, and non-formal learning. Every learning experience that an individual will ever have is part of their lifewide learning. While there are components of lifewide learning that can be evaluated, it is impossible to comprehensively capture every lifewide learning experience in a measurable way. Nevertheless, the impact of lifewide learning is not reduced as a result of not being able to holistically measure its scope. As Lindeman (1926) mentioned in *The Meaning of Adult Education*: "Educative experience spans the whole of life. And experience proceeds from any situation to which adjustment is made with accompanying mental release" (p. 110). Based on this knowledge, I recognize that lifewide learning should be viewed as organic and approached as a living experience. Recognizing learning as organic places an emphasis on overall growth, rather than metrics. The core of something being alive is that it is always changing and with change comes growth, causing a ripple effect. Each person's lived experience is as unique as they are and recognizing that lifewide learning is organic helps to eliminate the need to stamp a beginning and ending on every learning experience.

REFLECTION QUESTIONS

1. Differentiate between lifelong and lifewide learning. Provide some examples that foster both.

2. Have you intentionally provided relational and connected learning experiences for your students as a practitioner? In what ways can you commit to increasing your capacity in this area?

3. Learning synthesis (the ability to connect and apply lifewide learning experiences to opportunities) plays a pivotal role in the success of high-potential individuals. Two elements are necessary to strengthen this muscle: self-reflection and self-directed learning. How can you help students practice strengthening their self-reflection and self-directed learning abilities?

4. Having a strong support system helps to bridge equity gaps across backgrounds. What mentorship and professional development programs can you implement that will contribute to identity capital and social capital for your students?

5. What skill development strategies should be integrated in the K-12 gifted curriculum to prepare gifted students to transition into early adulthood as gifted or high-potential adults?

Notes

1 This study was completed as part of doctoral requirements for the dissertation, "When purpose calls: A grounded study on the lifewide learning experiences of high potential young adults." All research protocols, consent forms, permissions, and releases were collected at the

time of study and conferred by the Graduate Program in Adult, Professional, and Community Education (APCE) Program, Department of Counseling, Leadership, Adult Education and School Psychology, Texas State University, San Marcos, TX.

2 "The dream" is synonymous with one's view of what would constitute their ideal life.

References

Aktu, Y., & İlhan, T. (2017). Individuals' life structures in the early adulthood period based on Levinson's theory. *Education Sciences: Theory & Practice, 17*, 1383–1403.

Arnett, J. J. (2016). Does emerging adulthood theory apply across social classes? National data on a persistent question. *Emerging Adulthood, 4*(4), 227–235.

Berk, L.E. (2000). *Child development* (5th ed., pp. 27–33). Allyn and Bacon.

Birks, M., & Mills, J. (2011). *Grounded theory: A practical guide.* Sage Publications.

Bronfenbrenner, U. (1979). *The ecology of human development: Experiments by nature and design.* Harvard University Press.

Bronfenbrenner, U., & Morris, P. A. (2006). The bioecological model of human development. In N. Eisenberg (Ed.), *Handbook of child psychology.* John Wiley & Sons.

Brookfield, S. (1986). *Understanding and facilitating adult learning: A comprehensive analysis of principles and effective practices.* McGraw-Hill Education.

Charmaz, K. (2006). *Constructing grounded theory: A practical guide through qualitative research.* Sage Publications.

Corbin, J. M., & Strauss, A. L. (2008). *Basics of qualitative research: Techniques and procedures for developing grounded theory.* Sage Publications.

Côté, J. E. (1996). Sociological perspectives on identity formation: The culture-identity link and identity capital. *Journal of Adolescence, 19*(5), 417–428.

Côté, J. E. (1997). An empirical test of the identity capital model. *Journal of Adolescence, 20*(5), 577–597.

Côté, J. E. (2005). Identity capital, social capital and the wider benefits of learning: Generating resources facilitative of social cohesion. *London Review of Education, 3*(3), 221–237.

Côté, J. E., & Levine, C. (2002). *Identity formation, agency, and culture.* Lawrence Erlbaum Associates.

Dean, G. (2007). *An introduction to adult development.* Fieldnotes for ABLE staff. Department of Education, Bureau of Adult Basic and Literacy Education.

Dubois, D. L., & Silverthorn, N. (2005). Natural mentoring relationships and adolescent health: Evidence from a national study. *American Journal of Public Health, 95*(3), 518–524. https://doi.org/10.2105/ajph.2003.031476

Erikson, E.H. (1968). *Identity: Youth and crisis.* W. W. Norton & Company.

Erikson, E. H. (1980). *Identity and the life cycle* (vol. 1). W. W. Norton & Company.

Erikson, E. H., & Erikson, J. M. (1998). *The life cycle completed* (extended version). W. W. Norton & Company.

Gould, R. L. (1978). *Transformations: Growth and change in adult life.* Simon & Schuster.

Goulding, C. (2002). *Grounded theory: A practical guide for management, business and market researchers.* Sage.

Ito, M., Gutiérrez, K., Livingstone, S., Penuel, B., Rhodes, J., & Salen, K., & Watkins, S. C. (2013). *Connected learning: An agenda for research and design.* Digital Media and Learning Research Hub.

Jay, M. (2013). The defining decade: Why your twenties matter—And how to make the most of them now. Hachette, NY: Twelve.

Knowles, M. S. (1984). *Andragogy in action: Applying modern principles of adult education.* Jossey-Bass.

Kumpulainen, K. & Sefton-Green, J. (2014). What is connected learning and how to research it? International Journal of Learning and Media, 4(2), 7–18.

La Belle, T. J. (1982). Formal, nonformal and informal education: A holistic perspective on lifelong learning. *International Review of Education, 28*(2), 159–175.

Levinson, D. J. (with Levinson, J. D.). (1996). *The seasons of a woman's life.* Alfred Knopf.

Lindeman, E. (1926). *The meaning of adult education*. New Republic, Inc.

Merriam, S. B., Caffarella, R. S., & Baumgartner, L. (2007). *Learning in adulthood: A comprehensive guide* (3rd ed.). Jossey-Bass.

Otero, G. (2016). *Connecting school, family, and community: The power of positive relationships.* Centre for Strategic Education.

Paquette, D., & Ryan, J. (2001). Bronfenbrenner's ecological systems theory. Available at: http://www.floridahealth.gov/alternatesites/cms-kids/providers/early_steps/training/documents/bronfenbrenners_ecological.pdf

Reischmann, J. (2005). Andragogy: History, meaning, context, function. In L. M. English, *International encyclopedia of adult education* (pp. 58–63). Palgrave Macmillan.

Reischmann, J. (2014). Lifelong and lifewide leaning: A perspective. In S. Charungkaittikul (Ed.), *Lifelong education and lifelong learning in Thailand, Bangkok* (pp. 286–309). Available at: http://www.reischmannfam.de/lit/2014-Baifern.pdf

Spencer, R. (2007). Naturally occurring mentoring relationships involving youth. *The Blackwell handbook of mentoring: A multiple perspectives approach* (pp. 99–117). Blackwell Publishing.

Vaillant, G. E. (2002). *Aging well: Surprising guideposts to a happier life from the landmark Harvard study of adult development.* Little, Brown and Company.

Wang, V.C (2012). Handbook of research on technologies for improving the 21st Century Workforce: Tools for lifelong learning. Hershey, PA: IGI Global.

Index

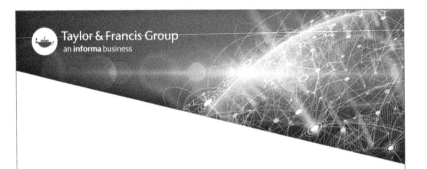